FRANCIS BACON: A POLITICAL BIOGRAPHY

The righte Honnorable Sr FRANCIS BACON Knight, Lorde keeper of the greate Seale of Englande and one of His Ma:ties most hon.ble priuie Counsell.

Simon Passæus sculpsit .L. Are to be sould by Iohn Sudbury & George Humble at the signe of the white horse, in Popes head Alley.

Francis Bacon   1561 - 1626

FRANCIS BACON:
A POLITICAL BIOGRAPHY

By
Joel J. Epstein

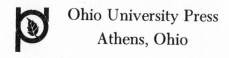
Ohio University Press
Athens, Ohio

DA358
B3
E67
1977

Copyright © 1977 by Joel J. Epstein
ISBN 0-8214-0232-3
Library of Congress Catalog Number 76-25617
Printed in the United States by
Oberlin Printing Company, Inc.

To Julia

ACKNOWLEDGEMENTS

The author's thanks are due to the following for permission to use copyright material:

Barrie and Jenkins for an extract from J. G. Crowther's *Francis Bacon: The First Statesman of Science*; University of California Press for an extract from Robert Zaller's *The Parliament of 1621*; Jonathan Cape Ltd. for an extract from David Harris Willson's *King James VI & I*; The Huntington Library for extracts from Joel Epstein's article "Francis Bacon and the Issue of Union 1603-1608", and from Robert C. Johnson's article "Francis Bacon and Lionel Cranfield"; The Institute of Historical Research for an extract from *Heyward Townshend's Journals*; Farrar, Straus & Giroux Inc. for an extract from Margaret Judson's *The Crisis of The Constitution*; Little Brown and Company in association with the Atlantic Monthly Press for extracts from Catherine Drinker Bowen's *Francis Bacon: The Temper of a Man* and *The Lion And The Throne*; McGraw-Hill Book Company for an extract from Thomas MaCaulay's *Critical And Historical Essays*; Martinus Nijhoff for an extract from Howard B. White's *Peace Among The Willows*; Methuen & Co Ltd. for an extract from J. W. Allen's *English Political Thought 1603-1660*; University of Minnesota Press for extracts from D. H. Willson's *The Parliamentary Diary of Robert Bowyer* and *Privy Councillors in the House of Commons, 1604-1629*; Oxford University Press for extracts from G. P. Gooch's *Political Thought from Bacon to Halifax*, Herford and Simpson's *Ben Jonson: The Man and His Work*, and Thomas L. Moir's *The Addled Parliament of 1614*; G. P. Putnam's Sons for an extract from *The Chamberlain Letters*; St. Martin's Press Inc. for an extract from J. E. Neale's *Elizabeth I and Her Parliaments 1584-1601*; The Viking Press Inc. for an extract from Hannah Arendt's *Eichmann in Jerusalem*; Wayne State

ACKNOWLEDGEMENTS

University Press for an extract from Jonathan Marwill's *The Trials of Counsel: Francis Bacon in 1621* and Yale University Press for extracts from Elizabeth Foster's *Proceedings in Parliament 1610* (II), Wallace Notestein's *The House of Commons 1604-1610* and Kelf, Notestein, and Simpson's *Commons Debates, 1621*, University of Southern California for Fulton Anderson's *Francis Bacon: His Career and His Thought*.

PREFACE

This study began as a doctoral dissertation under Margaret Judson at Rutgers University. It was Professor Judson who first introduced me to Francis Bacon's career in politics and ignited my interest in that subject. She has also influenced my view of the political-constitutional history of the period of English history in which Bacon functioned.

The task of converting a work on Bacon's career in Parliament into a broader study of his over-all political career proved slow but rewarding. The lion's share of the work was done during three summers, and my wife and children deserve credit for enduring my anxiety and short-tempered behavior during that period. Additional thanks go to my wife, Julia, for her proofreading and numerous suggestions for stylistic improvements.

My dear friend James Richardson of the University of Akron read the manuscript and made several useful suggestions. Thanks also go to Pat Abel, who typed the first draft; to Lisa Beverly, who proofread it; and to Susan Cooley, who typed the final manuscript. I should like also to express my gratitude to Dr. Kenneth Hance, former provost of Olivet College, for his encouragement about the project, and for giving me a reduced teaching load during the spring of 1973, thus allowing me to concentrate on completing the manuscript.

Finally, thanks go to Olivet College for a grant that paid for the typing of the final draft.

J. Epstein

CONTENTS

INTRODUCTION

This study is a purely political biography of Francis Bacon. Having studied his political career over the past several years, I became convinced that such a work is needed. Bacon has always attracted wide and varied attention; interest in him has ranged from the once popular absurdity that he authored Shakespeare's plays to the legitimate probing of his many intellectual achievements. Biographers have been attracted primarily to his intellect. Bacon has been admired as the great philosopher of scientific progress, the first modern mind. Those studying his life have focused on the positive achievements of that mind and have been lured to the man because of those achievements. Bacon's name most commonly calls to mind an eloquent line from one of the *Essays*, or perhaps the futuristic thoughts of the *New Atlantis*. He has been revered as one of the great minds of Western Civilization. The respect rendered him has been most justified.

But what of the Francis Bacon who served as Attorney-General and Lord Chancellor? Bacon spent most of his adult life in politics: He served in Parliament over a forty-year period, held at times the posts of Solicitor and Attorney, and exercised considerable power as a Privy Councillor. Bacon committed himself to the service of the Crown while in his early twenties and left it only when forcibly removed; his role in the legal and political history of late Elizabethan and Jacobean England is hardly without significance. Bacon was a key figure in several Parliaments as he sought to persuade the Commons to accept the proposals of the Crown. He struggled to rise in legal service of the government, encountering Edward Coke as his chief enemy. He rose ever so slowly, only to misuse the great power of Chancery and topple abruptly. This Francis Bacon, the one who courted power, the one who "turned on" Essex, the one who bitterly opposed the oracle of the Common Law, the one who defended an unpopular monarchy in Parliament—this individual has not been studied enthusiastically by biographers. Bacon has been looked upon rather consistently as a political failure. Some have condemned him; more sympathetic writers have attributed his shortcomings to weaknesses in his character. It has been common to admire Bacon the intellectual giant and to lament that he wasted himself in the treacherous world of politics. He has often been seen as the genius with profound ideas about the constructive use of power but for various reasons, was not able to apply them. The seemingly negative aspects of his career have been rationalized, apologized for, and seen as unfortunate imperfections, overshadowed by his great gifts. Four centuries of biographical study have seen diversity in interpretation. They have not, however, produced any study that has sought to focus solely on Bacon as a "political man." He was, to be sure, much more than that term implies. His active life was, however, spent primarily in pursuit of political ends, and his behavior was conditioned by the political standards of his society. Politics dominated him, however unhappy he may have been with the consequences it often brought.

I will examine the dimensions of that domination. I will therefore attempt to fill a gap in the biographical literature on Bacon which, despite some noteworthy twentieth-century scholarship, has continued to exist. No biographer has focused solely on Bacon as a political figure. No one has really tried to understand him as such without evaluating him in the broader perspective of the major intellectual figure. I use the term "political man," and will carefully define it. My book revolves around the theme that Francis Bacon was a "political man" saturated in and conditioned by the political structure of his society. He was neither a political demon nor an apostle of political virtue. To be certain, he was complex; gifted individuals usually are. His complexities have too often been neglected and need further scrutiny.

Admittedly, my study is a limited one. It pretends to be no more than an attempt to reinterpret Bacon as a political figure. There have been many comprehensive biographies, and some may feel that no work on Bacon should neglect treating his enormous intellectual accomplishments. I plead guilty to such a sin of omission. I have concentrated on what I believe to be a neglected area in Baconian scholarship. It is my hope that by helping to understand

Bacon's political career more clearly I may fill such a gap. My effort in no way seeks to preclude the need for a new, comprehensive, scholarly biography of Francis Bacon. On the contrary, that type of work is needed, and I only hope I am helping to establish a foundation for such a project.

CHAPTER I

FRANCIS BACON AS A POLITICAL FIGURE:
THE BIBLIOGRAPHICAL BACKGROUND

One noteworthy historian wrote that Francis Bacon led a "misused life."[1] Had Bacon devoted himself fully to the cultivation of knowledge and remained outside the political turmoil of late Elizabethan and early Jacobean England, he would certainly have emerged as a more appealing historical figure. The thought of an individual of almost unlimited intellectual capacity, who sought to revolutionize the process of learning yet chose to spend most of his mature life in the world of court and parliamentary politics, has disturbed even the most sympathetic interpreters. The view persists that Bacon did waste himself in politics, and his final public disgrace remains a blemish on his character. Defending his character has always been difficult even for his most enthusiastic admirers. The Essex affair, his behavior at Court, and his over-all conduct as Lord Chancellor have always stood as widely interpreted examples of deficiencies in his personality. Actually, few biographers have studied Bacon completely enough to understand the seemingly distasteful aspects of his long political life. The tendency has been to lament his "misused" life, to minimize the political side, and to emphasize the intellectual achievement.

It is not the purpose here to dispute the fact that it is more rewarding to explore the language of the Essays than to study the details of Bacon's Lord Chancellorship. Nor is it the intention to

1

make startling claims that Bacon should best be remembered as a statesman rather than as a writer-philosopher. The hope instead is to study fully his political life set against the circumstances of his time. The belief is that Bacon's character needs further probing, and while no new radical analysis is promised, I will attempt a thorough and objective study. Such an effort must aim at exploring the whole "political man." This means covering the much discussed subjects of his governmental career, legal career, and political and legal ideas, as well as the neglected subject of his career as an active member of the House of Commons. The "political man" in Bacon is a complex and fascinating topic in itself. It should be studied as such, free from the premise that his life was wasted in politics.

The biographical literature on Bacon is both varied and voluminous. The attitudes toward him have differed in every age, from his own to the present, and have ranged from hero worship to unfounded damnation, to a combination of both. Examining some of this literature is necessary to determine the various opinions, as well as to evaluate the degrees of thoroughness with which his political career has been studied. The problem of uncovering the whole "political man" in Bacon is crucial to this study.

Bacon's character provoked controversy among his contemporaries. As someone born into the familial political power structure he was immediately caught in the web of personalities that characterized the political life of the times. Bacon became politically involved early (he sat in his first parliament in 1581 at the age of twenty) and endured in government service for forty years until his impeachment in 1621. His varied career included lengthy tenure in the Commons, service before the bar as a Royal Counsel, the chief legal offices of Solicitor and Attorney, and membership on the Privy Council as Lord Keeper and Lord Chancellor. Such a career, together with the fact that his prolific pen made him well known, afforded him considerable public exposure. Diversity of opinion was therefore to be expected. Had Bacon's long career provoked only indifferent reaction, it probably would have meant that he was rather dull or mediocre.

Dullness or mediocrity were clearly not Francis Bacon's characteristics. Even his harshest critics grudgingly admire the intellect of this supposedly cold, sinister, and (in the eyes of some) "immoral" figure. Bacon has been subjected to the stereotyped characterization of a "cold" personality in every era, with even some of his admirers admitting the presence of some character deficiency. The development of such an attitude had been both gradual and uneven, and although Bacon received some severe contemporary criticism, his own century was generally not unkind to him. William Rawley, Bacon's chaplain and personal secretary, and the first compiler of some of his major works, presents the best example of extreme partiality. His brief *Life of Bacon* (1658) stands as the most complete seventeenth-century effort at a biographical portrait.[2] The work is a eulogistic chronicle written by someone who obviously held Bacon dear. Rawley's portrait stands in sharpest contrast to those who have emphasized the cold, ruthless characterization. "When his office called him," he writes, "as he was of the king's council learned, to charge any offenders, either in criminals or capitals, he was never of an insulting domineering nature over them, but always tenderhearted, and carrying himself decently towards the parties (though it was his duty to charge them home), but yet as one that looked upon the *example* with the eye of severity, but upon the *person* with the eye of pity and compassion." Rawley went on to assert that Bacon "was free from malice, which (as he said himself) *he never bred nor fed.*" Furthermore, "he was no revenger of injuries;" . . . and "no heaver of men out of their places, as delighting in their ruin and undoing." Neither was he a "defamer of any man to his prince."[3] Lord Bacon was not only the "tenderhearted" judge, but also the "free counsellor" who gave Essex "safe and honourable advice," the gifted essayist and biographer, the skilled parliamentarian. He was not lacking in "Christian virtues."[4] Significantly there is no mention in Rawley's portrait of Bacon's role in the Essex case, nor of his impeachment and fall from power. Rawley admitted that Bacon's fame was "greater . . . in foreign parts abroad, than at home," and was clearly writing to correct such a situation.[5]

Rawley's concise listing of selected facts in Bacon's life obviously cannot be judged by the same standards with which we evaluate the quality of modern biographies. His purpose was far different, and although the work is hardly a penetrating analysis of Bacon's character, it does possess sincerity of conviction. Rawley knew Bacon better than most men and believed what he wrote about him.

Other personal acquaintances were also generous in their words of praise. Peter Boener, Bacon's apothecary and secretary, surmised after his master's political fall "that whilst his fourtunes were so changed, I never saw any change in his mien, or his deeds towards any man. . . ." Boener is reported to have desired a statue to honor Bacon. "It would be desirable," he wrote, "that a statue or a bronzen image were erected in his country to his honour and name, as a noteworthy example and pattern for everyone of all virtue, gentleness, peacefulness, and patience."[6] One of Bacon's closest friends and confidants, Toby Mathew, remarked in 1618 that he

> never yet saw any trace in him of a vindictive mind, whatever injury were done him, nor never heard him utter a word to any man's disadvantage which seemed to proceed from personal feeling against the man, but only (and that too very seldom) from judgment made of him in cold blood. It is not his greatness that I admire, but his virtue: it is not the favours I have received from him (infinite though they may be) that have thus enthralled and enchained my heart, but his whole life and character. . . .[7]

But Mathew was hardly an impartial observer. He sustained a long friendship with Bacon which, although complicated by the former's conversion to Roman Catholicism, was apparently sincere.

Bacon had a host of friends among the notable subjects of the times. They included his secretary and later clerk of the Privy Council to Charles I, Bishop Lancelot Andrews; Thomas Meauthys and Henry Savile (both of whom helped translate the Bible for James); the antiquarians, Thomas Bodley and Robert Cotton; the lawyer, John Selden; the colorful Spanish Ambassador, Count Gondomar; and the famous Ben Jonson. Although not all of these individuals openly expressed their feelings towards the man, Jonson's pen was not to be denied. On the occasion of the Lord Chancellor's sixtieth birthday, he wrote:

> Haile, happie Genius of this antient pile!
> How comes it all things so about the (e) smile?
> The fire, the wine, the men! and in the midst,
> Thou standst as if some mysterie thou dids't.
> Some to the grave, wise keeper of the seale,
> Fame and foundation of the English Weale.
> What then his Father was, that since is hee,
> Now with a Title more to the Degree;
> England's high Chancellor: the destined heire
> In his soft Cradle to his Fathers Chaire,

4

> Whose even Thred the Fates spinne
> round, and fall,
> Out of their choysest, and their whitest wooll. . . .[8]

Even after Bacon's fall Jonson was emphatic in his praise. "My councel of his Person," he wrote, "was never increased toward him by his place or honours. But I have, and doe reverance him for the greatnesse, that was onely proper to himselfe, in that hee seem'd to me ever, by his worke, one of the greatest men, and most worthy of admiration, that had beene in many Ages. In his adversity I ever prayed, that God would give him strength: for Greatnesse hee could not want. Neither could I condole in a work, or syllable for him, as knowing no Accident could do harme to vertue; but rather helpe to make it manifest."[9]

The earliest biographical sketch of Bacon was written in 1631 by a Frenchman, Pierre Amboise.[10] This work, apparently unknown to Spedding, praised Bacon both as a man and as a government official. Amboise, who had a strong aristocratic bias, saw Bacon as a man free of the vices of "vanity, avarice, and ambition" and felt James "was one of the greatest Princes of his time, who understood thoroughly well the worth and the value of men."[11] He seemed anxious to praise Bacon in unlimited fashion. "Never was there a man," he wrote, "who so loved equity, or so enthusiastically worked for the public good as he." Bacon "was as truly as good a man as he was an upright judge," and Parliament's impeachment of him was "the working of monstrous ingratitude and unparalleled cruelty."[12] Amboise wrote with a compulsion to defend a servant of royalty, and his sketch, although interesting from a chronological point of view, can hardly be called an analysis.

Other seventeenth-century writers favorable in their opinion of Bacon were Thomas Tenison, Abraham Cowley, Peter Heylin, and one Dr. Sprat. Tenison edited a 1679 edition of Bacon's works and, relying heavily on Rawley, greatly admired Bacon's many talents.[13] Cowley, in a "poem to the Royal Society," wrote a flowery tribute to Bacon's intellectual ability:

> Bacon, like Moses, led us forth at last
> The barren wilderness he past,
> Did on the very Border stand
> of the blest promised Land, ...[14]

5

He appears to have recognized Bacon's contribution to the cause of learning. Heylin and Sprat in more modest remarks also recognized Bacon's intellectual talents.[15]

Although there appeared to be much sincere admiration and respect for Bacon, some contemporaries reacted differently. Other views ranged from more guarded praises, often tinged with pity, to open animosity. John Chamberlain, writing on occasion of the impeachment, lamented about the disgrace of "a man of so excellent parts" and asked that "God send him patience, and that he may make the best use of this affliction."[16] James Howell, genuinely grieved at Bacon's death, called him a "rare man . . . the most eloquent that was born in this Isle," adding that "the fairest Diamond may have a flaw in it." He compared Bacon to Cicero, Seneca, and Demosthenes, noting that the latter two individuals also succumbed to corruption.[17] In a historical study of noteworthy English figures, Thomas Fuller offered a brief biographical sketch in which Bacon is not condemned, but depicted as a Lord Chancellor who made some unfortunate mistakes. "Such who condemn him for pride," wrote Fuller, "if in his place, with the fifth part of his parts, had been ten times prouder themselves." Fuller also justified Bacon's behavior toward Essex by believing that he was "not the worse friend for being the better subject."[18]

Negative reaction to Bacon in the seventeenth century was not confined to the Edward Cokes, and those interested in embarrassing the monarchy. Perhaps no attack on him was as vicious as that leveled by the parliamentary compiler, Sir Simonds D'Ewes. D'Ewes in referring to Bacon's "gross and notorious bribery" asserted that while he may have been an eminent scholar "and a reasonable good lawyer . . . his vices were so stupendous and great, as they utterly obscured and out-poised his virtues."[19] Bacon's elevation to Viscount of St. Albans provoked the sarcastic reference by D'Ewes to "all bones" instead of Albans, coupled with the observation that all men were "wondering at the exceeding vanity of his pride and ambition."[20] D'Ewes' bitterness, however, was not confined to his feelings on Bacon's misbehavior as a public official. He virtually originated the often repeated accusation that Bacon was a homosexual. His contention was apparently based on his interpretation of some words written on the wall of a room frequented by Bacon at Gray's Inn. D'Ewes accused Bacon of intimacy with the Duke of Buckingham. He mentioned a "most abominable and daring sin" as proof that Bacon was "inflamed by wickedness and held captive by the devil."[21] While D'Ewes' venomous attitude does not appear to be grounded in direct dealings with Bacon, it should be noted that he himself admired Buckingham to the point that he was struck by the Marquis' "delicacy and handsome features" and his "especially effeminate and curious" face.[22]

D'Ewes' verbal outbursts together with Anthony Weldon's opinion that "never as many parts and so base and abject a spirit tenanted together in any one earthen cottage as in this man," constitute the extreme examples of written hostility toward Bacon in the seventeenth century.[23] John Aubrey, a biographical chronicler of the later century, superficially dismissed Bacon as an unworthy individual, and strongly hinted at homosexual behavior.[24] Bacon had yet to be subjected to solid analysis as a political figure. While such a task remained for later writers, the extreme prejudices of Rawley and D'Ewes provided a basis for future diversity of interpretation.

Eighteenth-century opinion about Bacon was highlighted by Alexander Pope's famous remark:

> If parts allure thee, think how
> Bacon shined (shin'd)
> The wisest, brightest, meanest
> of mankind.[25]

Pope indulged in no lengthy discourse on Bacon but merely depicted him with the harsh brevity of those famous words. They would ring loudly in Macaulay's ears a century later and provided the clearest foundation for the stereotyped portrait of Bacon as the brilliant but coldly sinister individual. David Hume in his work on English history reflected this attitude to some extent by disapproving strongly of Bacon's behavior toward Essex. "He did not scruple in order to obtain the queen's favor," wrote Hume as he portrayed a lack of humanity in Bacon's action. The same author, however, was somewhat more understanding of Lord Chancellor Bacon's impeachment. He called the sentence "dreadful," while concluding that the negligent Bacon lacked the "firmness of mind" for public affairs.[26] Hume's brief treatment of Bacon's character, although not one-sided, is too superficial to be of much value.

7

The eighteenth-century poet and pamphleteer, David Mallet, wrote a complete biographical sketch of Francis Bacon that was both balanced and reasonably perceptive.[27] Mallet appeared sensitive to the fact that Bacon was financially pressured into a public career and viewed his political behavior realistically. While he saved his greatest admiration for Bacon the scholar, he tried to understand the political man. The latter, although not sinister, did contain "blemishes" that one could not "conceal or palliate."[28] While Essex deserved his fate, and Bacon's conduct in the case was "moderate and decent," Mallet could not completely defend it. Bacon may have been wrongly accused of thirsting for vengeance, but even so he should not have taken such an active role against his former patron. Although the long struggle to rise was difficult and at times very frustrating, Mallet could not help being critical of Bacon's ambitious push from the Chancellorship. As Lord Chancellor, Bacon was used as a scapegoat by James (whom Mallet despised) to protect Buckingham from Parliament's wrath. His character was summed up as follows:

> Thus we behold him, a memorable example of all that is great and exalted, of all that is little and low, in man. Such inconsistencies in our human nature cannot but alarm and terrify even those who are most confirmed in a habit of virtue.[29]

Mallet did show some insight into the complexities of Bacon's character. He did not, however, develop his ideas thoroughly and appeared mainly interested in discussing Bacon's place in the European intellectual tradition. Although his work was superficial and selective in its coverage of Bacon's life, it stands as a sincere and thoughtful interpretation. It deserved the influential force which was generated instead by Pope's terrible epithet.

The nineteenth century saw the outflow of a large and assorted amount of biographical literature on Francis Bacon. The Victorian mind was attracted to his intellect and repelled by his politics. The laborious compilation of Bacon's assorted works carefully undertaken by men like Basil Montagu, James Spedding, Robert Ellis, and Douglas Heath laid the foundation for fruitful biographical study. In particular, Spedding's meticulous recording of letters and speeches, together with his running narration of the events in Bacon's life, furnished an invaluable source for interested writers.

The task of dissecting Bacon's profound residue of knowledge now stood as an exciting challenge to scholars, as did the opportunity to understand the political man within his character. The former challenge has been and continues to be dealt with more successfully than the latter one.

Basil Montagu began the serious investigation of Francis Bacon with a sixteen-volume compilation of collected works published between 1825 and 1834. Included was Montagu's own lucid biographical study.[30] The work, while flowery and overdramatic, is integrated with documents and written with true scholarly intent. Montagu was at his best in the intellectual area, as evidenced by his thorough probing of the main ideas in Bacon's major works. He was far less successful in treating his subject's political character. While the portrayal of Bacon as a cautious reformer who wished "in the true spirit of his philosophy to preserve; the next to improve the constitution in church and state," was perceptive, its plausibility was diminished by Montagu's over-all naïveté. Bacon emerges as an example of universal perfection, unjustly "accused of servility, of dissimulation for various base motives" by men "all unworthy of his high birth, and incompatible with his great wisdom."[31] He stood as unique in his all-around brilliance, incapable of doing wrong but openly and scandalously labeled by men like "D'Ewes and Weldon, whose falsehoods were detected as soon as uttered." Bacon, Montagu argued, drifted in a "capably unmindful" way into judicial corruption "careless" and "always poor" and innocently naive about the extent of his mistakes.[32] This apology was topped by a final laudation that makes it difficult to take Montagu seriously. "There is no record," he writes, "that he abused the influence which he possessed over the minds of men. He ever gave honest counsel to his capricious mistress, and her pedantic successor, the rash, turbulent Essex, and to the witty, avaricious Buckingham. There is nothing more lamentable in the annals of mankind than that false position, which places one of the greatest minds England ever possessed at the mercy of a mean king and a base court favourite."[33]

Despite a sensitivity to Bacon's intellectual talents, Montagu was not able to analyze objectively his subject's character. He sought mainly to administer a stern rebuke to any who dared to fault his hero. He did so eloquently and might have become the dominant influence in nineteenth-century Baconian studies had he not

9

been countered so sharply by Thomas Babington Macaulay. Macaulay's classic portrait remains an example of the power of articulate narrative over public opinion.[34] He specifically attacked Montagu's interpretation in his opening pages as a springboard for his lengthy indulgence in moralism. The great Whig historian had, in Bacon, the faithful and corrupt servant of the despotic Stuarts finally curtailed by parliamentary power, an ideal subject for condemnation. Even if there had not been some uncertainties about Bacon's character, Macaulay could not have dealt sympathetically with the political career of anyone who faithfully served the unreformed monarchy. The fact that there were some serious questions about Bacon's personal integrity, such as the Essex Case and the impeachment, however, generated a moralistic fervor in Macaulay which combined with that author's political bias, to expose Bacon to massive character assassination. Macaulay performed remarkably. "The moral qualities of Bacon were not of a high order. . . . "We do not say," he added, "that he was a bad man. . . . He was not inhuman or tyrannical." Bacon's "faults were—we write it with pain—coldness of the heart and meaness of spirit."[35] Although Macaulay tried periodically to temper his assault, the dominant tone of his essay left little doubt about the strength of his convictions. The Bacon of the Essex Case was the self-seeking opportunist who "exerted his professional talents to shed the Earl's blood, and his literary talents to blacken the Earl's memory."[36] Macaulay then went on to assert mistakenly that under James, Bacon "grew rapidly in fortune and favor."[37] All during this process a lack of principle dominated his character.

Macaulay, however, grudgingly admired Bacon the intellectual. In the temper of Bacon the philosopher, ". . . there was a singular union of audacity and sobriety. . . . Had his life been passed in literary retirement, he would, in all probability, have deserved to be considered, not only as a great philosopher, but as a worthy and good-natured member of society." "But," he laments, "neither his principles nor his spirits were as such as could be trusted, when strong temptations were to be resisted and serious dangers to be braved."[38] Macaulay clearly depicts a Bacon of two personalities. He is attracted to one of them and repelled by the other. Despite a genuine respect and admiration for Bacon's philosophic talents, Macaulay's over-all portrait remained framed by his strong bias. Had only Bacon's "civil ends continued to be moderate . . . he would have left not only a great, but a spotless name. . . ."

We should not then be compelled to regard his character with mingled contempt and admiration, with mingled aversion and gratitude. We should not then regret that there should be so many proofs of the narrowness and selfishness of a heart, the benevolence of which was yet large enough to take in all races and ages. . . . We should not then be forced to own that he who first treated legislation as a science was among the last Englishmen who used the rack, that he who first summoned philosophers to the great work of interpreting nature, was among the last Englishmen who sold justice. And we should conclude our survey of a life placidly, honorably, beneficently passed, . . . with feelings very different from those with which we now turn away from the checkered spectacle of so much glory and so much shame.[39]

Appropriately, in Macaulay's view, "shame" was the word most suited to conclude the essay. How unfortunate it was that Bacon could not have emerged as a more "virtuous" figure. And there was no doubt in Macaulay's mind that his characterization was flawless. He had captured the ugly political man in Bacon and poignantly conveyed it to the nineteenth-century reading public. While current students of Bacon may dismiss Macaulay's rhetoric by noting for example that "Bacon's political and social genius escaped him altogether" and that "this blindness vitiates" the entire essay, the over-all influence of the work remains very potent.[40]

Edwin Abbott, writing five decades after Macaulay, most strongly reflected the latter's influence and did so in a manner almost totally repulsive to the modern reader.[41] As one contemporary scholar puts it, Abbott "pursues Bacon through every incident of his life . . . with a 'moral' guile that sometimes appears malignant."[42] Such a description is hardly an exaggeration. Abbott depicted Bacon's political career as one that clearly revealed "an absence of healthy moral instinct, a deficiency which one might have expected . . . " and indicated "a cold, passionless, we may say crooked nature."[43] In his dealings with political contemporaries such as Essex, Robert Cecil, and Coke, Bacon was cast as the very incarnation of evil. Accepting Pope's description without question, Abbott, who appears to have researched his topic, was perplexed at how Boener, Rawley, and Mathew could consider the "meanest of mankind" a virtuous individual. Although admitting that Bacon was a complex and talented individual, Abbott was unable to appreciate his intellectual gifts. He suggested that Bacon's passion for science may explain "some of his moral derelictions," arguing that he can be compared to a religious enthusiast driven to extreme behavior.

11

Bacon's love of science, says Abbott, made him too rational and thus personally and politically cold. Even the fanatical Jesuits were "less vulgar" than this "selfish man of the world" who "on sufficient occasion . . . could creep like a very serpent."[44] Abbott's unfounded speculations were imaginatively stated. He did try to temper his criticism slightly toward the end of his work, by seeing something positive in Bacon's final five years and suggesting that they "may have chastened his moral character."[45]

Bacon's other leading nineteenth-century critics are easier to take. R. W. Church, while critical in his characterization, did not engage in Abbott's kind of moral castigation.[46] He admired Bacon's ability to give sound advice in political and legal matters and his sensitivity to the importance of Parliament. However, while Bacon "had the courage of his opinions," he lacked "the manliness and the public spirit to enforce them. . . ." Instead of doing "what a man of firm will and strength of purpose, a man of high integrity, of habitual resolution, would have done, . . . he was content to be the echo of and the instrument of the cleverest, the foolishest, the vainest, the most pitiably unmanly of English kings."[47] Church's prejudices were glaring and the unfortunate Bacon emerged as a political lackey, a parrot for James I.

Two mid-century critics (also exposed to Macaulay's influence) tried to be understanding in their opinions of Bacon. John Lingard, referring to him briefly in a general history, saw him as an "extraordinary man" who was the "victim of mistaken and disappointed ambition." He reflects strongly the view that Bacon wasted his life in politics without excusing his conduct as Lord Chancellor.[48] An English judge, John Campbell, in his voluminous study of the lives of Lord Chancellors, was particularly sensitive to Bacon's misconduct on the bench.[49] Campbell concentrates on Bacon's political and legal career, showing respect for his knowledge of the laws and regret that his ideas did not become dominant. "As a statesman," he remarked, "Bacon deserves high commendation. He was for governing constitutionally by parliament; . . . He had generally just views both of domestic and foreign policy . . . he was a reformer, yet he saw the danger of rash innovation."[50] Such views, had they been developed, might have produced some insight into Bacon's political character. Campbell, though not impressed by efforts to impeach Bacon's morals, was still primarily concerned with attacking his mishandling of Chancery. Bacon was a selfish individual, given to "instances of weakness and meanness by which he still tarnished his fame."[51] Although not vicious in his criticism, Campbell could not avoid contributing to the formation of a stereotyped portrait of Francis Bacon.

Pro-Bacon sentiment thrived in the nineteenth century despite these examples of hostility. The tradition of Montagu was both continued and enriched by the monumental work of James Spedding. No one individual devoted himself more to studying Bacon than Spedding. By collaborating with Ellis and Heath in compiling and editing Bacon's literary and philosophical works, and by compiling in chronological order Bacon's letters, speeches, and political writings, Spedding made what remains the foremost contribution to Baconian scholarship. The seven volumes of collected political documents is presented as a detailed biographical study, with the author's narrative and disclosures on the finding of documents tying together a wealth of source material. Although Spedding's profound admiration of Bacon was obvious in his undertaking such a study, he carefully maintained objectivity in presenting the material. Only upon concluding his study did he briefly, but staunchly, defend Bacon's character. He admitted that Bacon had been careless in managing money, but saw his conduct as Chancellor as understandable and hardly unique. Spedding was firmly convinced that Bacon had been purposely victimized by Parliament. He reacted sharply to Macaulay's type of moral condemnation and argued that Bacon had been attacked mainly because he supported an unpopular monarchy. Spedding was sensitive to Bacon's political gifts and to his painstaking efforts to preserve harmony in the state. He admitted that Bacon's efforts ended in disappointment. "As he looked round upon the world in the beginning of 1626," Spedding remarked, "it seemed that for any permanent benefit that his country was likely to derive from the labours of his political life, he might as well have spent it as an obscure student at Cambridge or Gray's Inn."[52] Bacon's political career was appreciated for its conscientious efforts, however, and not seen as a total waste. Spedding, despite a strong underlying partiality towards Bacon, did have insight into the political side of the man. He chose, however, to leave the task of thorough analysis to future scholars:

But when I attribute to a consciousness of moral elevation that "greatness" in Bacon which (though they would differ as to its na-

13

ture) most people feel; I am not to be understood as assuming to decide the question as to his moral *worth* . . . whether (in the phrase of the debating society) "the character of Bacon was deserving of the approbation of posterity," is a question which posterity must settle for itself.[53]

One asks whether Spedding himself should not have utilized fully the material he collected and attempted a full-scale biographical study.

Samuel Rawson Gardiner, the great parliamentary historian, sketched Bacon's political life and showed him as an individual of considerable ability.[54] Gardiner recognized Bacon's understanding of the main problems of his time and saw him as one committed to solving those problems through the maintenance of harmony between Crown and Parliament. No other nineteenth-century writer understood Bacon's ideas on government as clearly nor recognized his importance as a member of the Commons. "The one man who could have guided James safely through the quicksands," wrote Gardiner, "was Bacon. He had all the qualities of a reconciling statesman. . . . Above all, whilst he was the most popular member of the House, he had the highest ideas of the King's prerogative, because he saw in it an instrument for good."[55] While his portrait was brief, it was perceptive. Furthermore he refrained from passing moral judgments on Bacon's behavior towards Essex, and his conduct as Chancellor. Gardiner did feel strongly that Bacon's life was "misused" and although he classified him in "the first rank amongst statesmen," he believed that Bacon's "failure to recognize it was impossible for James and the Commons to work together "was a failure the cause of which lay in Bacon's moral as well as his intellectual nature. . . ." and "led to the great catastrophe of his misused life."[56] This loose usage of words is regrettable, since Gardiner did not define what he meant by Bacon's "moral" and "intellectual nature." Despite this flaw, his concise study commences thoughtful penetration into the political man in Francis Bacon.

John Nichol's intelligent study conveys an understanding of Bacon in the context of his age.[57] Nichol took into account the diverse views of his contemporaries, attempted to be moderate, and admired Bacon's political abilities. Bacon "tried to strike a balance between contentions" in politics and although he "came to regard politics as a game in which as in war and love, almost every-

14

thing is allowed," he "had considerable faith in political progress." Nichol saw him as the champion of a flexible paternalism, always respecting the role of parliament in government and sanctioning progress "by slow degrees."[58] A Machiavellian side of Bacon was seen by Nichol. "His moral faults, though common to his age, should be palliated rather than excused." Bacon lacked passions, and "some of his defects arose from the want of them."[59] Nichol, therefore, continued the practice of dabbling in value judgment without really probing Bacon's character. His work, however, was on the whole thoughtfully done.

The leading nineteenth-century positive studies of Bacon were not nearly so perceptive regarding his political character. Thomas Fowler admitted a great debt to Spedding as he sharply attacked the Pope-Macaulay image of Bacon. He chronicled his life briefly, presenting a moderate though superficial portrait, and devoted most of his book to studying Bacon's thought.[60] Henry Hallam in his constitutional history rejected Pope's smear and admired Bacon's political thought as well as his work in Parliament. "If all Lord Bacon's philosophy had never existed," he wrote, "there would be enough in his political writings to place him among the greatest men this country had produced."[61] Hallam, however, devoted little time to discussing Bacon.

No discussion of nineteenth-century historiography on Bacon should omit the flamboyant mid-century work of William Hepworth Dixon.[62] His "personal" history was almost as extreme in its defense of Bacon as was Abbott's moral condemnation. Dixon attacked what he called "the lie against nature in the name of Francis Bacon" which "broke into high literary force with Pope." "Before his day," he continued, "the scandal had only oozed in the slime of Weldon, Chamberlain, and D'Ewes. Pope picked it, as he might have picked a rough old flint, from the mud; fanged it, poisoned it, set it on his shaft." Dixon did not spare his pen on Bacon's nineteenth-century adversaries either. "Lingard paints him with a more unctuous hate." "Macaulay, in turn, is fierce and gay: his sketch of Rembrandt power: his lights too high, his smears too black: moon on the brow, dusk at the heart." Hallam (considered basically favorable to Bacon by this writer) and Campbell were also subjected to Dixon's wrath. "What Hallam left dark and Campbell foul should be cleansed as soon as may be from dust and stain. It is our due."[63] Dixon wrote as if he were ordained to admonish those guilty of "sins against Francis Bacon." "If it be true that the Father of modern Science was a rogue and cheat, it is also most true that we have taken a rogue and cheat to be our god." Dixon looked to Spedding's work (then in progress) with great optimism. "The lie," he noted, "it may be hoped, is about to pass away."[64]

Dixon's study, although based on some knowledge of the sources, showed no insight into Bacon's political character, and stands as a piece of flowery, empty rhetoric. It is an example of nineteenth-century biographical writing at its worst.

Twentieth-century scholarship on Bacon has materialized somewhat unevenly. While there has been a wealth of critical study of the *Essays* and the major philosophical writings, as well as efforts to evaluate him as a philosopher and contributor to the development of modern science, there has been only modest progress in subjecting his political career to complete analysis. Modern biographers, while discarding for the most part the Macaulayan prejudices, have not been attracted much to the exclusively political side of Bacon. More popular-type biographies have dominated. Quite often the emphasis has been on Bacon's great diversity of genius, with the intention of showing his many sides. His intellect, however, continues to be the main focus.

The flowery, popularly styled studies of such writers as Mary Sturt,[65] Bryan Bevan,[66] A. Wigfall Green,[67] and Charles Williams[68] are of little value to the serious student of Bacon. These works attempt to dramatize their subject's all-around virtuosity, without much insight into his character. All four biographies, and Sturt's in particular, are superficially praiseworthy in their characterizations. More scholarly, but somewhat archaically moralistic in its judgment of Bacon's character, is the brief study by Israel Levine.[69] Also scholarly but limited in scope is the capsule sketch by the Earl of Brinkhead,[70] and the incomplete study by Alfred Dodd.[71] The recent works of J. G. Crowther,[72] Fulton Anderson,[73] and Catherine Drinker Bowen[74] stand as the most thoughtful modern interpretations.

Crowther's intelligent biography revolves around the theme stated in its title; Bacon was the first statesman of modern science. "Bacon, who entered politics to obtain the political power to use science for the restoration of man to his position before the fall, struggled with problems of political behaviour which trouble the

16

scientists of today who wish to see their work used for the good of mankind." Bacon, Crowther believes, was "the first scientist to enter politics on a major scale primarily for scientific ends."[75] This interpretation, while open to challenge, is certainly worthy of interest. Crowther bases his theme around Bacon's statement that "power to do good" was "the true and lawful end of aspiring."[76] Bacon adhered to a strong belief in the constructive use of political power. Although he strove to impress James I with his plans for a new approach to learning, and hoped to spark realization of such plans from a position of power, one must question the accuracy of saying "he entered politics . . . primarily for scientific ends." Crowther appears fascinated by this theme, and makes it the main point of his study. He is not insensitive, however, to Bacon's self-seeking motives or his weaknesses. He is aware of the problem of studying Bacon's character and sees his personal psychology as "slightly abnormal." "Different activities of his mind," he added, "were kept in separate compartments" . . . and "this psychology of a divided mind may have contributed to the distrust in which he was held." Such psychology also led Bacon to "social isolation" and "restricted his intuitive understanding." Bacon, Crowther contends, "tried to make up for this by intellectual effort."[77] This view of Bacon as someone who failed to develop a completely integrated personality is worth more development than Crowther gives it. He is interested enough in Bacon's character to raise some interesting ideas, but is primarily committed to developing the "statesman of science" theme. His book is actually divided into two parts with the section "For Mankind" exclusively devoted to Bacon's scientific accomplishments. Crowther strives at uncovering the "whole man" in Bacon and this approach limits the effectiveness with which he can study his political character.

The most scholarly of the modern studies of Bacon is the one by Fulton Anderson. Anderson's main interest has been Bacon's philosophy, and he devotes a substantial portion of his book to interpreting it.[78] He is primarily interested in showing the systematic basis of Bacon's thought and applying it to both his intellectual and political careers. Anderson also subscribes (though not so completely as Crowther) to the view that Bacon sought to revolutionize learning via the use of political power. Bacon is studied mainly as a philosopher who functioned in politics. His actions are seen largely as products of his fundamental ideas. "When

17

judged by principles fit for reasoned ethical criticism," writes Anderson, "Francis Bacon's character is one of the most virtuous to be found among men of great political renown. Bacon was eminently virtuous in that distinctive part of man which is called the human reason, . . . Bacon displayed in his life Aristotelian magnanimity, Plato's four cardinal virtues: justice, wisdom, fortitude, and temperance, and the three theological virtues, faith, hope, and charity, not to mention the attribute of honor whose source, in tradition, was the King."[79] By his own admission Anderson uses Bacon's ideas as a basis for understanding his character. The result is that, despite his solid analysis of Bacon's career and his refutation of the stereotypes about his character as "reckless, uninformed, even at times malevolent," Anderson's Bacon emerges as more intellectual than human.[80] While he rightly chides the past efforts of hasty moral judgment, he is reluctant to explore the possible weaknesses in Bacon's character. Bacon's behavior towards Essex is totally justified without question as are his actions as Lord Chancellor. Anderson is more concerned about studying Bacon's intellect than his character. One gets the impression that he feels Bacon's greatness compensated for any human weaknesses. His study is noteworthy, perhaps even brilliant, but it does not orient itself toward uncovering the political man in Francis Bacon.

Catherine Drinker Bowen's stylish biography stands as the most penetrating study of Bacon's character to date. Mrs. Bowen, a gifted writer, is completely fascinated by his intellect and personality, and has probed both in an effort to "discover" this somewhat elusive human being. She has portrayed "the Temper of a Man" with its many complexities. Bacon emerges for the first time in biographical writings as a sensitive being. She writes of a complex man, who emerges as quite believable. Even though Bacon went too far in his behavior against Essex, his bitter piece "Of Deformity" written shortly after Robert Cecil's death is justified as an expression of deep hatred against a family that had frustrated his career. The Lord Chancellor who had lacked discretion, is depicted as a bewildered and pathetic figure at his impeachment. He is seen as someone whose many frustrations had made him unable to control the success he finally achieved. Bacon, Bowen believes, was caught between political and intellectual ambitions, or as she terms them, "the ambition of the will" and "the ambition of the understanding." "There is no doubt also that his nature craved both sides," even though she is convinced that Bacon was happiest as a scholar and would have preferred a career exclusively devoted to learning.[81] Mrs. Bowen herself is most attracted to Bacon the intellectual. She seems to enjoy most discussing the philosopher-scholar intrigued by nature's mysteries. The period of his life after impeachment, in which he retired to full-time intellectual pursuits, is termed "A Noble Five Years." Bacon, she feels, was never freer or happier than he was during this period. His mind was no longer restrained by the rigors of an all-too-busy political life.

Mrs. Bowen's biography, brief as it may be, has been the most successful attempt at exploring Francis Bacon's reality. It is not, nor does it pretend to be, a purely political biography. The author was too interested in Bacon's intellectual virtuosity to study him merely as a legal and political figure. Had she approached him with the exhaustive thoroughness with which she handles his adversary Coke, she might well have depicted the political man in Bacon. Her work remains invaluable, however, to anyone attempting that task.

Four centuries of literature on Francis Bacon have shown how elusive an individual of such scope can remain. A variety of approaches to his life have produced various insights into his career and thought. These works have varied in quality and orientation. It is the contention here that despite the vast amount of attention given him, Bacon has yet to be studied in depth as a political man. He was far more than that to be sure; however, most of his life was spent in the active pursuit of politics. Further dissection of that life is needed.

1. Samuel R. Gardiner, "Francis Bacon," *Dictionary of National Biography* (New York, 1885), II, 336.

2. The 1670 edition of *The Life of the Right Honourable Francis Bacon, Bacon of Verulum, Viscount St. Alban* is the first selection in the standard collection of Bacon's writings. *See The Works of Francis Bacon*, ed. James Spedding, Robert L. Ellis, Douglas D. Heath (15 vols., Boston, 1861-64), I, 35-58. Rawley originally published the work in a collection of Bacon's writings entitled, *Resuscitato*.

3. *Ibid.*, 50, 52.

4. *Ibid.*, 40, 53.

5. *Ibid.*, 53.

6. Peter Boener, *Life of Bacon*, "Baconiana" (July, 1906), Vol. IV, Third Series, No. 15, 141-45. This brief "life" was published originally in 1647 as part of Boener's edition of the *Essays*.

7. *The Letters and Life of Francis Bacon*, ed. James Spedding (7 vols., London, 1861-74), VII, 286.

8. Ben Jonson, *The Man and His Work*, ed. C. H. Hereford and Percy Simpson (11 vols., Oxford, 1925-52), VIII, 225.

9. *Ibid.*, 592. The statement is from *The Discoveries*.

10. Pierre Amboise, *Discourse on the Life of M. Francis Bacon, Chancellor of England* (Paris, 1631) trans. by G. C. Cunningham in "Baconiana" (April, 1906), Vol. IV, Third Series, No. 14, 72-78.

11. *Ibid.*, 75.

12. *Ibid.*, 75-76.

13. *Baconiana or Remains of Francis Bacon* (London, 1679), 6.

14. *Ibid.*, 270.

15. *Ibid.*, 263-66. Heylin's comments were made in *Life of Archbishop Laud* and Sprat's in *History of the Royal Society*.

16. John Chamberlain, *The Chamberlain Letters*, ed. Elizabeth M. Thomson (New York, 1965), 253-54. The date of the letter was March 24, 1621.

17. James Howell, *The Familiar Letters of James Howell*, ed. Joseph Jacobs (London, 1892), 218-19.

18. Thomas Fuller, *The History of the Worthies of England* (3 vols., London, 1840), II, 422-23. The work was first published in 1662.

19. Sir Simonds D'Ewes, *The Autobiography and Correspondence of Simonds D'Ewes*, ed. James O. Halliwell (2 vols., London, 1845), I, 187, 191. These remarks were made in 1621.

20. *Ibid.*, 168-69.

21. *Ibid.*, 191-92. The inscription reads as follows: "Within this sty a hog doth lie that must be hang'd for villany."

22. *Ibid.*, 166.

23. George Smeeton, ed., *Historical and Biographical Tracts* (1820), 39. Weldon's *Court and Character of King James* (1610) is reprinted here. Weldon's hatred of Bacon was overpowering and Spedding considers him "an authority of no value." (*Letters and Life*, VI, 477).

24. Oliver L. Dick, ed. *Aubrey's Brief Lives* (Ann Arbor, 1962), 10. Aubrey's work first appeared in 1681.

25. This was from the "Essay on Man," Ep. IV. See A. D. W. Ward, *The Poetical Works of Alexander Pope* (London, 1885), 224.

26. David Hume, *The History of England From the Invasion of Julius Caesar to the Abdication of James the Second 1688* (6 vols., New York, 1867), IV, 318, 327, 460. The work was originally published in 1754.

27. David Mallet, *The Life of Francis Bacon, Lord Chancellor of England* (London, 1740).

28. *Ibid.*, 2.

29. *Ibid.*, 111.

30. Basil Montagu, *The Works of Francis Bacon, Lord Chancellor of England* (3 vols., Philadelphia, 1842), I, 17-117. These pages contain his *Life of Bacon*. The complete edition of Montagu's work (16 vols., London, 1825-34) remained the standard collection of Bacon's works until publication of the more thorough and

better organized volumes of Spedding, Ellis, and Heath. Montagu's organization is somewhat haphazard. He sandwiches speeches and letters in between philosophical writings and doesn't present a complete collection of the letters and speeches.

A laudatory but limited study of Bacon published around the same time as Montagu's was Thomas Martin's *The Character of Lord Bacon* (London, 1835). Martin, a barrister, was mainly interested in Bacon's legal ideas.

31. *Ibid.*, 114-16.

32. *Ibid.*, 116-17.

33. *Ibid.*, 117.

34. The famous essay, *Lord Bacon*, appeared originally in the "Edinburgh Review," July, 1837. *See* Thomas B. Macaulay, *Critical, Historical and Miscellaneous Essays and Poems* (Boston, 1880), II, 142-254.

35. *Ibid.*, 173.

36. *Ibid.*, 174.

37. *Ibid.*, 178.

38. *Ibid.*, 244, 212.

39. *Ibid.*, 254.

40. H. Trevor-Roper, ed., T. B. Macaulay, *Critical and Historical Essays* (New York, 1965), 21-22. The essay on Bacon has been purposely omitted from this edition.

41. Edwin A. Abbott, *Francis Bacon, An Account of His Life and Works* (London, 1885).

42. Fulton H. Anderson, *Francis Bacon, His Career and His Thought* (Los Angeles, 1962), 207-8.

43. Abbott, 319.

44. *Ibid.*, 326-30.

45. *Ibid.*, 330.

46. Richard W. Church, *Bacon* (New York, 1901).

47. *Ibid.*, 146-48.

48. John Lingard, *A History of England* (13 vols., Boston, 1853), IX, 185.

49. John Lord Campbell, *The Lives of the Lord Chancellors and Keepers of the Great Seal of England* (7 vols., Philadelphia, 1851), II, 238-364.

50. *Ibid.*, 355.

51. *Ibid.*, 339.

52. *Letters and Life*, VII, 572.

53. *Ibid.*, 575.

54. *DNB*, II, 328-49.

55. Samuel R. Gardiner, *History of England, 1603-1642* (10 vols., London, 1883), I, 194.

56. *DNB*, II, 336.

57. John Nichol, *Francis Bacon His Life and Philosophy* (London, 1907).

58. *Ibid.*, 205-6.

59. *Ibid.*, 207-8.

60. Thomas Fowler, *Bacon* (New York, 1881).

61. Henry Hallam, *The Constitutional History of England From the Accession of Henry VII to the Death of George II*, 5th ed. (New York, 1867), 207. This work was first published in 1827.

21

62. William H. Dixon, *Personal History of Lord Bacon* (Boston, 1861).
63. *Ibid.*, 3-6.
64. *Ibid.*, 7, 11.
65. Mary Sturt, *Francis Bacon* (London, 1932).
66. Bryan Bevan, *The Real Francis Bacon* (London, 1960).
67. A. Wigfall Green, *Sir Francis Bacon* (New York, 1966).
68. Charles Williams, *Bacon* (London, 1933).
69. Israel Levine, *Francis Bacon* (London, 1925).
70. Earl of Brinkhead, *Fourteen English Judges* (London, 1949).
71. Alfred Dodd, *Francis Bacon's Personal Life Story* (London, 1949).
72. J. G. Crowther, *Francis Bacon: The First Statesman of Science* (London, 1960).
73. *Francis Bacon, His Career. . . ,*
74. Catherine D. Bowen, *Frances Bacon: The Temper of a Man* (Boston, 1963).
75. Crowther, 16.
76. "Of Great Place." *Bacon's Works*, XII, 113.
77. Crowther, 328-32.
78. Anderson also wrote *The Philosophy of Francis Bacon* (Chicago, 1948).
79. Anderson, *Francis Bacon. . . ,* 237.
80. *Ibid.*, 3.
81. Bowen, 112.

CHAPTER II

BACON'S EARLY POLITICAL CAREER

Francis Bacon was destined by birthright to be a political man. The society of that era was structured so that careers were seldom determined by choice. For a successful career in politics substantial familial status was essential, and as a son of Sir Nicholas Bacon, Elizabeth's Lord Keeper and a nephew of Lord Burghley, Bacon possessed strong credentials.[1] He was born into a world that would offer him opportunities to pursue both scholarly and political endeavors. A combination of necessity and ambition dictated his active pursuit of the latter, while the quest for knowledge remained his first love.

Bacon crammed diverse interests into an extremely active life, and while best remembered for his intellectual achievements, he spent most of his mature life in politics. From the time he entered Parliament at the age of twenty, in 1581, until his impeachment forty years later, Bacon was politically active. He was reared in a family that was close to England's governmental pulse and was groomed early for a public career. Queen Elizabeth knew him as a boy, and apparently took a strong liking toward him. She referred to him as "the young Lord Keeper" and was impressed by his intelligence. Bacon grew up in the splendor of Sir Nicholas' Gorhambury House, with its many ornaments, all symbolic of the wealthy, cultured, Elizabethan squirearchy. The atmosphere of his youth exposed him fully to the world of status, learning, and luxury. The experiences of two years at Trinity College, Cambridge, from ages thirteen to fifteen, followed by a period of continental travel, were all part of the careful nurturing of Bacon's younger years.

Despite the fact that Sir Nicholas and Lady Ann Bacon cautiously guided the upbringing of their sons with an eye toward solid futures, Francis Bacon spent most of his mature life struggling desperately to overcome financial turmoil. His father's sudden death in 1579 left Francis (for whom a substantial inheritance was probably intended) the only son not yet well provided for. He was left a small amount of property and an income of £300 a year. For a spendthrift young man used to opulence, this would hardly prove adequate. The reasons Bacon was not left comfortable and secure remain unclear. The result, however, was that he faced perpetual economic frustration as he struggled to achieve the public career he mistakenly thought would fall easily into his hands. He subsequently recorded the painful discovery that "the rising into place is laborious."[2]

Despite the disappointment of his father's will, the young Bacon faced the Elizabethan political world with vigor and confidence. He saw the Queen's memory of his father and his linkage to the Cecils as valuable assets to advancement. In 1579 he moved into his father's quarters at Gray's Inn, to begin his study of the law. Although little is known of his actual studies, he would develop a knowledge of English law as well as a profound legal philosophy. Bacon was confident of his capacity to master the law and equally certain that it would serve as a vehicle for advancement in the royal service. He certainly did not envision utilizing the luxury and prestige of his father's chambers merely to become a court barrister.

Instead of concealing his impatience to advance in government, Bacon expressed himself all too openly. He approached his uncle in the autumn of 1580 with a polite but overanxious plea for help in achieving a modest position in the Crown's legal service. Burghley apparently received an indefinite but favorable response from the Queen regarding the young Bacon's hopes. The latter, naive and premature in his desires, interpreted this as meaning certain advancement. He failed to realize that Elizabeth was always quicker to encourage one's hopes than she was to fulfill them.[3] Bacon had not even been admitted to the bar as yet. Although he remained apologetic about his age, and admitted that he was "prepared and furnished thereunto with nothing but a multitude of lacks and imperfections," he wrote with a definite confidence in his own abilities.[4] As a youth not yet twenty, he already displayed the articulate pen that would always distinguish him. Such an attribute was not enough, however, to convince a conservative Queen of the immediate value of an over-ambitious young suitor.

While Bacon's initial effort to enter government failed, we do know that he was admitted to the bar as an Utter Barrister in 1582.[5] Elizabeth was apparently instrumental in this action, and later (after Bacon had antagonized her by his conduct during the 1593 Parliament) angrily referred to having "pulled" him "over the bar."[6] It is also known that he succeeded in securing a seat in Parliament as early as 1581. His parliamentary career was previously thought to have begun with the session of 1584-85. Little was known of his activities between 1580 and 1584, other than his admission to the legal profession. We are grateful to John Neale for discovering that Bacon was returned for Bossiney in Cornwall in a by-election in early 1581 (probably January), and sat in the parliamentary session of that year (the third and final sitting of a Parliament first convened in 1572). Neale admits that he has been unable to uncover any further information regarding any of Bacon's activities during the session, and it is highly probable that, as an inexperienced upstart of twenty, he was not chosen for many parliamentary duties.[7] Since Bacon had only a minor role in the 1584-85 Parliament, there is little reason to believe he was active significantly four years earlier. It is likely that Burghley was influential in securing the seat for him, although details of the episode are not known.

The session of 1584-85 marked Bacon's first entry into a newly convened Parliament.[8] Amidst the tense atmosphere of the mid-1580s he stood as a parliamentary novice, observing the weighty issues of the day. As the complex Catholic threat to England neared culmination, Elizabeth faced the problems of internal subversion and the impending threat of Spain. Philip II, while watching the chaotic situation in France, was cautiously awaiting the opportunity to launch his crusade. The queen faced more than a Catholic menace, however. The Protestant "extremists," or Puritans, had been trying for years to revolutionize her church. She detested their radicalism, and stood firm against them despite their strength in Parliament. They stood as a popular rallying force against a Catholic threat and vehemently expressed their views in the Commons. The young Bacon, himself already exposed to his mother's Puritan sympathies, had an opportunity to observe these weighty and intricate issues as they were debated. The setting was dramatic as Elizabeth desperately needed new legislation to buttress her own safety as well as that of her kingdom. She required the assistance of the religious enthusiasts but was wary of encouraging them too much.

Bacon quietly and attentively absorbed these dramatic and critical events. The brief references to his rather sparse activities during the session indicate, however, that he was very much a novice in parliamentary matters. He served on two committees, both of which dealt with relatively minor legal bills.[9] He also delivered a speech (probably the first of his career) on a bill that sought to insure the Crown's right to wardship on land held by knight service and leased for over a hundred years. Wardship was an antiquated practice and House opposition to it was vehement.[10] Bacon's exact position on the issue is unclear, since the fragmentary account hardly reveals anything conclusive. The diarist William Fleetwood, recorder of London and an experienced parliamentarian, seems to have disliked young Bacon. He responded sarcastically to the short excerpts he recorded and was obviously irritated by the upstart's sharp tongue.[11] As Neale puts it: "Perhaps the generality of the House reacted in the same way to this debut of a genius."[12] It is possible, although not specifically recorded, that Bacon's age and familial connections did cause resentment among his colleagues. He remained primarily an observer during the session, withholding for the moment at least his reactions to the critical issues of the day.

It is likely that Bacon did express himself privately to the Queen on one aspect of the religious question during the winter of 1584-85. Both Spedding and Gardiner credit him with authorship of a letter advising Elizabeth how to deal with the internal papal menace.[13] The letter called for more scrutiny in the treatment of English Papists. It advised keeping them discontented but not desperate; desperation (a condition the author believed was being created by the government) would only make them more dangerous. On the other hand, a more moderate loyalty oath would be adhered to by most English Catholics and might divide them "from that great mutual confidence which is now betwixt the Pope and them." The tone of the letter stressed reconciliation rather than further alienation of this segment of the population. Bacon (assuming his authorship of the document) also advocated greater leniency toward Puritan preachers. While admitting that he was "not given over, nor so much as addicted, to their preciseness," he thought the Bishop's policy of persecuting them to be "a very evil and unadvised course." It succeeded only in furthering the disunity of Her Majesty's Protestant subjects during a period when the achievement of unity was critically important. The theme of necessity of religious unity runs throughout the letter.[14] Bacon demonstrated his ability to comprehend and reflect on an issue of great severity and showed an inclination toward moderate religious views. Throughout his long career he would staunchly advocate religious harmony. The view that complete harmony in the state was crucial to its survival would eventually lie at the heart of his political thinking. It is interesting to see him, still a very young man, already developing a reverence for harmony as he attempted to probe the difficult religious questions facing England in the mid-1580s.

Politically, Francis Bacon was still a novice. In 1585, he made another unsuccessful attempt to secure a government position. Little is known about his suit, but there were objections to Bacon on the grounds that he was too young for the particular position.[15] Bacon was apparently resented in the legal profession. Having been admitted to the Bar in 1582, he tried successfully through Burghley to have the customary five-year waiting period for practicing in the Westminster courts shortened.[16] Such an action was not popularly received, and Bacon reacted by defending himself to his uncle. "I know well and I most humbly beseech your Lordship to believe, that arrogancy and over-weening is so far from my nature, as if I think well of myself in anything it is that I am free from that vice."[17] He showed he was sensitive to criticism, but not frightened by it. Arrogance is a characteristic that many would find appropriate in describing Bacon throughout his life. We know too little about him, this early in his career, to determine whether he had earned such a label. He was indeed able, ambitious, and anxious. He was also already feeling frustrated in his attempt to enter Elizabeth's government.

Parliament met next in 1586-87, and again Bacon found himself

27

in a setting of developing tension.[18] The threat to Elizabeth and to Protestantism in England had reached a climax since Parliament convened four days after Mary Stuart had been found guilty of treason by a tribunal of commissioners. Elizabethan Parliaments had been calling for Mary's execution since the early 1570s and their wish now appeared close to fulfillment. While the Queen hesitated to issue the final execution order during the late autumn and early winter of 1586-87, Parliament pressured her out of indecision. We know that Bacon spoke out in favor of Mary's execution. The contents of his speech are not known, but it is reasonably certain that it echoed the general temper of the House.[19]

After the issue of Mary, religion and foreign policy dominated the business of the session. Bacon again appears to have stayed out of religious debates in the House. The Puritan fervor was even greater than last session, and the Queen remained adamant in her resistance to pressure. Despite his thoughts on the issue, Bacon was apparently content to remain uninvolved in what was already a highly complex and extremely bitter controversy. He did participate, however, in the debate over the handling of the subsidy. The Netherlands campaign had already been costly, and as of then, was far from won. Moreover, the threat of a Spanish invasion was now very great, since Mary's execution had all but guaranteed that Philip II would attack England. Parliament was willing to help, but sought to intensify the Queen's campaign in the Netherlands, arguing that this was the best way to stifle a Spanish attack. Elizabeth still wanted to proceed cautiously across the channel. Many in the House wanted any loan or benevolence to be granted only if the Queen pursued full-scale war, and some even sought to force her to accept an official title of ruler over the Dutch provinces. Bacon, appointed to the committee chosen to consider a loan or benevolence, appears to have advocated that no string be attached to any grant.[20] He debated on February 24 (before the committee actually met), and among the fragments of the speech recorded are the words, "preposterous the vale to judge of the hill; etcetera."[21] Such a remark suggests that Bacon believed the Crown's right to determine foreign policy should not be restricted by Parliament. The comment also suggests that Bacon favored Royal leadership as being natural to the makeup of the realm. The words are fragmentary, however, and cannot be taken as a comprehensive description of Bacon's political position. Neale apparently feels they justify his own contention that Bacon was "already a prerogative man."[22] In light of Bacon's later career, such a remark is perhaps understandable. It is questionable, however, whether Bacon can, as of yet, be "labeled" conclusively. If one is to judge him in 1587 by the fact that he spoke in favor of Mary's execution, then it must be assumed that he believed the Crown's action should be guided by Parliament's wishes in some matters. The sources describing Bacon's political activity are too fragmentary in this early period to allow us to categorize him rigidly. Furthermore, if he is to be termed "already a prerogative man" by 1587, then his maverick behavior during the Parliament of 1593 is most difficult to understand. Bacon was still a political novice, constantly observing, occasionally participating, and always seeking an opening that might lead to political power.[23]

The "Protestant wind" saved England in the summer of 1588 as Philip II's "enterprise" met its disastrous fate. Elizabeth, far from jubilant, immediately feared another Spanish effort. The Parliament that met in February, 1589, was summoned to provide a double subsidy for defense of the realm. Although the House was willing to grant this extraordinary sum, it disliked establishing the precedent of double subsidies, and insisted on a precautionary clause to safeguard against this practice in the future. Francis Bacon, sitting in his fourth Parliament, was selected to word the clause.[24] Although we do not know just what he wrote, he enthusiastically supported the measure and appears to have been significantly involved in the most important business of the session.[25]

The 1589 session marked Bacon's emergence as an active participant in the Commons. His name appears more frequently on committee lists, and, for the first time, as a reporter of committee business.[26] His skill as a speaker was also beginning to be recognized. It is known he spoke supporting a House effort "to reform disorders in purveyors."[27] Purveyance was an old medieval device by which the Crown could purchase products at below the market price. The government officials (known as purveyors) who did the purchasing were known to demand bribes for not buying more of a given product than the Crown actually needed. Since this meant that gentry and merchants alike were on occasion forced to sell goods at as little as a quarter of the market price, the dissatisfaction in the Commons was quite understandable. Bacon's speech on the measure, the details of which are again not known, was motivated jointly by a desire to support a just action and the hope of winning the trust of his colleagues. Neale says the bill threatened the prerogative because it sought to reform what had been an unlimited royal right. Apparently Elizabeth was of the same opinion, since she promptly killed the measure after the Commons had passed it.[28] Having stood in support of this bill opposed by the Crown, Bacon showed himself to be an emerging political figure as of yet fitting no rigid categorization. The Parliament of 1589 may be said, however, to mark the end of Bacon's apprenticeship period in Parliament. His more frequent role in business, and his apparent acceptance by his colleagues, indicate that he had (if nothing else) at least gained recognition as a capable member of the Lower House.

Although he had remained outside of the religious debates in Parliament, Bacon demonstrated concern and thoughtful observation in 1589. The defeat of the Armada had substantially defused the Puritan movement. An attempt to regain this fervor manifested itself in a furious pamphlet campaign characterized by the pen name "Martin Marprelate." This controversy, which reached its peak during the summer of 1589, interested Bacon enough to inspire him to write the tract, "An Advertisement Touching the Controversies of the Church of England."[29] He showed his understanding of the complex Puritan movement by advocating suppression of the more extreme Marprelate tracts. He did not believe that total suppression was the key to solving the over-all Puritan controversy, and again stressed the need for a conciliatory attitude on all sides. Religious harmony was still his goal as he appealed to the more moderate Puritans, "who, although they have not cut themselves off from the body and communion of the church, yet do they affect certain cognizances and differences, wherein they seek to correspond among themselves, and to be separated from others."[30] These people could, he believed, still be reconciled to the Church; the Bishops must, however, display a willingness to compromise heretofore in evidence. "Quiet, moderate and private assemblies and conferences of the learned" should discuss the issues; meetings burdened with emotion were doomed to failure. "I repeat," wrote Bacon, "that a character of love is more proper for debates of this nature than that of zeal."[31] This tract argues that moderation could solve even the most intricate problems, and that men naturally sought a condition of harmony. While these precepts are fundamental to Bacon's over-all philosophy, the attempt to apply them here suggests possible naïveté about the emotional quality of Puritanism. It is true that Elizabethan Puritanism was still an embryonic movement, without the over-all strength that tore through England after Bacon's death. There perhaps was reason to think in the late 1580s that removed from its own extremes and treated differently by the Elizabethan hierarchy, the movement could still be reconciled with the official Church. Bacon studied the Puritan tracts and saw this possibility as feasible. Although he had also been exposed to his own mother's Puritanism, it still remains questionable whether he ever understood the depth of the Puritanical convictions. His efforts in the 1580s to advise on religious affairs should perhaps be seen as the thoughtful attempts of a concerned man, a gifted writer, and a developing philosopher. It remains questionable, however, whether he ever fully grasped the character of radical Protestantism.

By the close of the 1580s Francis Bacon still found himself outside the structure of political power. His familial status had opened the doors to legal practice, to a career in Parliament, but as of yet had not proven to be the key to governmental position and financial security.[32] As he developed his views, he was most eager to impress those in power with his ability to speak and write intelligently. Bacon was not yet deeply frustrated in the struggle to rise. Aware of Elizabeth's caution in advancing people, and still confident he would convince her of his worthiness to follow along his father's path in serving the Crown, Bacon had taken these first steps toward becoming a political man. He had bred some resentment, won some respect, and showed a youthful eagerness and a gifted pen. He had not yet learned how brutal the struggle for power could be. The 1590s were to provide him with that lesson.

1. Sir Nicholas Bacon had five sons. Edward, Nicholas, and Nathaniel were by his first wife, Jane Fernley, and Anthony and Francis by Ann Cooke. Lady Ann Bacon, as she was known, was a sister-in-law to William Cecil (Lord Burghley).

2. "Of Great Place," *Bacon's Works*, XII, 112.

3. *Letters and Life*, I, 12-15. The first letter to Burghley, dated September 16, 1580, implied that Bacon had already discussed the subject of his advancement with his uncle. The second, dated October 18, 1580, indicated that Bacon believed he had practically been assured a position by the Queen. He graciously thanked

Burghley, noting that he felt "exceeding comfort and encouragement . . . setting forth and putting myself in way towards her Majesty's service."

4. *Ibid.*, 14.

5. *Ibid.*, 15. The date was June 15.

6. *Ibid.*, 348. Bacon refers to this statement by the Queen in a letter to his brother Anthony, January 25, 1595.

7. I am most grateful to Sir John for permission to use this material. It was granted in a personal letter of September 15, 1964, after the knowledge of his discovery had been made available to me by Mrs. Elizabeth Foster. Mr. Neale specified that he knew of no new material concerning any role Bacon may have played in the 1581 session. He asked me to credit his discovery to the *History of Parliament Trust*. The latter will be publishing the information in the Elizabethan section of its *History of Parliament*. It should be added that this discovery is confirmed by two standard parliamentary sources. In a speech delivered in Parliament, November 28, 1601, Bacon mentioned that he had "been a member of the House these seven Parliaments," and that he had been present when one Arthur Hall was committed to the Tower. That incident occurred in 1581. See Heywood Townshend, *Historical Collections* (London, 1680), 260. In a parliamentary address of May 22, 1610, Bacon referred to specific activities that occurred in the House in "a °23 Eliz." This would again be the year 1581. See *Parliamentary Debates in 1610*, ed. Samuel Gardiner (London, 1862), 38.

8. *Letters and Life*, I, 37. He sat as a representative from the borough of Melcombe in Dorset. Spedding points out that Burghley had also secured a seat from Gatton, but Francis obviously chose to sit for Melcombe instead. Apparently the latter seat was obtained with the help of another maternal uncle.

9. On December 9, 1584, Bacon served on a committee that considered a bill "for redress of disorders in Common Informers." "On March 5, 1585, he was appointed to a committee selected to treat a bill concerning 'The Latitats of the Peace in the King's Bench.' " The recorder refers to this latter measure as being "of no great moment." There is no record of his activities on either of these bodies. See Sir Simonds D'Ewes, *The Journals of All the Parliaments During the Reign of Queen Elizabeth of Both Houses* (London, 1682), 337, 363.

10. For an adequate discussion of the bill *see* J. E. Neale, *Elizabeth I and Her Parliaments, 1584-1601* (New York, 1958), 91-94.

11. British Museum, Landsdowne MS 43, fol. 175. This brief diary (fols. 164-75) is made up of remarks by three members of the 1584-85 Parliament, Francis Alford, Thomas Digges, and William Fleetwood.

To Bacon's remark, "I will open plainly to you that this Bill is harsh in some points," Fleetwood responded: "If he had as substantially answered as he confessed it plainly!" Bacon, speaking of the Queen's worthiness then said that "his father had received by her, ability to leave a fifth son to live upon: but that is nothing to the matter." The annoyed Fleetwood retorted, "Then you should have left it alone."

12. *Elizabeth I. . .* , 93.

13. Spedding explains thoroughly why he believes the paper was possibly and not improbably his (Bacon's) composition." See *Letters and Life*, I, 43-46. Gardiner attributes the letter to Bacon without qualification. He considers it an important work showing Bacon's advanced thinking on the subject. See *DNB*, II, 329.

14. *Letters and Life*, I, 47-56.

15. *Ibid.*, 57. The only information about this quest for office is contained in a brief letter to Sir Francis Walsingham, August 25, 1585.

16. *Ibid.*, 58.

17. *Ibid.*, 59-60. This letter to Burghley was written May 6, 1586.

18. *Ibid.*, 63. Bacon sat this time for the Borough of Tauton in Somersetshire.

19. D'Ewes, 393-94. Bacon spoke on November 4, 1586, and was appointed to committee dealing with the issue on the same day.

20. *Ibid.*, 410. The date was February 23, 1587.

21. Neale, *Elizabeth I . . .* , 175-76.

22. *Ibid.*, 175.

23. D'Ewes, 410, 417. Bacon also served on two other committees during this session. On February 25, 1587, he was appointed to a body selected to discuss a bill of Attainder after its second reading. On March 20 he was put on a committee chosen to confer with the Lords about a bill for the Continuance of Statutes.

24. *Ibid.*, 431, 433. Bacon sat for Liverpool this time. He was chosen for the job on February 17, 1589, and at the same time offered his services to read the clause to the Queen's Counsel. This job, however, was reserved for the Speaker. These events occurred in a committee first chosen to consider the subsidy on February 11.

25. Neale says that "the mild, ineffective words finally incorporated in the preamble appear to have been composed by Burghley." *Elizabeth I . . .* , 205.

26. On February 25, Bacon reported to the House (from a committee to which he had been appointed on February 22) on a "bill for the Assurance of the Jointure of Ann the Wife of Henry Nevill esquire." On February 26, he reported on the framing of a bill concerning forestallers, regrators, and ingressors (D'Ewes, 437-39). Bacon also served on a committee (February 10) chosen to consider motions made for Burgesses returned for the session but who were "sick and wish to have others serve in their place," on one (February 12) selected to consider a privilege case of a member (Mr. Aylmer) who had been subpoenaed by the Star Chamber, and on a committee (February 25) appointed to confer with the Lords on a bill for the abridgement of proclamations to be had upon fines levied at the Common Law (*Ibid.*, 430, 432, 439).

27. *Ibid.*, 432. The date of the speech was February 15.

28. *Elizabeth I . . .* , 209-11. Neale discusses the progress of the purveyance bill, but does not mention Bacon's speech.

29. *Letters and Life*, I, 73-95. Spedding points out that the document, written "for circulation in manuscript" during the summer of 1589, was not published until 1640.

30. *Ibid.*, 90.

31. *Ibid.*, 94.

32. *Ibid.*, 102-3. Burghley did secure Bacon's appointment to the reversion of the office of Clerk of the Counsel in Star Chamber in October, 1589. The post was worth some £1,600 per year, but it would be twenty years before it fell vacant and Bacon could claim it.

CHAPTER III

THE STRUGGLE TO RISE: THE PARLIAMENT OF 1593 AND ITS CONSEQUENCES

The early 1590s would prove crucial in shaping Francis Bacon's political behavior. He would find himself struggling desperately for high office, driven by both a desire for power, and what had become chronic financial insecurity. Bacon was also developing his thoughts on legal reform and learning as he seriously tried to penetrate the structure of government. Thus he was motivated by both the necessity to advance personally, and a growing desire to utilize power for progress. An analysis of the motivation behind Bacon's prolonged effort to advance politically is relevant to this study. It is always difficult to evaluate the curious combination of self-seeking and idealistic motives that push an individual. In Bacon's case the early 1590s were a furious period during which he found himself important in Parliament, but still frustrated vocationally and financially, and beset with a strong desire to expand intellectually. Bacon was now searching for some kind of fulfillment, and the search would indeed prove agonizing.

Bacon sought any avenue to Elizabeth's good graces that seemed available. There was still the Cecil family, even though Burghley had thus far been of little help. Bacon apparently never perceived that his uncle saw his advancement as a possible impediment to that of his own deformed son, and thus would never champion his cause with enthusiasm. In a letter to the elder Cecil in 1592, Bacon showed how desperate he had become by combining flattery with an open admission of his financial troubles. He referred to his uncle as "the Atlas of this commonwealth, the honour of my house," admitting that "the meanness of my estate doth somewhat move me." The letter stressed Bacon's destitute position while offering his services humbly and sincerely. It also contained an expression of what may be termed his deeper thoughts:

> Lastly, I confess that I have as vast contemplative ends, as I have moderate civil ends: for I have taken all knowledge to be my province; and if I could purge it of two sorts of rovers, where of the one with frivolous disputations, confutations, and verbosities, the other with blind experiments and curricular traditions and impostures, hath committed so many spoils, I hope I should bring in industrious observations, grounded conclusions and profitable inventions and discoveries; the best state of that province.[1]

Bacon indeed showed his dilemma; he eagerly sought help to advance politically, yet craved a contemplative life that would be best pursued by someone freed from the pressure to which he was subjected. Burghley still might help in some way—or so he thought.

While he may not have fully grasped the Cecil family's reasons for not furthering his career, he did not continue to rely solely on their support. He turned to the Earl of Essex as his principal patron, launching a relationship that was eventually to reverse itself full course. From 1591-1595, however, Bacon and Essex were on close terms. Much has been written about their relationship, and Bacon's role in prosecuting Essex has often been cited as evidence of his "cold, sinister" character. Their friendship was for some years quite cordial, and although they were of different temperaments, each recognized the utility of a friendly relationship. Bacon met Essex through his brother Anthony. Although he lacked the Earl's flamboyance, the two became friends very quickly. Bacon probably saw Essex as his most likely channel to advancement. The Earl was the rising favorite at Court, and while he stood as the Cecils' potential rival (the lines of rivalry were not yet clearly drawn in the early 1590s), Essex possessed an appreciation of intellectual pursuits and seemed interested in popularizing Bacon's contemplated innovations in learning at court. Bacon was most attracted by Essex's sympathetic attitude toward his ideas, and was convinced that the Earl's influence was rising so rapidly that he would be an excellent

35

influential link to the Crown. Essex was himself a born innovator, interested also in conquering the conservative minds of the government. He had the mentality to understand Bacon's plans to revolutionize learning. He was also fascinated by the latter's scholarly inclinations and might have considered an "idea man" useful in penetrating the heights of political power. "If Essex seemed like a man expressly made to realize the hopes of a new world," writes Spedding, "so Bacon may seem to have been expressly made for the guardian genius of such a man as Essex."[2]

The relationship was so firmly established by early 1593 that Francis Bacon would write:

> I applied myself wholly to him, in a manner which I think happeneth rarely amongst men. For I did not only labour carefully and industriously in that he set me about, whether it were matter of advice, or otherwise; . . . I did nothing but devise and ruminate with myself, to the best of my understanding, propositions and memorials of anything that might concern his lordship's honour, fourtune or service.[3]

Bacon believed he had found the key to rising. What he had actually done was to thrust himself into the struggles and intrigues of political life.

Since a gifted man could also use his talents to impress his superiors, Bacon tried flattering Elizabeth with an eloquently written "Discourse in the Praise of His Sovereign." He composed it for a court celebration in 1592 marking the anniversary of the Queen's accession.[4] "How admirable is her discourse;" wrote Bacon "whether it be in learning, state or love, what variety of knowledge; what rareness of conceit; what choice of words; what grace of utterance."[5] He praised each characteristic of the Queen. With respect to statesmanship, he portrayed her as the great champion of Protestantism's struggle against Spain. Most revealing was his praise of her handling of domestic affairs. He referred to "her exquisite judgment in choosing and finding good servants; . . . her profound discretion in assigning and appropriating every one of them to their aptest employment; her penetrating sight in discovering every man's ends and drifts; her wonderful art in keeping servants in satisfaction, and yet in appetite."[6] Bacon obviously sought to show Elizabeth that he respected her discretion in making appointments, hoping that she would see this as a sign of his own worthiness. Despite such praise, and despite the fact that Bacon demonstrated a sound understanding of matters of state, Elizabeth was not immediately moved to upgrade the aspiring Bacon. He remained very much "in appetite," and "dissatisfaction."[7]

In February, 1593, Essex became a Privy Councillor. That same month the Attorney-Generalship fell vacant, and two men began contesting for the position: Edward Coke and Francis Bacon. Thus began the long and bitter rivalry between the two. Coke, nine years Bacon's senior, and already Solicitor-General, was the obvious choice. There was no doubt that he was far better qualified than the legally inexperienced Bacon. The latter's main asset in this effort was Essex's persistent support. The Earl, whose influence at court was formidable, was confident he could persuade the Queen in favor of his candidate. Coke won out, but was not appointed until April, 1594. It is possible that Elizabeth never seriously considered Bacon's candidacy; however, Essex did manage to convince her to hesitate for a year before disclosing her decision. Since both aspirants could participate in the Parliament convened on February 19, 1593, the Queen could observe their behavior during the session.[8] Bacon was perhaps not aware just how closely his performance in this Parliament would be observed.

As usual, Elizabeth urgently needed money, and the session of 1593 was summoned primarily for that purpose. Philip II had gained the allegiance of several powerful Scottish nobles and again posed a threat to the security of England. Aside from having to guard against such a danger, the Queen was still sustaining armies in both France and the Netherlands. The subsidies granted in 1589 had run out, and she had already been forced to sell Crown lands to obtain revenue. Parliamentary funds were now a necessity.

Because the Puritan movement had been substantially defused since the Armada, the Queen had good reason to expect relatively little difficulty with the body convened in 1593.

> With the Parliament of 1593 comes a change of complexion. The previous assembly of 1589, though also a war-Parliament, had been stiffened by a national synod of Puritan ministers, meeting in London to organize and stimulate agitation in the House of Commons. In this respect it had been like its predecessors. But in 1593, there was no national synod and the Puritan classical movement was defunct. In the course of their hunt for Martin Marprelate, the ecclesiastical authorities had uncovered this

37

secret ministerial organization, and fortified by the refulsion against the Marprelate excess and by the sterner mood of wartime, had ventured to strike out at its leaders.[9]

Despite such a situation, islands of protest in the personages of the redoubtable Peter Wentworth and a certain James Morice remained to assure the session of some significant controversy. Bacon too provided something of an obstructionist voice during this Parliament. While he can never be categorized as a "rebel" against government policy, his stubborn independence during this session, particularly in his stand on the subsidy, represents a curious twist in the pattern of his political behavior.

This is the first of Bacon's Parliaments for which the sources provide a clear picture of his activities. He played important roles on several committees and was of course a most significant speaker. Early in the session, he served on a committee that dealt with liberties and privileges of members and their servants. Its task was to examine and report all cases dealing with elections, returns and privileges. Freedom of action in the House was wanting and the re-election of such a committee shows the great concern for internal liberty.[10] Although little is known of the committee's activities, it is not unreasonable to assume that Bacon was in agreement with its purpose.

Sir Robert Cecil made the Crown's initial request for supply and Bacon endorsed it immediately. He went on record at once as a government supporter in this important business, emphasizing the need to protect the realm from a three-sided Catholic menace— Spain, the Pope, and the Holy League—and pointing out that Philip had also been conducting treacherous activities in Ireland, the low countries, France, and Scotland.[11] This is all that is known about the main part of the speech, but an important fragment of its introduction has been preserved. Bacon prefaced his plea to support the Crown with remarks stressing Parliament's role as a lawmaking body. He apparently was concerned that finance was becoming that body's main function and saw the need to emphasize what he felt was one of its traditional roles:

> The cause of the assembling of all Parliament hath been heretofore Laws or Money; the one being the sinews of peace, the other of war. To the one I am not privy; but the other I should know. I did take great contentment in her Majesty's speeches the other

day delivered by the Lord Keeper, how that it was . . . a thing
not to be done suddenly nor at one Parliament; nor scarce a
whole year would suffice, to purge the statute book not lessen the
volume of law; being so many in number that neither common
people can half practice them, nor the lawyer sufficiently understand them; then the which nothing should tend more to the eter-
nal praise of her Majesty.

The Romans appointed ten men who were to correct and recall
all former laws, and set forth their twelve Tables, so much of all
to be commended. The Athenienes likewise appointed six to that
purpose. And Lewis IX of France did the like in reforming of
laws.[12]

In these remarks Bacon expressed a great concern for the necessity
of law reform, a subject upon which he was to speak frequently
in future Parliaments, and to philosophize about in his writings.
Neale's view that this statement showed that Bacon "was as irrele-
vant as old recorder Fleetwood, without the latter's humor or sense
of timing," and his comment "it looks as if he were showing off,"
is harsh.[13] There was perhaps a flamboyant tone to Bacon's remarks, and it is possible that he also sought to impress upon his
colleagues that he was not an unqualified supporter of the government proposal. His subsequent maverick behavior on the subsidy
issue convinces me that Bacon was sincere in his remarks. He
would in the future always display a genuine concern for Parliament's lawmaking role.

Bacon immediately became involved in formulation of the subsidy. He and several other lawyers were chosen to draw up a preamble to the bill guarding against costly precedents.[14] The Crown
then demanded a triple subsidy, and both houses were thrown into
joint conference to discuss the larger grant. Bacon again directly
involved himself by speaking out for the Commons on what became
a privilege dispute.[15] The Commons traditionally initiated monetary
grants, and joint action by both houses was deemed a blow to precedent. By agreeing with this view, Bacon told his colleagues that
while he supported the grant, he felt the right of the House had to
be maintained. He said,

The custom and privilege of this House had always been first to
make offer of the subsidies from hence, then to the Upper House,
except it were that they present a Bill unto this House, with desire
of our assent thereto, and then to send it up again. A reason it is,
that we should stand upon our privilege, seeing the burthen rest-

eth upon us as the greatest number; nor is it reason the thanks should be theirs. And in joining with them in this motion, we shall derogate from ours; for the thanks will be theirs and the blame ours, they being the first movers.

To avoid friction with the peers, he suggested adherence to a precedent of Henry VIII's time, "where four of the Lords came down into the House of Commons, and informed them what necessity there was of a subsidy."[16] Bacon's stand and his proposed compromise were popular with his colleagues. He had defended the Commons' privilege and displayed a formidable legal knowledge of popular parliamentary precedents. It was an unusual stand for one competing for high office, and although there is no evidence of any official reaction to Bacon's speech, it certainly could not have improved his standing with the Queen. After a lengthy debate, the Lower House finally agreed to a joint conference with the Lords; the subsidy, however, was to be initiated solely by the former. Bacon had been instrumental in effecting a compromise, had won the respect of his colleagues, and showed a determination to proceed cautiously on this rather expensive request.[17]

Bacon's most dramatic and significant action on subsidy was yet to come. Although the Crown modified its demand by allowing payment of the triple subsidy to span four years instead of the three-year term originally requested, many in the Commons, including Bacon, believed that even the revised term was still too burdensome on the Queen's subjects. In objecting to payment that would span less than six years, Bacon took the boldest stand yet on the subsidy issue. He was no longer merely bickering with the Lords, but standing in actual opposition to the policy of the Crown itself. His speech remains one of the most famous and important of his parliamentary career.

> Mr. Francis Bacon assented to three subsidies, but not the payments under six years. And to this propounded three questions, which he desired might be answered. The first impossibility or difficulty; the second danger or discontentment; and thirdly, a better manner of supply than subsidy. For impossibility; the poor men's rent is such, as they are not able to yield it, not to pay so much for the present. The gentlemen must sell their Plate, and farmers their Brass Pots, ere this will be paid. And for us we are here to search the wounds of the realm and not to skin them over; therefore not to persuade ourselves of their wealth more than it

is. The dangers are these. We shall first breed discontent in paying these subsidies, and in the cause endanger her Majesty's safety, which must consist more in the love of the people than in their wealth; and therefore not to give them discontentment in paying these subsidies; Thus we run into a double peril. In putting two payments into one, we make double subsidy. For it maketh four shillings in the pound a double payment. The second is this, that this being granted in this sort, other Princes hereafter will look for the like; so we shall put an evil precedent upon ourselves, and our posterity. And in Histories it is to be observed, that of all nations the English are not to be subject, base or taxable. The manner of supply may be by Levy or Imposition, when need shall most require; so when her Majesties Coffers are empty, they may be fitted by this means.[18]

Although the account is incomplete, the recorded words reveal much. Bacon believed that the proposed term was both economically unfair and politically unwise.

What compelled him to take such a stand? He did not persist in his opposition, since the House passed a triple subsidy "to be made in four years," the day after Bacon's speech, and there is no record of any further statement by him.[19] Neale is shocked by Bacon's behavior. He calls it "a strange blunder . . . for so astute a person." "If he foresaw its repercussions . . . Then he was a courageous man: but perhaps he had merely become intoxicated by popularity —an unaccustomed experience for him."[20] Was it only a desire to enjoy the momentary benefits of newly won popularity that caused Bacon to take the position? Bacon knew that Elizabeth would be watching him, and perhaps felt she would admire and respect the honesty of his views. He was still politically naive enough to believe that he could speak his conscience on important matters without damaging his governmental ambitions. He may have been somewhat "intoxicated by popularity," but he was primarily inspired by his own convictions. He would always believe in utilizing power constructively, and in this case he felt it was wrong to overburden the people with a highly concentrated tax. The year 1593 marks the high water mark of Bacon's idealism in Parliament.

Besides being involved in several other issues, Bacon made another major speech during the session.[21] He hoped to impress the Queen with his unselfishness by speaking against a "Bill for the Better Expedition of Justice in the Star Chamber."[22] Bacon held the reversion of the clerkship of that court; had the bill passed, it

41

probably would have meant that the present clerk would have been removed in his favor since the measure directed itself against the former's alleged abuses. His opposition to the bill, however, was vehement. "Neither profit nor peril shall move me to speak against my conscience in this place," he remarked, adding that one of the reasons for his opposition was that the bill "offered also some kindness to myself; for it gave a present forfeiture of the office upon sundry causes."[23] The measure was, in fact, rejected and Bacon lost an opportunity to obtain a position that would have brought him £1600 per year. He obviously hoped that his stand on this matter might be admired by the Queen sufficiently enough to cancel any misgivings she may have had toward him.

His problems were not to be rectified that simply. Bacon learned from Burghley shortly after his subsidy speech that the Queen was displeased with him.[24] His reply was interesting, for although labeled an "excuse," it was more of a justification than an apology:

> I was sorry to find by your Lordship's speech yesterday that my last speech in Parliament, delivered in discharge of my conscience and duty to God her Majesty and my country was offensive. If it were misreported, I would be glad to attend your Lordship to disfavour anything I said not. If it were misconstrued, I would be glad to expound my words, to exclude any sense I mean not. If my heart be misjudged by imputation of popularity or opposition by any envious or officious informer, I have great wrong; and the greater, because the manner of my speech did most evidently show that I spoke simply and only to satisfy my conscience, and not with any advantage or policy to sway the cause; and my terms carried all signification of duty and zeal towards her Majesty and her service. It is true that from the beginning, whatsoever was above a double subsidy, I did wish might (for precedent's sake) appear to be extraordinary, and (for discontent's sake) might not have been levied upon the poorer sort; though otherwise I wished it as rising as I think this will prove, and more. This was my mind, I confess it. And therefore I most humbly pray your Lordship, first to continue me in your opinion; and then to perform the part of an honest friend towards your poor servant and ally, in drawing her Majesty to accept of the sincerity and implicity of my heart, and to bear with the rest, and restore me to her Majesty's favour.[25]

The words support the contention about his naïveté at this stage of his career. He seemed confident that Elizabeth would understand and appreciate his sincerity. On the contrary, the Queen became infuriated enough to forbid Bacon the free access to her person that he had enjoyed. Forbidden to see her, he began to realize the painful consequences of his activities in Parliament. He tried appealing to her directly, begging to be restored to favor, and asking "to have means to deserve your benefit and to repair my error." Without specifically referring to his actions in Parliament, he offered his submission to the Queen, assuring her that if she bypassed him for office, he would "be glad there is such choice of abler men than myself."[26] The tone of this letter is markedly different from the one written earlier to Burghley. Although Elizabeth was supposedly pleased, she was not moved to a hasty advance of Bacon's career.[27] Bacon was at last learning "the way to please."[28]

Persistently, Essex continued to push Bacon's futile suit for the Attorneyship until late March, 1594.[29] Then, to no one's surprise, came news of Edward Coke's impending appointment to the post. For Bacon, this ended one endeavor at advancement and ushered in another. Coke would be vacating the lesser but still important office of Solicitor-General, and Bacon, again enthusiastically supported by Essex, offered himself as a candidate for the job.

Bacon's suit for the Solicitorship, which lasted from the spring of 1594 until November, 1595, was also to end in failure. While Elizabeth considered him more seriously this time, she had not forgiven his insolence. He was still denied the right of access and so could not plead his case in person. Essex, again his main source of support, was cautiously optimistic that he could persuade the Queen in favor of Bacon, who did not relish this long period of uncertainty.[30] He practiced for the post by examining prisoners in the tower, but as time elapsed he became disillusioned. He expressed the desire to give up politics for the scholarly life and in January, 1595, actually declared that if he were not appointed soon, he would drop the suit and travel abroad. Elizabeth was furious at such behavior. She remarked angrily that she had hereto advanced his legal career, but might "seek all England for a Solicitor" rather than appoint him.[31] In November of that year, Bacon was officially rejected. Elizabeth culminated two and one-half years of displeasure with Francis Bacon by again refusing him political and financial power.

The first half of the 1590s had been sorely frustrating years for Bacon. His period of "searching" had thus far come to nought. Having stated in 1592 that "all knowledge" was his "province," he chose to pursue a public career both as a vehicle to develop such knowledge, and a means to satisfy his complex needs. Bacon sought to realize his ambitions in combination. He pursued two high legal positions in the 1590s because they were available, and because Essex promoted him. He had an increasing need for the recognition he felt was due him by birthright, and the Earl seemed the best channel toward its realization. In Parliament, he gained recognition in 1593 as a thoughtful spokesman on important issues and was not yet the staunch defender of the royal prerogative that he would later become. His ideas on the Crown-Parliament relationship were still developing and would be significantly affected by the impact of these experiences. The session of 1597 would see Bacon emerge as a political realist.

Despite the frustrations of two unsuccessful suits for office, and the fact that at age thirty-five he was without "place" or money, Bacon still kindled hope for future success. He wrote to Essex shortly after failing to gain the Solicitorship: "I have lost some opinion, some time and some means; this is my account: but then for opinion, it is a blast that goeth and cometh; for time it is true it goeth and cometh not; but yet I have learned that it may be redeemed."[32] Bacon thus persevered. He would not be immune from future frustration and despair, but he would remain committed to political life.

1. *Letters and Life*, I, 108-9. Although this letter is undated, Spedding places it in early 1592 since Bacon mentioned that he was "one and thirty years."

2. *Ibid.*, 106.

3. Thomas Birch, *Memoirs of the Reign of Queen Elizabeth from the Year 1581 till Her Death* (2 vols., London, 1754), I, 73. The exact date of this letter to the Earl of Devonshire is not given.

4. *Letters and Life*, I, 119-43. The full title was "Mr. Bacon's Discourse in the Praise of His Sovereign."

5. *Ibid.*, 138-39.

6. *Ibid.*, 139.

7. A somewhat more famous work, also written in 1592, was Bacon's tract, "Certain Observations Made Upon a Libel. . . ." It was written in answer to a Jesuit document that had strongly castigated Elizabeth and her government. Bacon tried to disprove these allegations and to persuade the more moderate English Catholics that the Jesuit charges were false. The "Observations. . . ." is a long, eloquent defense of Elizabethan foreign policy written in a patriotic tone. Although the "Discourse in Praise of His Sovereign" was designed for flattery, the "Observa-

tions" was written to show loyalty. The fact that Bacon wrote it at his own initiative suggests he was most eager to impress the Queen. *See ibid.*, 143-208.

8. Birch, I, 93. Coke was in fact Speaker of the Commons and Bacon sat for the important county of Middlesex.

9. Neale, *Elizabeth I . . .* , 241-42.

10. D'Ewes, 470-71. The committee was appointed on February 26, one week after the opening of Parliament. On February 24, Peter Wentworth, among others, had been sent to the Tower for proposing that the succession issue be the session's first business.

11. *Ibid.*, 471. The date again was February 26.

12. *Letters and Life*, I, 214. Spedding believes Bacon meant Louis XI and not "Louis IX."

13. *Elizabeth I . . .* , 299.

14. D'Ewes, 474, 478. The committee convened on February 26.

15. D'Ewes, 481. Bacon was appointed to a committee on March 1 to discuss the Crown's demand with the Lords.

16. *Ibid.*, 483, 484. Bacon made these remarks on March 2.

17. *Letters and Life*, I, 220-22. *See* also D'Ewes, 484-90, Neale, 303-9.

18. D'Ewes, 493. The date given for the speech is March 7.

19. *Ibid.*, 495. D'Ewes says March 8 was the date of House action on the measure.

20. *Elizabeth I . . .* , 309.

21. Bacon's other activities during the 1593 Parliament were numerous. He was active along with his brother Anthony in helping mitigate the harshness of a bill against recusants. Although no details of what they did are available, it is again interesting to witness Bacon's moderate stand with respect to religious problems (*Letters and Life*, I, 226). No reference to the exact date of this business is given by Anthony Bacon in his letter to one A. Standen, March 14, 1593.

On March 12, he was appointed to three committees. Two concerned legal matters and dealt respectively with a bill concerning exemplifications of fines, recoveries, and the matter of the continuance of laws giving poor relief (D'Ewes, 499). The third body was selected to consider a bill for the relief of maimed soldiers and mariners. Bacon reported to the House on this measure on April 3, proposing several amendments (*Ibid.*, 503, 516).

On March 16, he served on a committee chosen to consider "The Bill for Mr. Anthony Cook" (*Ibid.*, 501), and on March 19, reported to the House from still another committee (one treating the continuance of statutes) on that group's conference with the Lords (*Ibid.*, 499).

A minor committee, to which Bacon was appointed on March 24, considered a twice-read bill "touching Clapboards and Casks" (*Ibid.*, 509).

On April 3, he spoke briefly on a legal matter involving the jurisdictional rights of the Commons. The dispute concerned a rather complicated case on the eligibility of one Thomas Fitzherbert. Bacon advocated cooperating with the Lords on this issue without surrendering the Commons' privilege. *See ibid.*, 515 and Neale, 313-18. The latter discusses fully the intricacies of the case.

On April 4, he served on a committee treating a bill explaining the branch of an older statute concerning the reducing of disloyal subjects to their due obedience (D'Ewes, 517). This obviously involved the matter of internal security.

Finally, on April 6, Bacon served on a committee dealing with "Restraint of new buildings, and converting of great houses into several Tenements, and for restraint of Inmates and Inclosures near London" (*Ibid.*, 519). No further details are known about what was obviously an issue of some importance.

22. *Letters and Life*, I, 226-28. The date was March 20.

23. *Ibid.*, 227.

24. Birch, I, 97. Bacon learned about her Majesty's feelings during a conversation with his uncle in early March, 1593.

25. *Letters and Life*, I, 233-34. While the exact date of his letter is not known, Spedding feels it was probably written in March, 1593.

26. *Ibid.*, 240.

27. *Ibid.*, 241. Anthony Bacon in a letter to his mother, June 2, 1593, related that Essex found the Queen, "thoroughly appeased, and that she stood only upon the exception of his years for the present preferment."

28. Mrs. Bowen, in discussing Bacon's mistakes in the Parliament of 1593, observes that "from now on, Bacon would study the way to please" (*Francis Bacon* . . . , 71).

29. *Letters and Life*, I, 254-55, 258-59; Birch, I, 152-53. Essex apparently refused to give up the suit despite the fact that it appeared rather hopeless.

30. *Letters and Life*, 289-90.

31. *Ibid.*, 348. Bacon tells of the Queen's reaction to Anthony, January 25, 1595. Although he was not present when Elizabeth showed her disgust for him, he received an accurate account of what she said.

32. *Ibid.*, 372. Although this letter is undated, Spedding places it in November, 1595, a few days after the Queen's decision on the Solicitorship.

CHAPTER IV

ELIZABETHAN FINALE:
BACON EMERGES AS A LEADER
IN PARLIAMENT; ESSEX

Politically, Bacon became a realist during the final Elizabethan years. Personally, he would remain frustrated in his quest for officialdom and reach near financial destitution. He had already learned the necessity of tempering idealism and would now become a loyal spokesman for the Crown. The importance of his political career during this period lies in two areas. First, Bacon rose to a position of prominence in the Parliaments of 1597 and 1601. He became a strong supporter of the prerogative, establishing the basis of his more important parliamentary role under James. The other area concerns his break with Essex, and subsequent role as a prosecutor of the unfortunate Earl. This latter business had a lasting effect on his political reputation.

Having painfully learned how not to please the Queen, Bacon concerned himself with regaining royal favor. He did have an official position as a Learned Counsel of the Crown, which brought him nominal fees.[1] By the spring of 1596, he was again admitted in the Queen's presence, and by December, appears to have won back her good graces.[2] Early in 1597, the first edition of the *Essays* appeared. Bacon had no intention of stagnating and still expected to combine amibitious intellectual pursuits with a public career. This twenty-pence little book, the contents of which have helped

47

immortalize Bacon, brought no immediate boon, financial or otherwise. His prolific pen had displayed a profound insight into many aspects of knowledge and had made clear his genius. Recognition, however, was modest at best, and the financially destitute Francis Bacon remained committed to the struggles of politics.[3]

Parliament again met during the autumn and winter of 1597-98 with Bacon playing his most important role to date.[4] He has been called "if not the official, the semi-official leader of the House."[5] Bacon was not a Privy Councillor and thus was not a government official. Although he strongly championed government positions, the session was relatively harmonious. The Puritan protest no longer echoed loudly since the movement apparently had been temporarily driven underground. "Elizabethan Puritanism, of the heroic, revolutionary kind, was destroyed."[6] The mood of Parliament being cooperative, it responded complacently to the Crown's request for money and concerned itself with major social and economic problems. The last two Elizabethan Parliaments would deal extensively with such issues, with the 1597 session showing specific concern about growing social unrest among the poor. Shortages in grain had provoked food riots in several parts of the country, causing an outcry for anti-enclosure legislation. Sentiment for and against enclosures varied as the state of the grain supply increased and decreased.[7] Sensitivity among the ruling classes to disorder in society was great, and as Neale puts it, "with the eclipse of Puritanism, a vacuum existed into which rushed concern for the economic disorders of the day."[8] The House would thus be concerned with legislating against enclosures, and for the maintenance of tillage. While the Crown sympathized with such feelings, it would allow the Commons to take the initiative in formulating legislation. It was Francis Bacon who served as chief manager of this business.

On November 5, 1597, Bacon moved against enclosures, depopulation of towns, and houses of husbandry, and for the maintenance of tillage. He presented two bills "not drawn with polished pen but with a polished heart, free from affection and affectation." "Because former laws are medicines of our understanding," he added, that he "had perused the preambles of former statutes, and by them did see the inconveniences of this matter, being then scarce out of the shell, to be now fully ripened."[9] Bacon had studied the issues carefully and articulated his reasons for moving the legislation:

And though it may be thought ill and very prejudicial to lords that have enclosed great grounds, and pulled down even whole towns, and converted them to sheep pastures; yet considering the increase of the people and the benefit of the commonwealth, I doubt not but every man will deem the revival of former motheaten laws in this point a praiseworthy thing. For in matters of policy, ill is not to be thought ill which bringeth forth good. For enclosures of grounds brings depopulation, which brings forth first idleness, secondly decay of tillage, thirdly subversion of houses, and decrease of charity and charge to the poor's maintenance, fourthly, the impoverishing the state of the realm. A law for the taking away of which inconveniences is not to be thought ill or hurtful unto the general state.[10]

Such a view reflected the general opinion of both government and membership on this subject. Bacon's stated belief in the importance of social peace and order in the commonwealth can hardly be called unique. While his concern for basic social harmony was shared by those with vested interests in political and economic power, Bacon's motivations were infinitely more profound and idealistic than those of his colleagues. Having already shown a concern for religious peace, he now spoke on the importance of general order in society. Bacon would go on to develop his ideas on learning and science always stressing the importance of political, religious, and social stability in creating an atmosphere conducive to progress. The attempt to link Bacon's reverence for peace and his essential political conservatism to his quest for utopian progress constitutes an interesting approach to his political thought and will be duly discussed. Although in 1597, he had not yet matured as a philosopher or politician, his mind was alive with ideas and he had already begun to develop the notion of perfecting knowledge. Knowledge would need a suitable climate to expand and an orderly society was essential to creating such an atmosphere. Although Bacon hardly ranks as an advanced social thinker, his reverence for harmony among the populace is important to understanding his thinking.

Was Bacon also politically motivated to introduce this legislation? Neale maintains that although Bacon was "an independent member," he "stood in close relationships with the government, and it may well be that there was official inspiration behind his initiative." The Crown, however, the same writer maintains, did not attempt to push through passage of these bills immediately after Bacon's motion.[11] The measures, on the contrary, underwent

49

a thorough examination and were altered considerably in the process. Spedding calls Bacon their "chief manager" during the substantial committee work required to work out the legislation.[12] As he played a major role translating the measures into clear and acceptable language, he became concerned that proposed amendments for the tillage bill threatened to exempt some areas from the act's restrictions. He remarked angrily during the bill's second reading that he "was as glad to be discharged of it as an ass, when he hath laid down his pack." The revised measure, he added, "was like the cock, which, though it do no good in punishing offenders past, yet it cuts short the like offense to come."[13] This suggests that Bacon may well have been reflecting the government's displeasure over the limitations imposed on the bill. He continued, however, to partake in this complicated business until February, 1598, when a bill curbing enclosures and maintaining tillage, and another prohibiting the decaying of towns and houses of husbandry emerged from the House. Bacon had been a party to important legislation, apparently motivated by both conviction and expediency.

The social issues of penal and charitable legislation were also dealt with in 1597-98. It is known that he served on a committee discussing a bill for erecting houses of correction and punishing rogues and sturdy beggars, and on one considering bills on poor relief.[14] Little is known of Bacon's exact role in this business, yet it is safe to assume that he favored passage of these significant statutes. Later, during the Parliament of 1601, he would refer to the numerous bills that had been proposed to deal with poor relief in 1597 as "a feast of charity."[15] His support of poor relief can only be said to have been motivated by his strong desire for social peace.

Forestallers, regraters, and ingressors were people who hoarded commodities (particularly corn) in order to control the market and maintain a profitable price. Not only were they a repulsive breed of monopolists but they were, in fact, helping to starve the poor. The government introduced legislation to curb their practices, and Bacon took part in the committee work.[16] Again his exact role is not known. With respect to the general issue of monopolies, Bacon favored petitioning the Queen for relief.[17] Elizabeth verbally promised redress and thanked Parliament for approaching her respectfully. The issue would of course be of greater importance in 1601.

It was his stand on the subsidy in 1597-98 that showed Bacon's conversion to political realism. His speech of November 15, in support of the government's appeal, was the only one of his Elizabethan parliamentary speeches to be prepared in advance.[18] He was most anxious to make certain that this subsidy speech made a more favorable impression upon official circles than did his last one. His words left no doubt that he had abandoned his maverick practices of four years earlier:

> Neither will I make any observation upon her Majesty's manner of expending and issuing treasure, being not upon excessive and exorbitant donatives, nor upon sumptuous and unnecessary triumphs, buildings, or like magnificence; but upon the preservation, protection and honour of the realm: for I dare not scan upon her Majesty's actions, which it becometh me rather to admire in silence, than to gloss or discourse upon them.

Bacon then blended humility with an eloquence for which he was already famous:

> Sure I am that the treasure that cometh from you to her Majesty is but a vapour which riseth from the earth and gathereth into a cloud, and stayeth not there long, but upon the same earth it falleth again; and what if some drops of this do fall upon France or Flanders? It is like a sweet odour of honour and reputation to our nation throughout the world. But I will only insist upon the natural and inviolate law of preservation. It is a truth, Mr. Speaker, and a familiar truth, that safety and preservation is to be preferred before benefit or increase, insomuch as those counsels which tend to preservation seem to be attended with necessity, whereas those deliberations which tend to benefit seem only accompanied with persuasion.[19]

It was by the use of such language that Bacon appealed for unquestioned support of the subsidy. He attached no qualification as he outlined the great dangers faced by the realm. The Crown again asked for three subsidies, this time to be paid within a three-year period. Although there was some brief criticism of this short-term payment, none of it came from Bacon.[20] The bill passed smoothly, receiving the emphatic backing for which Bacon had called. His obstructionist behavior was behind him and he could be counted upon as a Royalist supporter in the Commons.

Aside from participation in legal matters, these activities consti-

51

tuted Bacon's major role in this session.[21] The Parliament had been free from crises and had given Bacon an opportunity to temper his beliefs with political realism. Although it is premature to assume that he already had developed a philosophy of the proper role of Parliament, the atmosphere that prevailed during this session most definitely influenced his later views. A Parliament tactfully led by the Crown, in which the membership cooperated and contributed as a "junior partner," would be Bacon's ideal in the future. He was in the process of developing this view as the Elizabethan period approached its finale.

In 1601, Bacon emerged even more significantly as an "unofficial" government spokesman in the Commons.[22] This brief but important climax to the parliamentary history of the reign was highlighted by a famous monopolies dispute that was to be successfully resolved by the Queen in one of her last important political acts. In this dispute, as in most major business of the session, Bacon played a leading role as a Crown supporter.

Parliament had been satisfied in 1597-98 with the Queen's promises to grant relief from monopolies and allow their legality to be tested in the Common Law Courts. As the need for money grew, however, the Crown found it less easy to keep its pledge and, in the words of Neale, "more new patents seem to have been created than were rescinded."[23] In 1601, many in Parliament sought something more than a promise of relief. On November 20, a bill was introduced entitled "an act for Explanation of the Common Law in certain cases of Letters Patents."[24] This measure would have declared the most odious monopolies illegal according to the Common Law and thus would have constituted a direct threat to the prerogative. A dispute arose over whether to proceed in what was surely to be interpreted by the Crown as an antagonizing fashion, or whether to rely again on the more traditional approach to petitioning the Queen for relief. Francis Bacon was vehement in his defense of the latter course. His opposition to the bill was his strongest defense of the prerogative to date:

> For the prerogative Royal of the Prince, for my part I ever allowed of it: and it is such as I hope I shall never see discussed the Queen, as she is our Sovereign, hath both an enlarging and restraining liberty of her Prerogative: that is, she hath power by her Patents to set at liberty things restrained by statute law or otherwise: secondly, by her Prerogative she may restrain things that are at liberty.[25]

52

The House, Bacon believed, must moderate its tone and restrain its attack. He reminded his colleagues that "the use hath been ever by petition to humble ourselves to her Majesty and by petition to have our grievances redressed; especially when the remedy touch her so nigh in point of Prerogative . . . all cannot be done at once, . . . neither was it possible since last Parliament to repeal all." He ended his speech by reiterating his strong belief:

> I say, and I say again, that we ought not to deal, or meddle with, or judge of her Majesty's prerogative. I wish every man, there-fore, to be careful in this point. And humbly pray this house to testify with me, that I have discharged my duty, in respect of my place, in speaking on her Majesty's behalf; and do protest, I have delivered my conscience, in saying what I have said.[26]

Bacon's political conservatism was emerging. Tradition was to be upheld and relief was to be sought without disrupting govern-mental harmony.

In the monopolies debate that followed, Bacon continued as chief spokesman for what must be termed the position of the gov-ernment and restated his opinion that Parliament proceed only by petition. He emphatically declared that the proposed bill "sweep-eth away her Majesty's Prerogative."[27] He spoke yet another time on November 25 as the issue threatened to stagnate Parliament.[28] The Queen, however, with the tactful assistance of Robert Cecil, agreed to grant relief from monopolies by royal proclamation before the deliberation of the House reached the crisis stage. This wise intervention by the Crown not only buttressed the preroga-tive, but was graciously received by Parliament. Elizabeth made her promise in what was to be her last and best known speech. A sense of harmony, superficial as it may have been, prevailed in this final act of a great monarch. Bacon must have been satisfied. He had been of substantial help to the Crown in upholding its status. The cooperative setting of 1601 would always be cherished by Bacon. He was unaware that he would never witness such cooperation again.

While the monopolies question was the most volatile subject of the session, Bacon also partook in other important matters. Parlia-ment was told at the outset that it had been summoned solely to provide funds for defense. Although supply would obviously take precedence over other issues, Bacon chose to introduce bills respectively on abuses in weights and measures, and the repeal of superfluous laws. He knew that these measures, constructive as they may have been, would stand no chance of being considered until after the subsidy was granted. Why did Bacon choose to speak at length on these measures at what was clearly an inopportune time? Spedding says that Bacon felt "it was important to the health of the relation between Crown and Parliament, that Parliament should never seem to be called for money only, but always for some other business of estate besides." In 1593, he adds, "he endeavored in the same way, by interposing a discussion on some topic of popular and legislative character, to cover the nakedness of the appeal for pecuniary help."[29] Was Bacon "officially inspired" to dupe his colleagues into believing they had been convened for purposes other than the granting of aid? There is no evidence of this, and his remarks on the proposals suggest his sincerity.[30] Perhaps, as Spedding's observation implies, Bacon wanted to convince his colleagues that he was not a government lackey, and was genuinely concerned with the legislative function of the House. He had won the esteem of Commons in 1593 and obviously sought to maintain it.

While his motion on weights and measures was totally rejected a day after it was made, he persisted in pushing the other bill by moving to establish a committee to take up the repeal of superfluous laws. His concern for legal reform was clear. "Laws be like pills all gild over, which is they be easily and well swallowed down, one neither bitter in digestion nor hurtful to the body. Every man knows that time is the true controller of laws, and therefore there having been a great alteration of time since the repeal of any number of laws, I know and do assure myself there are many more than I know laws both needless and dangerous."[31] Bacon would always be concerned with this problem, and we should not look for any deceptive motive behind his action. He saw Parliament as an important vehicle for legal reform and hoped it might treat his motion later in the session. His effort failed; there was no discussion of his bill and all that emerged was the standard type of continuance act. It is interesting to note that Bacon actually spoke out against the act in the hope that the House might take more constructive action.[32]

The subsidy matter was disposed of with little difficulty. There was some dispute as to whether those subjects who owned land assessed at £3 or under should be subject to the tax. Bacon supported inclusion of the so-called "three pound men." Such a policy was "dulcis tractus apri jugo (a pleasant course to go in equal yoke) and therefore the poor as well as the rich not to be exempted."[33] We know of no other action by Bacon concerning the subsidy. Although there was some debate over the scope of the bill, the measure when passed included the "three pound men." The final Elizabethan subsidy provoked comparatively little controversy.

Bacon's other activities during the Parliament of 1601 included participation in matters of moderate importance. He reported a bill from committee, reforming abuses in the office of Remembrancer of the Exchequer.[34] Since the post had been established under the Crown's Privy Seal, Parliament's desire to meddle could be interpreted as an encroachment on the prerogative. Bacon was careful not to use offensive language in his report. He pointed out that although "the Committees have reformed some part yet they have not so nearly eyed every particular, as if they would pare to the quick an office of her Majesty's gift and patronage." He then added that "her Majesty's Learned Counsel were in sentinel to see that her Majesty's right might not be suppressed."[35] It appears that the House sought to correct abuses in an office created by royal patent. Bacon apparently realized the possibility of collision with the Crown and retracted somewhat by asking that the matter be handled more slowly and cautiously.[36] Parliament, believing (and rightly so) that the bill was a safeguard rather than an encroachment on the Crown's rights, ignored this plea for caution and ultimately passed the bill.[37] We do not know whether Bacon withdrew his early support of the measure. Neale remarks that while this bill touched the prerogative, it was "sponsored by that champion of the prerogative, Francis Bacon." "If substance alone mattered," he adds, "the Queen could safely grant her royal assent. She vetoed the bill, giving a final demonstration of her inflexible adherence to principle."[38] Bacon vacillated on the issue, believing on the one hand in the bill's constructiveness, yet reluctant to provoke royal displeasure. His political sensitivity was ever so obvious.

In his stand on social issues in 1601, Bacon surprisingly opposed a move to repeal an act concerning charitable trusts that had been passed during the previous session. Although this measure was supposed to guarantee against the misuse of the funds of charitable institutions, it was felt that under it the bishops enjoyed too much financial power. The House therefore sought to substitute a new statute armed with stricter guarantees against the mishandling of funds. Just why Bacon opposed such action is not clear. Spedding appears surprised and calls such behavior contrary to Bacon's "traditional reputation."[39] The fragmentary account of the speech does not reveal his motives, and we have only Townshend's comment suggesting that Bacon's opposition was based on what he felt were legal grounds. Bacon did offer a substitute measure that would have amended the existing statute without totally repealing it.[40] His effort failed and the House passed the repeal and the new act without any opposition from the Crown. There is every reason to believe that he was motivated solely by his own conviction and not by government pressure. He seems to have become upset over the issue, particularly when his speech was coldly received by the House. There is evidence that his temper flared up more than once during the debate, suggesting the egoism that was to reveal itself more and more.[41] Finally, he did acquiesce to the will of his colleagues.

It was also conviction that moved Bacon to defend the continuance of the tillage statute (motion for repeal had been made) that he had helped secure in 1597-98. Some argued that the act overburdened the husbandman whenever the price of corn was low (as it was then). Bacon disagreed, arguing that it still protected small farmers. "It stood not with the policy of the Kingdome," he stated, "that the wealth of this Kingdome should be engrossed into a few Pasturers' Hands."[42] The law, Bacon felt, was still basically sound and should not be repealed. Apparently it was not.[43]

Such were the major issues in which Bacon was involved during the session of 1601. The Elizabethan phase of his parliamentary career had ended. He had emerged as an ardent and tactful spokesman for royal leadership in the Commons. He had further developed his belief that unanimity in government could be achieved only if Parliament accepted the Crown's leadership in the handling of all major business of the realm. Such a view did not imply, however, that the House should refrain from initiating legislation that it deemed important. Bacon himself had repeatedly demonstrated his conviction that Parliament should fulfill such a function provided it did not attempt to challenge the prerogative in the process. Although Parliament had the ancient privilege to seek redress of grievances, it did not possess the right to defy the

56

Crown's traditional position. It followed therefore that an issue which threatened to create a direct conflict, such as the monopolies dispute, could not be resolved unless the House humbled itself accordingly. Such an attitude was, to Bacon, the key to effective compromise and to the maintenance of a sense of balance in government. Even though he thought such a balance should favor the Crown, he saw Parliament as a necessary partner whose advice should always be sought, and whose legislative and judicial functions should be recognized. Bacon's belief in a "balanced constitution" was shared by virtually all Englishmen; they would, however, begin to disagree sharply over just how such a balanced polity should function specifically. The question was to intensify over the next forty years until the outbreak of civil war; could harmony between Crown and Parliament survive as the latter steadily desired greater political power?[44] Bacon would revere a stable and balanced political order in which the Crown tactfully maintained its position without causing parliamentary dissension. He would strive tirelessly, if fruitlessly, to maintain such a condition under James I. The view that political peace was essential to material progress was already a crucial basis of Bacon's developing philosophy. Harmony in the state was a vital condition for the advancement of learning. The prerogative, cautiously used, was still the best instrument to preserve such harmony. Francis Bacon had become a prerogative man for reasons both of conviction and political expediency.

Bacon's role in the Essex case is notorious. Did he betray his one time patron when in the courtroom? Opinions differ. The details of Essex's path toward treason are well known and need not be intricately restated. Essex himself remains a fascinating and puzzling character, and the rationale behind the futile London rebellion is still difficult to explain. The purpose here is to take another look at Bacon's relationship with the Earl and the Queen during the former's long period of impetuous behavior which culminated in treason and death. Bacon's part in this complicated story illustrates his steadily changing attitude towards Essex, as well as his own political character. Many biographers have seen something disloyal, unethical, or cruel in Bacon's prosecution of his onetime patron. Anderson, among others, has convincingly vindicated Bacon's behavior in the case, and the view which seeks to condemn Bacon appears discredited.[45] The opinion professed here is that Bacon was compelled to act against Essex in order to function within the Elizabethan system as a political man. His role in the case stands as another example of his coming to grips with reality.

Despite the difference in temperaments, the two men found friendship mutually advantageous in the early 1590s. After the failure of the Solicitorship suit, the Earl presented Bacon with a generous gift, an estate at Twickenham worth £1800. Although Bacon wrote his friend, thanking him, he stressed in the letter that he was most interested in pleasing the Queen, in any way she wished.[46] The implication was that while he appreciated Essex's generosity, he was not automatically at the Earl's disposal. Bacon apparently was already a little wary of Essex's potential for impetuous behavior. Essex briefly promoted Bacon for the post of Master of the Rolls in 1596 and helped in the latter's abortive quest for the hand of Lady Hatton in 1597. Despite these efforts, he no longer served as Bacon's patron after 1596. As the Earl grew more ambitious and daring, Bacon became more convinced that his own ambitions could only be realized by pleasing Elizabeth. He had been sobered by his frustrating experiences, and while he had relied on Essex's guidance just previously, he now began to assume the role of advisor to his overly ambitious friend. By late 1596, Essex's military exploits, coupled with his rare personality, had raised his popularity to heights which many people, including Bacon, believed dangerous. There was already deep animosity towards the Earl within the Privy Council, particularly from the Cecils. Bacon realized that Elizabeth's infatuation with this dashing man would not blind her to his insolent individualism. As early as October, 1596, a few months after Essex's bold assault on Cadiz had earned him unlimited popularity, Bacon wisely advised the Earl in the following manner: "A man of a nature not to be ruled; that hath the advantage of my affection, and knoweth it; of an estate not grounded to his greatness; of a popular reputation; of a military dependence: I demand whether there can be a more dangerous image than this represented to any monarch living, much more to a lady, and of her Majesty's apprehension?" Bacon was as perceptive as he was blunt. "A man . . . not to be ruled" could not but bring about his own ruin. "Win the Queen" with "agreeableness," he pleaded.[47] He already realized Essex was flirting with danger and tried seriously at this early date to caution him. The wheels had turned in their relationship.

58

The complex events of the next few years saw a steady deterioration of Essex's relationship with Elizabeth. Bacon continued to drift further apart from his former patron. As Essex contemplated an Irish expedition, Bacon again cautioned against bold adventurism. "Ambitious men," he wrote, "if they rise not with their service, they will take order that their service fall with them."[48] In March, 1598, Bacon advised the Earl to "cool" his desires to go to Ireland, and concentrate instead on fully regaining the Queen's favor at home. "Your Lordship," he warned, "is too easy in such cases to pass from dissimulation to verity."[49] Intrigue at court followed, with the Earl increasingly wary of a Cecil plot to destroy him. Essex finally amassed a force to confront Tyrone's rebellion in Ireland, but cautiously withheld from leaving until he received the Queen's permission to return whenever he wished. He finally left in March, 1599, and suffered a bad defeat within two months. Furious, Elizabeth forbade his return; the Earl returned anyway, and threw himself at her mercy. Essex was now (autumn 1599) under detention and Bacon managed to involve himself in the case as a Queen's Counsel, taking part in examinations of the Earl. The evidence shows that Bacon involved himself in the case to try to plead with Elizabeth on Essex's behalf. Ugly rumors circulated, however, that he was speaking against the Earl to the Queen.[50] On the contrary, Bacon was still trying to help his onetime patron regain royal favor. He took a minor part in the York House proceedings against Essex in June, 1600, and then, after the Earl was put under virtual house arrest, wrote a detailed account of the proceeding for the Queen in an effort to persuade her to rescind the sentence and restore him to full favor at Court.[51] He failed in this effort, although Essex was released from detention within a month. Bacon wrote him in July, assuring him of his continuing friendship, but stressing that his loyalty to the Queen stood above his loyalty to any friend. "I confess," he wrote, "I love some things much better than I love your lordship, as the Queen's service, her quiet and contentment, her honour, favour, the good of my country and the like, yet I love few persons better than yourself, both for gratitude's sake and for your own virtue's, which cannot hurt but by accident or abuse."[52] Thus, he made it clear that while he still cherished Essex's friendship, he was firmly committed to serving the Crown, and would not condone the Earl's disloyal behavior. He continued, however, to try to help Essex. In an effort to improve the latter's relationship with the Queen he

59

even framed apologetic letters from the Earl to Elizabeth, trying to convince him to submit to her completely.[53] His good intentions toward Essex, cautious as they may have been, were still very much in evidence a scant half year before the Earl's fatal treason.

The events of Essex's folly in London are well known. There remained the trial, and Bacon's famous role as a prosecutor. As a Queen's Counsel and one previously involved in the Examination of Essex, Bacon would assist Coke in handling the prosecution. Did Bacon desire a dominant role in the case to win the Queen's favor? He had been in close contact with her regarding Essex's behavior. There is no evidence that he specifically requested the job, and would later state emphatically in his famous "Apology" on the case that the role was assigned to him. On the other hand, we know of no effort on his part to be relieved of the task. The truth is that Bacon was overwhelmingly convinced of Essex's guilt. He had investigated the case thoroughly, and had no doubts about his onetime friend's plans against the Queen. Bacon had shown in his letters that he feared his friend might be driven to commit treason. He reacted almost as if he had expected this kind of finale from Essex, and now had to stand by and defend the Crown as he had warned the Earl he would. "For God hath imprinted such a majesty in face of a prince that no private man dare approach the person of his soverign with a traitorous intent," he told the court. "With like pretences of dangers and assaults," he added, "the Earl of Essex entered the City of London and passed through the bowels thereof, blanching rumours that he should have been murdered, that the state was sold; whereas he had no such enemies, no such dangers: persuading themselves that if they could prevail, all would have done well." "Me-thinks," he concluded, "it were best for you to confess, not to justify."[54] Without displaying personal malice, Bacon confronted his former patron with what he honestly believed to be the truth.

Essex attempted to detract the Court from the issues stated by Bacon by charging him with personal betrayal. He intimated there had been deceit and trickery by Bacon in the letters "artificially framed" in his name; and by totally misrepresenting the intent of these letters, tried to portray his former protégé as a Judas. "To answer Mr. Bacon's speech at once I say thus much; and call forth Mr. Bacon against Mr. Bacon."[55] These were moving words, spoken by a man who already knew he was doomed. This scene constituted a high drama in which Bacon emerged the villain. Catherine Drinker Bowen focuses on Essex's poignant utterance, and without actually accusing Bacon of betrayal, asserts that "there must have lingered in his breast that cry from the prisoner's box—the voice of a onetime friend who thought himself betrayed: 'I call forth Mr. Bacon against Mr. Bacon.' "[56] Although Bacon may have thought about the case over the years, the facts exonerate him and Mrs. Bowen's statement is perhaps a bit overdramatic. In spite of his personal feelings, Bacon, having made his political commitment, could only act as a faithful servant of the Crown. He certainly realized that many of his contemporaries would think him cold and hypocritical. He always defended his role in the case, however, and in his "Apology" of 1604 (which will be discussed in the context of Bacon's position upon James's accession) offered what has to be considered a convincing explanation of his actions. Bacon had gone as far as he could in helping Essex. It should be noted also that he received no unusual reward for his role in the case, nor was Elizabeth moved to offer him any high-ranking position. He had served his Queen faithfully in a nasty business and if doing so meant acquiring an unfavorable reputation in the eyes of other political persons, so be it. One contemporary, Thomas Fuller, defended Bacon's behavior towards Essex by remarking that Francis "was not the worse friend for being the better subject."[57]

Bacon had emerged by 1601 as an able royal servant experienced in Parliament and law. His commitment to royal service had been made, and he had learned with difficulty the type of behavior expected of political aspirants. Yet, at age forty, he was without high government office or financial security. As the Elizabethan curtain drew near, his future as a political man was still very much in doubt.

1. Bacon had served as a Learned Counsel since 1594.

2. Birch, I, 468, II, 241.

3. Bacon was in fact arrested for debt in the autumn of 1598, but avoided imprisonment. *See Letters and Life*, II, 106-8.

4. He sat this time for the borough of Southampton.

5. A. F. Pollard and Marjorie Blatcher, eds., "Hayward Townshend's Journals," *Institute of Historical Research Bulletin*, XII (1934), 11. The remark is that of the editors. These journals cover the 1597-98 session.

6. Neale, *Elizabeth I* . . . , 326.

7. *Ibid.*, 337. Neale points out that in 1593 grain had in fact been too plentiful. The government thus saw to it that Parliament repealed the main clauses of an antienclosure act of 1563.

8. *Ibid.*

9. *Letters and Life*, II, 82-83.

10. *Ibid.*

11. *Elizabeth I* . . . , 338.

12. *Letters and Life*, II, 83. Bacon was involved in committees dealing with social and economic matters from November to February. I have spelled out the details of his work in "The Parliamentary Career of Francis Bacon," unpublished doctoral dissertation, Rutgers, 1966, Appendix IV.

13. *Townshend's Journal*, 15-16. The date was Nov. 24.

14. D'Ewes, 559, 561, 579.

15. Heywood Townshend, *Historical Collections* (London, 1680), 290.

16. *Ibid.*, 102; D'Ewes, 552. The committee was selected on November 7.

17. D'Ewes, 555, 570. He supported the motion of Sir Thomas Cecil on December 8.

18. *Letters and Life*, II, 84.

19. *Ibid.*, 85-86.

20. D'Ewes, 559.

21. His abilities were used in handling several issues. On November 5, he was appointed to a committee dealing with privileges and returns. That same day he was appointed to a body seeking to reform abuses in the granting of marriage licenses (D'Ewes, 552, 557).

Bacon also worked on legal reform. On November 8, he seconded a motion "for the abridging and reforming of the excessive number of burthensome penal laws." This bill appears to have been quickly killed and three days later he was appointed to a committee chosen to take up the matter of continuance of certain statutes. Passage of a "continuance act" was the usual substitution for any attempt at far-reaching legal reform (*Historical Collections*, 102-3, 104; D'Ewes, 555, 580).

Finally, he also served on committees dealing with Tellers and Receivers, the due performance of a will, the repeal of a town charter, the taking possession of a Bishopric and several even less weighty matters (D'Ewes, 553, 562, 565-66, 568, 570, 572, 581, 593; *Historical Collections*, 102, 112, 115).

22. Bacon was returned for both Ipswich and St. Albans and chose to sit for the former (D'Ewes, 622).

23. *Elizabeth I* . . . , 376.

24. *Historical Collections*, 229.

25. *Ibid.*, 231-32. The date was November 20.

26. *Ibid.*

27. *Ibid.*, 238. The date was November 21.

28. *Ibid.*, 252. The contents of this speech are not known.

29. *Letters and Life*, III, 17.

30. D'Ewes, 626-27. He introduced both bills on November 5.

31. *Historical Collections*, 194.

32. *Ibid.*, 197, 290. He spoke against a "Continuance Act" on December 7.

33. *Ibid.*, 290. Bacon spoke on November 9.

34. *Ibid.*, 223. The date of the report was November 18.

35. *Ibid.*

36. *Ibid.*, 237.

37. *Ibid.*, 323.

38. *Elizabeth I . . .* , 419.

39. *Letters and Life*, III, 37.

40. *Historical Collections*, 291. Bacon spoke on December 7.

41. *Ibid.*, 297. During the debate on December 8, Sir Francis Hastings pointed to Bacon and said, "If he be so hot as he was yesterday, then put me out of doors."

42. *Historical Collections*, 299. He spoke on December 9.

43. *Letters and Life*, III, 36. It was amended exempting Northumberland from jurisdiction.

44. The basic theme of a "balanced constitution" is developed thoroughly by Margaret A. Judson in *The Crisis of the Constitution* (New York, 1964).

45. *Francis Bacon . . .* , 53-70.

46. *Letters and Life*, I, 372-73. The letter was written in November, 1595.

47. *Ibid.*, II, 40, 41. This letter is dated October 4, 1596.

48. *Ibid.*, 105.

49. *Ibid.*, 98-101. This was in a letter written in late March, 1598.

50. *Ibid.*, 159-63. Spedding says these rumors circulated in late 1599 at which time Bacon apparently often saw the Queen. He wrote to Lord Howard and Robert Cecil denying them.

51. *Ibid.*, 172-89. Bacon wrote his account in mid-June, 1600, just after the York House proceeding had ended.

52. *Ibid.*, 190-91. The letter is dated July 20, 1600.

53. *Ibid.*, 192-201. Bacon composed several letters of this type. Spedding doesn't say whether the Queen ever saw any of them.

54. *Ibid.*, 225-26. This was during the trial in February, 1601. Spedding doesn't indicate the exact date.

55. *Ibid.*, 226.

56. *Francis Bacon; . . .* , 80.

57. *History of the Worthies . . .* , II, 422.

CHAPTER V

THE POLITICAL MAN AT THE
ACCESSION OF JAMES I

At the time of Elizabeth's death, Bacon was still desiring political status. His public career had thus far brought little in the way of satisfaction. Rawley bluntly described the situation:

> Nevertheless, though she cheered him much with the bounty of her countenance, yet she never cheered him with the bounty of her hand; having never conferred upon him any ordinary place or means of honor or profit, save only one dry reversion of the Register's Office in the Star Chamber, worth about 1600 £ per annum, for which he waited in expectation, either fully or near twenty years.[1]

How, then, did Bacon view the great Queen whom he had served so faithfully, but who had never bestowed upon him the status he had sought so long? He was to reveal his feelings only years later, and would show both great admiration and a touch of bitterness. In his "In Felicem Memoriam Elizabethae Angliae Reginae" (On the Fortunate Memory of Elizabeth Queen of England), written in 1608, he had great words of praise for his late monarch.[2] He wrote of her statesmanship, of her ability to overcome the obstacle of being a woman ruler:

> The government of a woman has been a rare thing at all times; felicity in such government a rarer thing still; felicity and long

continuance together the rarest thing of all. Yet this Queen reigned forty-four years complete, and did not outlive her felicity. Of this felicity I proposed to say something; without wandering into praises; for praise is the tribute of men, felicity, the gift of God.[3]

He recalled her expert handling of her many complex problems, never letting up in his admiration in what appears to have been a nostalgic look at the past. Nowhere in the work does Bacon refer to his own frustrations during the past.

While he could display a genuine reverence for the great lady, Bacon showed also that he still harbored other feelings as well. In a fragmentary unfinished work, "The Beginning of the History of Great Britain," written in the period 1609-10, he pointed out that many people were eager for a change by the end of Elizabeth's reign.[4] "Many were glad," he wrote, " . . . that the fears and uncertainties were overblown and that the dye was cast." Those "that had made their way with the King or offered their service in the time of the former Queen, thought now the time was come for which they had prepared." "And therefore it rejoiced all men," he also wrote, "to see so fair a morning of a kingdom, and to be thoroughly secured of former apprehensions; as a man that awaketh out of a fearful dream."[5] In this brief writing, Bacon recalled the weariness that had captured many men by 1603 and pointed to the fresh optimism that accompanied the successful transition to a new reign. That he was recalling a personal attitude is quite obvious. He might remember the glories and virtues of the famous Queen, but he could not hide the fact that he himself had welcomed the new possibilities that her passing might bring.

Upon James's accession, Bacon looked immediately to the future. His thoughts were to win the monarch's favor as quickly as possible. He wrote to his cousin, one Robert Kempe, expressing satisfaction over the orderly manner in which the succession had taken place, as well as cautious optimism on the prospects of his own future. "It is in vain to tell you with what wonderful still and calm this wheel is turned round. . . . It is hoped that as the State here hath performed the part of good attorneys to deliver the King quiet possession of his kingdom, so the King will redeliver them quiet possession of their places; rather filling places void, than removing men placed."[6] Believing his chances for advancement would be increased if he could make an early impression on the new monarch, he also wrote several letters to Scottish gentlemen who were likely to be influential during the new reign.[7] While it was important to utilize discreetly important contacts, Bacon was also interested in impressing James directly. He wrote to the new King only a few days after Elizabeth's death, humbly offering his services:

> I was not a little encouraged, not only upon a supposal that unto your Majesty's sacred ears (open to the air of all virtues) there might perhaps have come some small breath of the good memory of my father, so long a principal counsellor in this your kingdom; but also by the particular knowledge of the infinite and incessant endeavours . . . which appeared in my good brother toward your Majesty's service . . . there is no subject of your Majesty's who loveth this island, and is not hollow and unworthy, whose heart is not set on fire, not only to bring you peace-offerings to make you propitious, but to sacrifice himself a burnt-offering to your Majesty's service: amongst which number no man's fire shall be more pure and fervent than mine.[8]

He was cautious in not referring specifically to any particular office. "I must leave all to the trial of further time," he concluded humbly. He sought merely to assure James of his complete willingness to serve, wasting no time in establishing contact.

Bacon had his first meeting with the King before the latter arrived in London.[9] He would write shortly afterwards that James was "a prince the farthest from the appearance of vain glory that may be, and rather like a prince of the ancient form than of the latter time."[10] While he hoped flattery might be appreciated, he knew he would have to work hard to secure significant advancement. Immediately he was continued "of the learned counsel in such manner as he was to the Queen"; however, there was no hint of a quick promotion to something more desirable.[11] Bacon would again find himself generally frustrated, and again in specific financial trouble. His cousin, Robert Cecil, would from the outset be dominant in James's government, and although Bacon had already been deeply disappointed when seeking help from this family, he had little choice but to try again. Perhaps he thought that his cousin, about to experience his greatest political success, would be more sympathetic now that Bacon could no longer be considered a serious rival. Cecil did help financially during the summer of 1603. Bacon was some £500 in debt and appealed for a £300 loan. Cecil appears to have graciously obliged, hinting also that he might use Bacon in some unnamed capacity.[12] Even though Bacon expressed thanks, his words showed a growing impatience. He expressed particular dissatisfaction at his proposed knighthood. Bacon had been assured of the rank; however, he was less than happy about receiving it as one of three hundred at James's coronation. He told Cecil that he wished "the manner might be such as might grace me, since the matter will not; I mean that I might not be merely gregarious in a troop."[13] Thus Bacon's position in 1603 was hardly enviable. Past forty and deeply in debt, he would have to play up to a relative who had been no help in furthering his career, and whom he would come to despise increasingly. Even though he may have become weary, he was far from ready to give up. The King might still be impressed directly.

Bacon decided to write to James about critical issues in an effort to reassure the King of his loyalty, and to display his knowledge of political questions. Specifically, he wrote three important tracts for the King in 1603. He explained his role in the Essex Case in the famous "Apology," and wrote thoughtful treatises on the questions of union with Scotland, and on religion. An eloquent pen was a precious asset, and Bacon hoped James recognized it as indicative of his value to the Crown.

James's affinity for Essex was well known.[14] The King was openly favorable to former members of Essex's party and had even made one of them, Lord Montjoy, the Lord Lieutenant of Ireland. Montjoy had been conclusively implicated in the rebellion and had been spared only because Elizabeth still desired his services.[15] In deciding to write the "Apology" late in 1603, Bacon shrewdly chose to address it directly to Montjoy, believing that if the King was suspicious of his role in the Essex affair, the best way to remove such suspicions was to write a full account of his story to someone deemed least likely to be persuaded.[16] The tract is a concise, but careful summary of Bacon's role in the case. In truth, although labeled an "Apology," it was in fact an explanation and justification of his action. As one would expect, Bacon emphasized his loyalty to the Crown repeatedly throughout the tract. Although he sought to erase general misconceptions about his behavior in the Essex business, he wrote this document at this particular time specifically to boost his political standing with the new king. Although there is no evidence that James was suspicious of Bacon because of the latter's part in the Essex Case, the "Apology" brought no immediate change in Bacon's fortunes. He was convinced, however, that it was good politics to write such a document.

In his letter to Northumberland, written after his first meeting with the king, Bacon reflected on the question of uniting the two kingdoms. He remarked with skepticism that the King "hasteneth to a mixture of both kingdoms and nations, faster perhaps than policy will conveniently bear."[17] James had obviously told Bacon that he sought to enlist his support in such an undertaking. Bacon would of course become the Crown's leading advocate of union in Parliament during the next several years.[18] Initially, he decided to express his views on this question in "A Brief Discourse Touching the Happy Union of the Kingdoms of England and Scotland," written probably in late 1603, and dedicated to James.[19] In it, he sought to show the King how union might be successfully accomplished. He was determined to convince James that while he believed in the idea, he understood the problems involved in its realization. By approaching the King as a scholar rather than as a politician, Bacon showed his awareness of James's taste for intellectual interests. He was hopeful that a philosophical tract on this pertinent topic might be viewed with royal favor.

Bacon showed profound insight into the problem. Arguing primarily from a theoretical point of view, he attempted to show that the merger of any two bodies, and particularly that of "two mighty and warlike nations," was an extremely difficult goal.[20] He concerned himself with two types of union. In one form, the nations "retain the ancient forms still severed," and were "only conjointed in sovereignty." In the second type the nations could "superinduce a new form agreeable and convenient to the entire estate." The first of these, Bacon asserted, "hath been more usual, and is more easy; but the latter is more happy." In citing the union of Aragon and Castile as an example of the first type, he pointed out that even though the two kingdoms were united "by marriage and not by conquest" they continued "in a divided government" and were not "cemented" to each other. He noted that recent rebellions in Aragon signified that kingdom's dissatisfaction with the union. The second form had been successfully achieved only by the Romans; he supported his argument with concrete examples from Roman history.[21]

A formula for perfect union was sketched with four conditions

68

(besides sovereignty itself) cited as being necessary: "Union in name, Union in language, Union in laws, and Union in employments."[22] Union in laws was the most difficult to achieve, and was the more thoroughly discussed. Bacon called for a moderate approach to the problem by pointing out that it would be inconvenient "to seek either to extirpate all particular customs, or to draw all subjects to one place or resort of judicature or session." He added that "nothing amongst people breeds so much pertinency in holding their customs, as sudden and violent offer to remove them. . . . It is sufficient that there be an uniformity in the principal and fundamental laws both ecclesiastical and civil."[23] Bacon confined his treatment of the problem of unifying laws to a theoretical discussion. He obviously felt that James would well understand his thoughts without his probing the specific problem of how to merge the legal systems of England and Scotland.

The tract stands as a plea for patience and moderation. It is the duty of man, he wrote, "to make a fit application of bodies together, but the perfect fermentation and incorporation of them must be left to Time and Nature; and unnatural hasting thereof doth disturb the work, and not dispatch it."[24] These words again reveal Bacon's reverence for order and harmony in the body politic. For two kingdoms to achieve such a condition in their union was essential if they hoped to survive and prosper. However, the realization of such a "perfect fermentation" was most difficult to attain. Bacon's wisdom on the problem was profound. While his doubts were obviously not understood by a hasty James I, they were to be validated by the subsequent history of the problem.

Bacon further echoed his quest for order in the advice he gave James on religious problems. In 1603, the King's attitude toward religion was yet unclear, and Bacon thought the situation ripe to offer advice.[25] He believed that a monarch entering a country with different and far more complex religious problems than previously encountered would welcome opinions on the subject. Also, religion was not unrelated to the problem of union. If it was to be realized, both Presbyterian and English Puritanism would have to be dealt with tactfully and fairly. Bacon, a careful observer of the Elizabethan religious scene, had not been satisfied with the way in which the Puritan problem had been treated, and "could not but be anxious that the chance should not be missed of taking up the right position now, when everything lay so fair and open for it."[26] He may not have been fully aware of James's hope for religious unity, but thought it appropriate to express his own ideas on how to achieve peace in this volatile area.[27]

The tract "Certain Considerations Touching the Better Pacification and Edification of the Church of England" was written in 1603 prior to the famous religious conference at Hampton Court.[28] While Spedding accurately calls it "a worthy sequel" to Bacon's 1589 religious tract, its tone is more general and philosophical. The work does not discuss in detail the problem of reconciling the Puritans with the English Church. "The unity of your Church, excellent Sovereign, is a thing no less precious than the union of your kingdoms being both works wherein your happiness may contend with your worthiness."[29] His plea was a general call for church unity, with the hope that such a policy would simplify the task of reconciling dissident factions. Believing that reform was a necessity, he attacked the opinion "that it is against good policy to innovate anything in church matters." He asked, "Why the civil state should be purged and restored by good and wholesome laws made every third or fourth year in Parliament assembled, devising remedies as fast as time breedeth mischiefs, and contrariwise the ecclesiastical state should still continue upon the dregs of time, and receive no alteration now for these five and forty years and more?"[30] While he did not advocate doctrinal changes, he saw no reason for rigidity on such matters of "rites," "ceremonies" and "the particular hierarchies, policies and disciplines of church." Unity, he argued, meant "one faith, one baptism, and not one hierarchy, one discipline." For although "Christ's garment was without seam, . . . the Church's garment was of diverse colours."[31] Bacon was advocating a more comprehensive church. Anglicanism should be broadened so that the seeds of Puritan dissent would not ripen again and cause graver religious problems than those witnessed during the previous reign.

Bacon argued against the arbitrary power enjoyed by the bishops, and for a more learned ministry and reforms in the liturgy.[32] Furthermore, he thought bishops were excommunicating too freely and saw nonresidence and pluralities as serious abuses.[33] He showed an understanding of many of the complex problems facing the Church, and advocated (as he had previously) a moderate approach in dealing with them. Bacon remained an Anglican committed to compromise, who saw religion largely as a state matter to be handled harmoniously by the monarch. While the Puritans were not discussed specifically in this work, it must be remembered that their cause had been in abeyance for several years and was just on the verge of surfacing again. He had reflected philosophically on the importance of religious peace for the general well-being of a state. It was hoped the King would appreciate these contemplations.

Thus Bacon approached James I as both a politician and a scholar. His overtures were carefully conceived and motivated by conscience, ambition, and desperation. Although he may have made a favorable impression, there was to be no quick alteration of his own fortunes. He remained a frustrated political man who would still have to prove his value. The convening of Parliament in 1604 would offer such an opportunity.

1. *Bacon's Works*, I, 40-41.

2. *Ibid.*, XI, 443-61.

3. *Ibid.*, 443.

4. *Ibid.*, 405-10.

5. *Ibid.*, 408-9.

6. *Letters and Life*, III, 74. This letter is undated.

7. *Ibid.*, 55-77. Spedding includes these letters, as well as those to other important persons, all written between the date of Elizabeth's death (March 24) and April 10, 1603. They all show how much Bacon sought to win the new King's favor. He knew the Scots mainly through his late brother Anthony.

8. *Ibid.*, 61-63. The letter was entitled "An offer of service to his Majesty K. James upon his first coming in." It was dispatched to the King through his friend Toby Mathew on either March 28 or 29, 1603.

9. *Ibid.*, 76. Although Spedding cannot date the interview exactly, it is known that James took one month to progress from Edinburgh to London. Their first meeting therefore probably took place in late April, 1603.

10. *Ibid.*, 76-77. Bacon wrote this to the Earl of Northumberland shortly after his first meeting with the King.

11. Francis Egerton Ellesmere, *The Egerton Papers* (London, 1840), XII, 368. This information is contained in a warrant to Lord Keeper Egerton, April 21, 1603.

12. *Letters and Life*, III, 79-81. Two letters to Cecil, dated July 3 and 16, 1603, reveal this information.

13. *Ibid.*, 81. He expressed this feeling in the second letter.

14. For a discussion of James's relationship with Essex, *see* D. H. Willson, *King James, VI & I* (London, 1956), 149-54.

15. *Letters and Life*, III, 137-38.

16. *Ibid.*, 138-62. The document was printed in early 1604.

17. *Ibid.*, 77.

18. For a discussion of Bacon's role in the union question, see Joel Epstein, "Francis Bacon and the Issue of Union, 1603-1608," *The Huntington Library Quarterly* (February, 1970).

19. *Letters and Life*, III, 89-99.

20. *Ibid.*, 92.

21. *Ibid.*, 94-96.

22. *Ibid.*, 96.

23. *Ibid.*, 97-98.

24. *Ibid.*, 98.

25. Willson expresses this view clearly and concisely. "There was a moment of breathless uncertainty" about what James would do with respect to religion. *See King James* . . . , 197.

26. *Letters and Life*, III, 100. I agree with Spedding's conclusion.

27. For a thorough treatment of James's quest for religious unity, *see* Willson, 197-243. I have found no evidence showing that Bacon was aware of James's views.

28. *Letters and Life*, III, 102-27.

29. *Ibid.*, 103.

30. *Ibid.*, 105.

31. *Ibid.*, 107-8.

32. *Ibid.*, 114-19.

33. *Ibid.*, 121-24.

CHAPTER VI

THE POLITICAL MAN IN PARLIAMENT, 1604-1610

It would be under James that Bacon would finally reach great heights in political life. The road to status and power, first as Attorney-General and ultimately as Lord Chancellor, was, however, still to be painfully long. Salisbury was the key figure in James's conciliar government during these first years, and Bacon's career would not progress significantly until after Salisbury's death. Until then, Bacon remained under the shadow of the hunched Lord Treasurer. The Cecil name continued to dominate and the new King would hardly recognize the aspirations of Francis Bacon. The publication of *The Advancement of Learning* in 1605 marked an unsuccessful effort to win the favor and respect of the scholarly-minded monarch. While Bacon was quite serious about his hopes to revolutionize learning, he was also politically stagnant and sought to use his intellectual talents to break that condition. In 1607, he would gain the Solicitor-Generalship, and while this was an office of respectable status, it hardly constituted great success for a forty-six year-old man of proven universal ability. Frustration still characterized Bacon's public career, yet he persisted in demonstrating to his King his worth as a political servant.

It is in the Commons that we again see Bacon functioning as a political man. During the five sessions of James's first Parliament 1604-1610, he served as the Crown's leading servant in the Lower

House, trying to champion the government's causes while still maintaining the trust and respect of his colleagues. Bacon had revealed to the King his thoughts on union and religion. James had already displayed a rigidity on religion at Hampton Court, and union was bound to be a primary goal of the Crown during this first session of Parliament. What Bacon did not know, was how the new monarch would relate to Parliament. Moreover, the attitudes and aspirations of that body now that a new reign was beginning were also unclear. Although the Elizabethan "finale" of 1601 had been superficially harmonious, it was not clear how Parliament would react to the new King. While Englishmen greeted their new ruler optimistically, the behavior of the landed and commercial interests that dominated Parliament was yet to be seen. There were several complex issues that involved financial power, and the Crown was hardly in a position to be independent. What was needed was continuation of the "reconciling spirit" of the Elizabethan period. The achievement of such a goal could only be difficult.

If James I had understood the need for cooperation in government, the parliamentary history of his reign might have begun more favorably. The key individual in any sustained effort to establish harmony between Crown and Parliament could have been Francis Bacon. Bacon, according to one noted historian, had "all the qualities of a reconciling statesman" and was perhaps "the one man who could have guided James safely through the quicksands."[1] Although this may be a speculative statement that assumes one man could have altered parliamentary history, Bacon certainly could have functioned more effectively had royal leadership been more enlightened. For one thing, if he sat in the House as an official instead of just a private member speaking for the Crown, he conceivably would have had more influence. Perhaps then, he could have used the prestige of officialdom together with the standing he enjoyed in the Commons to help launch James on a happier course with Parliament. By 1610, when Bacon finally sat as Solicitor, a spirit of confrontation had already nullified the real possibilities of reconciliation. We may never know how real the chances were for greater political harmony, however, Bacon, for one, worked for such a goal. He tried at once to advance his own position, while striving to persuade Parliament to be cooperative. Under conditions that would grow increasingly difficult, he would try to play what became for him a more difficult role.

James never understood the basic need for cooperation in government. He arrived with a concept of Parliament totally alien to England. In Scotland, that body was "a court and an advisory council which could debate nothing but what the King propounded to it." "How abysmal," James's biographer adds, "was his ignorance of the English House of Commons! It was, he discovered, a formidable body that challenged his prerogative; but he never fathomed the source of its strength, and growing effectiveness of its procedure and leadership, or the inevitability of its advance to power."[2] Bacon's views on government would never mirror those of his king. Although he became a proponent of a strong prerogative, he always retained a basic belief in the importance of Parliament that James was never able to develop. Bacon was English and part of a heritage that accepted Parliament as an integral part of political life.

While virtually all Englishmen agreed on the permanence of Parliament, they would begin to differ sharply over the extent of its power within the unwritten English constitution. Unsettled was the question of how strong the royal prerogative was in relation to the so-called ancient rights and privileges of the people as represented in Parliament. Men agreed on the existence of a prerogative power; they would begin to differ sharply, however, over the extent to which that power should be exercised without encroaching on the rights of the subject. Francis Bacon always believed in the necessity of preserving agreement in this area. His effort to do so, while defending a prerogative power that fell increasingly under attack, constitutes his major role in the Jacobean Parliaments.

The growth of an "opposition" in the Commons during the first half of James's reign is also a dominant theme in the political history of this period. No modern scholar would deny that Parliament's development into a revolutionary political force during the first four decades of the seventeenth century was gradual and sometimes uneven. Although a forceful "opposition group" existed as early as 1604, a closely knit party determined to challenge the sovereignty of the Crown did not emerge until the eve of the Civil War.[3] The early Jacobean "opposition," rather than trying to abolish or even stifle the royal prerogative, sought to clarify its legal limitations. Even as the unwritten constitution made such an effort impossible, Englishmen still drifted cautiously toward revo-

75

lutionary confrontation. Political men on both sides were slow to realize the developing incompatibility of Crown and Parliament. Just how clearly Bacon ever understood the growth of "opposition" to the Crown is a somewhat controversial point to be dealt with later. In reality, he would be defending the Crown against an emerging political dissent and would be trying to neutralize opposition to James. Bacon saw his role as one committed to a governmental harmony in which Parliament remained the junior partner. Balance in government was necessary, but that balance must remain in favor of the Crown. Parliament, to be sure, stood for the rights of the subject, but it must function only under the guidance of royal leadership. Bacon entered his first Jacobean Parliament not aware that this leadership was to prove itself to be substantially weakened and thus susceptible to a growing challenge. He encountered this challenge from the outset as a political man trying harder than ever to prove his value as a royal servant.

Without fully realizing how controversial the matter of union with Scotland was, James I convened his first Parliament primarily to consider this very issue. He quickly learned that he was dealing with a body determined to raise issues it considered at least as important as the question of merging with the Scots. The Commons sought further relief from abusive monopolies and revision of the outdated practice of wardship. It did not hesitate to obstruct James's plans by vehemently pressing both these issues, and eventually utilized the second as the basis for its defiant "Apology" at the end of the session. In addition to these basic grievances, a serious dispute arose at the session's outset over the eligibility of a member of Commons. This issue delayed consideration of other business and immediately brought the conflict between prerogative and parliamentary privilege into sharp focus. Bacon quickly found himself as mediator in this dispute. This was a role he would more or less play throughout the 1604 session of James's first Parliament.[4] In fulfilling such a function, he sought to use his political abilities to compromise with an "opposition" for the first time in the new reign. It marked a challenging beginning to an extremely active and frustrating phase of his long tenure in Parliament.

The Goodwin-Fortescue Case involved the conflicting claims of Parliament and Chancery to judge the validity of election returns of Commons members. Sir Francis Goodwin saw his election to the House voided by Chancery on the grounds that he had been outlawed. The court acted under a new royal proclamation allowing it to judge the validity of all returns. One Sir John Fortescue, a Privy Councillor, was then elected in Goodwin's place. The House immediately decided that the latter had been rightfully elected and voted him seated.[5] It pointed out that the two debts for which he had been outlawed had been paid and also cited Elizabethan precedents where the House had seated members charged with outlawry.[6] Obviously, Parliament greatly feared a dangerous precedent by which Chancery could control the composition of the House. James defended (the reply was conveyed to the Commons by Bacon) Chancery's action by also citing precedent and asked Commons to confer with the judges who had handed down the decision. His reply showed contempt for the House's challenge of a prerogative court.[7] The stage was now set for confrontation.

Bacon's role here is quite interesting. I would agree with Notestein's contention that "he would have liked to have been the honest broker, stating the case for each side with skill and bringing opposing groups together."[8] In attempting to avoid confrontation, he advised conferring with the judges, remarking that "by it we shall lose no privilege, but rather gain, for the matters of the conference will be two; satisfaction of the King, and putting in certainty our privilege." He advised further not to oppose the King, stating that "we are not to contest with one that is governor of 30 legions."[9] Despite this, however, he did not want the House to relinquish its privileges. The Commons, he believed, was judge of its own returns once it had convened. He cautioned that no precedent existed for a man being "put out of the House for outlawry. . . . Therefore, it had been fit we should have desired to inform the King that he was misinformed."[10] Bacon hoped the King might be satisfied that he was not being challenged, and the House might still retain its privileges. Perhaps a joint conference might convince the judges to withdraw Fortescue's name honorably. His colleagues rejected a conference, however, on the grounds that holding one did in fact breach their privilege.[11]

Although his own effort to resolve this issue had failed, Bacon does not seem to have lost favor with the House. He tried to assure them that James wanted to settle the Goodwin case in good faith. Moreover, he assured them how he tried to convince the King that the House was sole judge of its own returns. Finally, Bacon told his colleagues that in order not to prolong the dispute, James decided that neither Goodwin nor Fortescue should be seated. The King promised that he would confirm all Parliament's just privileges, but appears to have avoided specifically supporting its claim to have complete control over its own composition. Bacon seemed satisfied that James's nullification of both returns showed his desire to avoid confrontation and told his colleagues that "his Majesty did meet us half way."[12] Many in the House were, of course, not pleased with such a solution since parliamentary privilege had not been clearly affirmed. The seriousness of the dispute indicated that the session could expect future conflicts. Bacon had tried to play the "honest broker"; such a role promised to become increasingly difficult.

If future "opposition" to the Crown materialized, Bacon knew he would be faced with the continuing task of trying to neutralize it. He would always have to act cautiously in order to maintain the trust of his colleagues while still convincing James that he was a loyal servant worthy of high office. It is not clear whether Bacon realized at this point the potential obstructive capacity of the budding "opposition." One can only assume he was shrewd enough to recognize that his own parliamentary career promised to become increasingly complicated.

Wardship, purveyance, monopolies, and, of course, union were the main substantive issues of the session. The grievance of wardship was eventually used by Edwin Sandys as the basis of the "Apology" of 1604. Bacon appears to have played little or no role in the actual consideration of this long-standing grievance. While he served on the committee considering the problem, he stated that he had been "merely a relator" and "no actor" in the discussion. This remark, together with his strictly objective report of the meeting, indicates he was not directly involved in the dispute.[13] In the protest against the practice of purveyance, Bacon served as the House's main channel to the Crown.[14] He presented the grievance to James in a carefully prepared speech that showed his obvious desire to mollify the King before unleashing the substance of the complaint. "We may acknowledge," he stated, "that we have found in your Majesty great cause both of admiration and commendation." He then praised the King for his handling of the Goodwin case, his promotion of union, and his efforts to effect unity in religion.[15] Bacon wanted to flatter James before presenting the House's strong outcry against purveyance. He made it clear that he agreed the complaint was serious and totally justified. "There is no grievance in your Kingdom so general, so continual, so sensible, and so bitter unto the common subject as this whereof we now speak." Bacon went on to enumerate in detail the abuses of officials in support of this contention. He spoke carefully and humbly, assuring the King that Commons in no way sought to "derogate" from the prerogative.[16] His hope was to reassure James of his loyalty while at the same time arguing a case for Parliament that he felt entirely justified. It marked an effort on his part to resolve an important issue via cooperation. The King reacted favorably to Bacon's speech; however, the House could not agree on how to compensate the Crown for loss of revenues.[17] Further discussion was postponed until the next session and purveyance remained an unresolved grievance.

The problem of monopolies was again a major issue in Parliament, with Sandys the main architect of the protest. Bacon, who in the past favored appealing to prerogative for relief on this issue, did not play a major role in the Commons' effort to legislate against patents. He did report on a bill for free trade and appears to have favored compromise legislation during the next session.[18] His involvement, however, in this serious controversy was hardly extensive.

We know Bacon pleaded unsuccessfully for a subsidy, remarking toward the end of the session that Parliament should not end "like a Dutch feast in salt meats but like an English feast in sweet meats."[19] Apparently, James was advised that it might set a bad precedent if the session were allowed to end without at least some financial aid being voted. The effort came, however, just as an angry Commons began formulating its "Apology" for the King. This document, which sought to advise James how to conduct affairs in England, marked the complete failure of this first parliamentary session. Although it is not surprising that Bacon opposed the measure, no record of his remarks remains to show his argument.[20] He tried hard in 1604 to get Parliament and the King to cooperate, and must have been disturbed by any action carried out in a spirit contrary to the one he sought to promote. The "Apology" was not written in the spirit of harmonious government, even though James deserved such a "lesson" in 1604.

The most important political issue that Bacon was involved in from 1604 to 1607 was the royal effort to unite the two kingdoms.

79

This was James's primary political goal during these early years and no one worked harder to help him achieve it than Francis Bacon. The frustrating attempt at union began in 1604, was tabled during the session of 1605-1606 because of a preoccupation with the Gunpowder Plot, and ended with a sustained but unsuccessful effort to effect a merger during the session of 1606-1607. The latter session was almost completely concerned with the issue. Despite the cautious advice about the feasibility of a successful union he rendered to James in 1603, Bacon served as the Crown's leading proponent of the project both in and out of Parliament. He knew how important it was to the King and committed himself completely. Here, Bacon would attempt to utilize his prestige in the House to the utmost, in order to convince his colleagues to join with a historically hostile nation.

The effort began in April, 1604, after the atmosphere of the session had already been strained by the Goodwin dispute. Consideration of the issue stagnated immediately over the question of what aspects of union to discuss first. The Lords suggested and Bacon agreed that a name be chosen for the combined kingdoms before the more difficult problems of establishing common government and common laws were considered. Commons, however, was influenced by Sandys' strong statement of opposition to the project and insisted on debating the entire issue. Bacon sensed a growing mood of opposition, but told the House that James insisted on immediate consideration of a new name as well as acknowledgment of a union in substance. The King, he said, offered guarantees against Scottish and against alteration of the laws of the realm. James apparently realized, however, that the project would not be passed upon immediately, and called for a commission to work on it between parliamentary sessions.[21] The House grew more hesitant as Sandys developed his opposition. Bacon persevered but his confidence appears to have been shaken by the growing reluctance to support the idea of union. "The more we wade, the more we doubt," he told his colleagues as he continued to defend James's scheme.[22] Perhaps some of the reservations that he himself had held now appeared justified by the hesitation of his fellow members. As Sandys intensified his attack, Bacon's task grew more difficult. While he stood committed to union, he probably began to question whether the majority of literate opinion in England actually favored a merger with the Scots. The display of national pride shown by the Commons' stubborn refusal to consider a new name for the joint kingdom must have made him wonder whether he was pursuing a hopeless endeavor. The debates and conferences dragged on, however, until the inevitable postponement of the issue. It was agreed that a select commission be appointed to study the matter during the interim. For Bacon, the session of 1604 had been a frustrating political experience.

Bacon served on the commission as the Crown's key agent.[23] This body's recommendations, which became the basis of royal policy, were made known when Parliament resumed deliberation of the subject during the 1606-1607 session. In addition to playing an important decision-making role, Bacon made certain to assure James of his continued devotion to the cause. In the tract, "Certain Articles or Considerations Touching the Union of the Kingdoms of England and Scotland," he summarized the major issues discussed by the commission. The document dealt objectively with problems of laws, courts, religion, and names, as well as with several other important subjects. Although Bacon echoed his plea for a basically cautious approach to the over-all problem, he sought primarily to demonstrate the complexities of the topics considered.[24] He did not attempt to write a letter of advice to the King. On the contrary, he made clear his intention not "to presume to persuade or dissuade anything" and to follow James's "royal directions" in his future handling of the matter.[25] His political sensitivity was obvious.

Despite intensive preparation by the commission, the union question would face renewed and more vigorous opposition in Parliament. Because of his position as channel to the Crown and architect of compromise, Bacon's role would again be critical. Initially, he revealed the commission's recommendations which called for a comparatively moderate plan instead of James's initial one for immediate creation of a perfect union. Bacon called for resolving the problems of border violence, hostile laws, commerce, and naturalization. All of these were major obstacles to be overcome before any advanced concept of union could be realized. In asking for specific consideration of each of these issues, he cautioned that by proceeding too generally "it will be temptation to lead men to ingratiate themselves sometimes for favour, often for fame, both vices; and to speak as operators only, and not as lawmakers." "The thing," he said, "divided itself into three parts: 1. Laws of Hostility; 2. Com-

81

merce; 3. Naturalizing. These are of great consequence. Of the two first, the one included in streams of water, the other of blood; and the third of both." He urged cooperation with the Lords, hoping that the matter would proceed more smoothly via a joint approach.[26]

The House was not inclined to endorse this approach to union enthusiastically. It agreed to consider it, but soon showed strong opposition on the issues of commerce and naturalization. These were the serious controversies that would show just how strong the resentment toward the Scots actually was. The commission had advised that the *postnati* (Scots born after James's accession) were already naturalized by common law and were thus eligible to hold office in England.[27] This conclusion was based upon the premise that such persons, born under allegiance to James since 1603, were automatically subjects of both Scotland and England. There was considerable opposition to both the "automatic" naturalization of the *postnati* as well as to their supposed right to hold royal offices. Apparently, there were strong fears that naturalization would mean the encroachment by Scots upon the rights and privileges of Englishmen. Bacon delivered a long and eloquent speech that tried to diminish such fears, and convince his colleagues of the fairness and wisdom of the proposed "Article of Naturalization."[28]

This speech marked the culmination of the sustained effort he had made on behalf of this cause. He dealt with the main objections individually, arguing that the professed "inconveniences" that would result from naturalization had been exaggerated and that there would be greater "inconveniences" if the policy were not adopted. In refuting the claim that naturalization would lead to a "surcharge of people," he answered that England was "not yet peopled to the full," and contended that an added population would add to her stature and greatness as a nation.[29] The high point of the speech came when he answered the objection against invoking naturalization prior to the creation of one legal system. "Naturalization," he said, "is in order first and precedent to union of laws; in degree, a less matter than union of laws; and in nature, separable not inseparable, from union of laws. For naturalization doth but take out the marks of a foreigner, but union of laws makes them entirely as ourselves. Naturalization taketh away separation; but union of laws doth take away distinction."[30] With such language, Bacon urged a gradual approach toward complete union. With the same eloquence, he went on to explain further advantages of naturalization. He emphasized that union would mean a greater and more secure England, appealing to the members' growing national pride. "I think a man may speak it soberly and without bravery," he remarked, "that this kingdom of England, having Scotland united, Ireland reduced, the sea provinces of the Low Countries contracted, and shipping maintained, is one of the greatest monarchies, in forces truly esteemed, that hath been in the world."[31] With such prophetic language, Bacon hoped to broaden the appeal of the proposal and break through the opposition.

This speech ranks as one of Bacon's masterpieces of parliamentary oratory. It was, however, a failure. Bacon remained in favor with the House and was obviously admired for having studied the union issue so thoroughly. The fact remains, however, that the Commons refused to accept the contention that the *postnati* were naturalized by common law.[32] The issue dragged on and Bacon agreed to relate the objections to the Lords and report back on their views. He assured his colleagues that he would report "truly and nakedly" and "not add or diminish, nor express anything with unequal advantage."[33] Despite his commitment to union, he appears to have still sought to play the "honest broker." Maybe so. However, Bacon had also become somewhat disgusted with the persistent obstructiveness of the House. He finally told his colleagues that he "prayeth the House, that at other times they would use some others, and not oppress him with their favours."[34] Obviously, he had grown tired of representing a membership that continuously opposed him. His deep involvement in this matter finally necessitated a response to the Commons' uncooperative attitude.

The dispute dragged on and, despite his feelings, Bacon remained active. Sandys, in a move designed to thwart the Crown's plan, called for an immediate union of laws or "perfect union."[35] Although approval of this plan would end the dispute over naturalization, Sandys and his supporters realized that the government would not abandon its own plan. Bacon stated that Sandys' proposal was "moved out of zeal" and was thus "moved out of time." He refuted it, and again tried in vain to persuade the House to accept naturalization.[36] Deliberations lingered on over this stalemated issue until mid-June, 1607 (the session was prorogued on July 5), with Bacon remaining the Crown's chief spokesman. Although the Commons did agree to pass a vaguely worded act abolishing hostile laws, it refused to act more comprehensively. The only concession made to the government was that the statute's preamble indicated hope "for the furtherance of the happy Union, already begun in his Majesty's royal person, to be enacted."[37] Such a statement was general enough to be both harmless and meaningless. Union, as far as Parliament was concerned, was a dead issue; it would remain so for a century.

Francis Bacon's doubts about the political possibility of promoting union had been borne out. During the 1606-1607 session, he exhausted his persuasive talents while failing to guide the commission's work to successful passage. It is perhaps questionable whether he fully understood the intensity of the opposition to this controversial question. Although he had long been aware of the complex problems involved in union, he had convinced James to proceed moderately, hoping that Parliament would support a cautious approach to the issue. He appears to have been startled by the wholly obstructive attitude he encountered. The opposition, well organized in this matter, continually rebuffed Bacon, and at the same time expected him to serve as its spokesman. As he grew tired of being used by the House, it became clearer that he could no longer occupy an intermediate position. In all probability, the members' trust in Bacon declined during the union debates of 1607. Although he had argued discreetly, he had staunchly opposed the majority on the issues of naturalization and the proposed union of laws. His value as a conciliator had declined.

The first three Jacobean parliamentary sessions had been most frustrating for Bacon.[38] He had tried from an unofficial position to engender the harmony between Crown and Parliament necessary for effective government. The complex barriers to such a task, including his own political ambition, had proven too great. In June, 1607, Bacon's own status finally changed. With the stagnated session still in progress, Bacon was appointed Solicitor-General of England.[39] While he had long since proven himself worthy of higher officialdom than this, the appointment marked the end of a long drought in his quest for advancement. At least, James had shown some recognition of his ability.

It would be as Solicitor-General that Bacon would again serve James in the cause of union. Parliament's refusal to cooperate on naturalization led James to the courts for a favorable decision. Francis Bacon delivered one of the Crown's arguments before the Exchequer Chamber in the famous *postnati* case of 1608.[40] Bacon's speech, called by Spedding "probably the greatest of his forensic speeches," stressed allegiance to the King as taking precedence over allegiance to any law. Submission to a monarch, he argued, was "natural and more ancient" than submission to law.[41] Although Kings were not "owners" of the people (God is the sole owner), they governed as fathers did their families, and protected them in the way shepherds cared for their flocks. "The word, sacred, hath been attributed to kings," he stated, "because of the conformity of a monarchy with a divine Majesty: never to a senate of people."[42] Even though Bacon is not regarded as an exponent of the more extreme Divine Right theory, these words, read out of context, might lead one to believe he favored that point of view. Bacon, however, was emphatic about the importance of law. "Law, no doubt, is the great organ by which the sovereign power doth move. . . . Towards the king himself the law doth a double office or operation: the first is to entitle the king, or design him." "The second," he added, "is to make the ordinary power of the king more definite or regular." "But I demand," he continued, "do these offices or operations of law evacuate or frustrate the original submission which was natural? Or shall it be said that all allegiance is by law? No more than it can be said that *potestas patria*, the power of the father over the child is by law." He went on to conclude that he could "hardly consent that the King shall be esteemed or called only our rightful sovereign, or lawful sovereign, but our natural *liege sovereign*; as acts of Parliament speak: for as the common law is more worthy than the statute law; so the law of nature is more worthy than them both."[43] Thus, while Bacon recognized the significance of law and did not sanction government without it, he believed that submission to a Monarch was "natural" and did not have to be confirmed by any man-made law. The belief that the Sovereign derived his power from natural law was basic in Bacon's thinking. It was the basis for his view that naturalization might rightfully precede the union of laws. It might also be considered a philosophic foundation for his belief in a strong royal prerogative.

The emphasis on natural law and its relevance to the subject of naturalization constituted the core of Bacon's argument in this monumental case. He proved his value as a legal official by helping James gain a verdict from the courts that he had been unable to secure from Parliament. Thus, he successfully climaxed his arduous efforts in this politically ill-timed project.

85

For Bacon, the Solicitorship was a long-sought step toward higher office. It was not, however, a final goal, and might only have been considered a noteworthy achievement had Bacon gained it in the 1590s. He could only hope that arguments like the one he gave in the *postnati* case would impress the King sufficiently. The far more important post of Attorney-General was now within reach and he would do anything possible to convince James of his worthiness. While Bacon must have realized that he might have to wait some time before even being considered for that office (he would in fact wait until 1613), he had by necessity learned political patience. His endeavors for James during the struggles of these first years made clear that his commitment to the Crown had deepened. In his mid-forties and still financially insecure, Bacon knew there was no escape for him from political life. He was already what may be termed a seasoned politician; his greatest rewards and frustration, however, lay ahead.

Sitting as a royal official in the Commons for the first time in 1610, Bacon would enter a new phase of his parliamentary career. He was now an "official" spokesman for the Crown, and while such a position might have given him more prestige with the House in 1604, it would now prove a liability. The two sessions of 1610 ended James's first complete Parliament and climaxed the first phase of the reign's turbulent political history. The attitude of defiance toward the royal prerogative that had been developing since 1604 would now be expressed openly. As a ranking government official Bacon supported the Crown's efforts to bargain a "Great Contract" with Parliament and vigorously defended the prerogative during the dramatic debate over impositions. He acted in such capacity mainly out of duty for he sensed the futility of the session from its outset, and tried in vain to avoid the direct confrontation that eventually took place over impositions. Hardly in a position to mediate in 1610, Bacon still hoped for a harmonious session. He thought Salisbury's attempt to bargain via a "contract" to be a misguided effort and engendered contempt for such a scheme. It would only be after the death of his cousin in 1612, however, that he would openly express this feeling to the King. In 1610, the politically sensitive Bacon served the Crown faithfully, unable to alter the tactless course pursued. The strongest challenge yet to a high-handed prerogative would be made.

Since 1604, the parliamentary "opposition" had concentrated

on attacking the Crown's arbitrary and distasteful policies primarily on the basis of precedents found in the law and in past constitutional practices. James's adversaries strove to define the limits of the prerogative and clarify its relationship to Parliament within the constitution. The culmination of this type of opposition came during the debate over the legality of impositions in 1610. Here, the opposition manifested itself in a loud protest against the practices of legal absolutism and in the failure to achieve a financial settlement through the process of bargaining. By brilliantly refuting the royalist arguments for arbitrary impositions and refusing to help the Crown out of its financial straits, the House intensified the strained atmosphere that had been developing since 1604. As Solicitor-General, Bacon would find himself more firmly on the side of the government in a sharply divided Parliament.

Bacon knew at the outset that he might find himself in sharp conflict with the House. He tried, however, to assure his colleagues that he would serve them faithfully despite his official capacity. In reporting Salisbury's statement of the Crown's needs, he preluded with a dramatic appeal of his own:

> I know you will remember you are not in a theatre, but in a parliament, house of counsel, and that you will consider the most flourishing branches cannot be maintained without the root be nourished. And therefore though with less delight both to you and myself I shall, I know not *quo fato* but it falls out ever that pain is my portion, and by the grace of God whilst my breath and power will serve I will willingly undergo any labor this House shall impose upon me.[44] [Ital. mine]

He hoped he might maintain the trust of the membership even though he expected immediate difficulty for the Crown. The substance of his report showed the bad condition of the royal treasury and immediately put the Crown in a weak bargaining position. Bacon not only realized this, but knew that the Commons would insist on determining quickly what grievances the government was willing to redress.[45] After Salisbury indicated that James was willing to abolish purveyance and was considering (although without having made a commitment) the main issues of tenures and wardship, Bacon began the Crown's intensive plea for money.[46]

At first, the Solicitor stressed the traditional pattern of rendering aid without emphasizing the idea of a bargain. Perhaps, he hoped (wistfully, it could be said) that in the interest of harmony the House might settle for the standard promise of redress in return for a large subsidy.[47] Knowing the general mood of the Commons, however, he soon realized its determination to pressure for abolition of tenures and wardship. The contract scheme would have to be pursued. Bacon agreed to represent the House in asking the Lords to join in petitioning James for extinction of these two grievances in return for an annual grant. He hoped to persuade the Peers that asking the King to abolish two of his ancient privileges would not constitute an infringement upon the prerogative:

> We acknowledge that this tree of tenures was planted into the prerogative by the ancient common law of the land; that it hath been fenced in and preserved by many statutes; and that it yieldeth at this day to the King the fruit of a great revenue. But yet notwithstanding, if upon the stem of this tree may be raised a pillar of support to the Crown permanent and durable as the marble, by investing the Crown with a more loving dowry, than this of Tenures; we hope we propound no matter of disservice.[48]

He spoke similarly about wardship, stating that it was "not an incident inseparable of the Crown."[49] These remarks showed that Bacon still believed the King could rightfully "departe with anie part of his prerogative" which was not "inseparable" (as was his right to "judge or do justice"), and "nevertheless remaineth a King as before."[50] Throughout the speech he cautiously stressed that Parliament was not trying to pressure the King into responding hastily, but merely hoped he would act "according to his good times and royal pleasure."[51] By convincing the Lords to agree to the petition, Bacon was still playing the reconciling statesman. He knew, however, that as a royal official he could continue in this role only as long as open confrontation was avoided. Bacon was desperately trying to avert the crisis that was building from the start of the session.

His hopes and efforts were, of course, doomed to failure. The question of the contract's price remained unsettled since the House had come to understand that the annual fee would be £100,000 instead of the £200,000 originally requested. While Bacon supported the higher fee, he realized the futility of the government's position.[52] As a stalemate developed over the contract, the House proceeded to take up the grievance of royal impositions (it had not been covered in their petition) thereby unleashing the most significant issue of the session.

The great dispute in which Parliament strongly challenged the legality of the decision rendered in Bate's case dominated business from mid-May until the prorogation in late July, 1610. The struggle was highlighted by a dramatic five-day debate in late June, during which the lines between prerogative and parliamentary privilege were sharply drawn. A series of complicated stages led up to this debate during which Bacon tried unsuccessfully to neutralize this hostility. He told a committee of the whole convened to treat impositions that while he did not believe "the King's prerogative" was "infinite" (there were those "that would have said that loudly," he inferred), "the partition wall between the King and the subject must stand." He then added:

> If in the question in hand we only complain of the inconveniences, I think there is a great and full latitude for us to seek and obtain our ends. But you object that we admit the right. Though it is fit to reverence legal judgments yet to wrap ourselves in a mere acknowledgment and confession that the House is right is needless, neither am I so unknowing in the use and carriage of words, but that I conceive an answer may well be penned without direct confession of the right.[53]

Bacon implied that he had never believed the prerogative was limitless. His general belief in a balanced government, as well as the numerous references to the rights of the subjects made throughout his career, support this remark. He did believe, however, that the right to levy impositions was legally part of the prerogative, and could never be challenged. Although he was firm in the belief that "the partition must stand," he pleaded that Parliament confine its complaint to the inconveniences caused by the impositions. If the latter course were pursued, then perhaps the grievance could be resolved without a direct conflict over the question of right. Redress, he felt, was a distinct possibility.

As the debating continued, Bacon again had the opportunity to comment on the relationship between Crown and Parliament. His remarks stand as one of the most revealing statements he ever made on the subject:

> The King's Sovereignty and the Liberty of Parliament are as the two elements and principles of this estate; which, though the one

89

be more active, the other more passive, yet they do not cross or destroy the one or the other, but they strengthen and maintain the one the other. Take away liberty of Parliament, the griefs of the of the subject will bleed inwards: sharp and eager humors will not evaporate, and then they must exulcerate, and so may endanger the sovereignty itself. On the other side, if the King's sovereignty receive diminution or any degree of contempt with us that are born under an hereditary monarchy (so as the motions of our state cannot work in any other frame or engine) it must follow that we shall be a *meteor* or *corpus imperfecte mistum*; which kind of bodies come speedily to confusion or dissolution.[54]

This plea for harmony in government showed Bacon's continuing belief in a balanced constitution. His recognition of Parliament as a junior but necessary partner of the Crown again demonstrated that he did not believe the prerogative to be "infinite." Bacon retained his Tudor view of cooperation between these basic institutions; each had its specific purpose as part of the whole organism. Any disruption of these purposes would upset the balance and cause chaos in the state. Such a view implied that Parliament should recognize its functions and its limitations, and should not attempt to contest the prerogative power. Bacon's reference to the "active" and "passive" places of the King and Parliament respectively showed that he could never really approve of the two bargaining as equals. The entire concept of the contract was contrary to his basic political thinking. Although the purpose of the speech was not to attack the proposed bargain, the implications of his remarks are worth noting.

Despite further efforts by Bacon to persuade the House not to challenge the prerogative, the session drifted toward open confrontation.[55] The great debate on impositions took place in a committee of the whole from June 23-28, 1610. The legality of the decision handed down in Bate's case, by which the King claimed the right to levy nonparliamentary impositions on movables related to commerce as part of his prerogative, was now strongly challenged on the basis of legal and constitutional precedent.[56] The opposition, claiming that the King's right to impose on any commodity had depended on the consent of Parliament since the reign of Edward I, openly contested the victory James had won in the courts. The direct attack on the prerogative was answered by royalist arguments also based on historical precedents. As Gardiner remarks: "In looking back to the past history of their country, both parties allowed their view of the constitution to be tinged with colours which were derived from their political opinions."[57] The use of past decisions to buttress legalistic arguments, already a common parliamentary practice, was employed extensively during this controversy. The debate "was left almost entirely in the hands of the lawyers," and sounded very much like a series of court arguments.[58] While Bacon and the other royalists sought to defend the prerogative, the leading opposition spokesmen were determined to refute their arguments, and to prevent the Crown "from registering any legal victories in Parliament."[59]

Bacon delivered an eloquent speech in which he utilized extensively his knowledge of precedent. His involved argument "proving the king's right of impositions" relied heavily on examples from medieval statutes. It was a systematic, carefully organized defense of the prerogative.[60] Although he agreed with two other leading royalist spokesmen that only Parliament had the power to tax, he did not believe impositions fell into this category.[61] The fact that tonnage and poundage were always granted in Parliament, Bacon argued, did not mean that all impositions must necessarily be levied by that body. "It is not strange with kings," he added, "for their own better strength and the better contentment of their people, to do those things by Parliament, which nevertheless have perfection enough without Parliament." He argued that the king's right to impose established "by the fundamental laws of this kingdom," was not totally abolished either by 25 Ed.I, or by 14 Ed.III.[61] The former statute (the Confirmation of the Charters of 1297), Bacon said, only limited the King's power with respect to the commodity of wool. The latter act pertained to impositions on woolfells and leather. Bacon maintained that Edward III's silence on the grievances against lead and tin (also included in the petition) implied that these two duties were to continue. Thus, neither of these statutes put any total limitations upon the imposing power of the royal prerogative. "Kings," he remarked, "shall not be bound by general words." Bacon continued:

> The reason for the imposition is whatsoever concerns the government of the kingdom as it hath relation to foreign parts—the law hath reposed a special confidence in the King. . . . Though you have no remedy by law, yet you may complain in Parliament, as your ancestors have done by petition. And God and nature hath provided a remedy.[63]

These words constituted the heart of the royalist opposition on this delicate issue. Bacon attempted to be both convincing and conciliatory in his approach. He again tried to convince the House, that while it had no legal right to challenge the prerogative, it did have the right to petition for relief.[64]

The arguments of Bacon and the other royalists were refuted brilliantly by the two leading spokesmen of the opposition, Hakewill and Whitelocke.[65] According to one writer, these individuals put forth "such telling and effective arguments . . . that the royalists might well have wished that they had left the question of absolute prerogative as a matter of policy and government, and had never argued it in a court of law."[66] Hakewell skillfully answered the portion of Bacon's argument based on the statutes by citing passages from these same documents which showed the existence of ambiguity. "Even as an interpretation of the mere letter of the statute," Gardiner adds, "Bacon's view of the case is manifestly inferior to that of Hakewell."[67] Whitelocke, called "the most forceful and profound of all the parliamentary debaters and thinkers in these years," delivered the most potent argument against the prerogative.[68] He was the only opposition member to grasp the concept that the power of the King in Parliament was supreme, and that the King's prerogative was, in fact, subordinate to this power. In recognizing that the King in Parliament was sovereign, and that the legislative power of that body was its most important function, Whitelocke was more advanced in his thinking than any of his contemporaries. No other opposition spokesman recognized "the extent of Parliament's sovereignty."[69] Even though the parliamentary attack would have been more effective had Whitelocke's ideas prevailed, the opposition scored a noteworthy triumph during these debates in 1610. The royalists had been soundly attacked on the basis of the law and the constitution and had been put very much on the defensive within Parliament. The House had displayed its distaste for legal absolutism, and had defended what it believed to be its basic rights under the constitution. Without advancing anything that could be termed a revolutionary position, the Parliament of 1610 had sharply attacked the fundamental policy of the time. One can assume that Bacon was most disturbed during those late June days.

Despite further reconciling efforts by Bacon during the summer and autumn of 1610, the June debates doomed the session to total stagnation.[70] There was to be no "great Contract" nor even an ordinary grant of financial aid. The House failed to secure a legal prohibition of impositions, but had dealt a serious blow to the Crown's prestige. Governmental harmony in Jacobean England was farther from reality than ever before.

In discussing Bacon in 1610, Notestein claims that he "had little conception of the slow but steady accretion of influence and power by Parliament." He calls this "a strange want of insight on the part of a man of philosophic outlook." Notestein goes on:

> It is the more strange because he had long experience in the House of Commons. In 1593, he had stood stubbornly for the rights of the Commons against the Lords in initiating money grants and had lost for the time being the favor of the Queen. At that stage of his life he seems to have valued the historic rights of the Commons and to have been willing to throw his cap over the wall for them. But although he wrote a brilliant biography of Henry VII, he had not the historian's interest in orderly change. At this time, he was eighteen years older and had lost some of the zeal of his early thirties. Now he was examining precedents largely to make a case for the King. His ambitions had been thwarted time and again: the position he deserved, he would win soon or never. He had come to believe that the power of the gentry (as shown in the Commons) was a menace to the good subject (as Gardiner has pointed out) and thus that royal power hand in hand with wise Councillors such as himself was best. He knew how the Commons might be manipulated. The leaders of the Commons had their price, in offices and honors, which they should be given. His advice to the King, more often proffered than accepted, was judicious and often farseeing. He was the English Machiavelli with a difference.[71]

Such an extensive comment necessitates reaction as one attempts to understand Bacon as a political man. The contention that Sir Francis had "little conception" of Parliament's accumulation of greater power is unjustified. His rich parliamentary experience encompassed development of opposition factions during these early Jacobean years. He had witnessed the hostility expressed over both privilege and wardship in 1604, had debated the union issue with an unyielding opposition group in 1607, and had defended the Crown in the great impositions dispute in 1610. Bacon negotiated with the opposition extensively as it developed 1604-10, experiencing the many frustrations just explained. It is difficult to believe that someone of his mentality and experience was blind to the fact that the government would face continued hostility from Parliament. His subsequent advice to James on the subject (to be discussed later) demonstrated that he was aware of the deteriorated political situation and did not pretend that a solution would be easy or automatic. Bacon's views on solving these complex problems may be questioned as to their feasibility. He was hardly ignorant of the existence of a growing obstructive attitude in Parliament, however, even though he never discussed the "opposition" explicitly in his writings. It must be understood that Bacon was a contemporary of this "opposition" as it was first developing an awareness of its own existence and potentialities. Opposition to the Crown was not yet taken for granted as an accepted fact of political life. Would it not be asking too much to expect Bacon to have analyzed this "opposition" with the perception of a modern observer? His attitude would be one of awareness of future political stagnation and hardly indicates "a strange want of insight."

The changes in Bacon's views from 1593 are also quite understandable. They indicate not so much a loss of "the zeal of his early thirties" as the development of an attitude of political realism. Despite his defense of the prerogative, Bacon never really abandoned the view that the Commons had "historic rights." Further discussion will reinforce this evaluation. It also is a bit rash to contend that the author of the *Novum Organum* and the *New Atlantis* did not have an interest in "orderly change." Notestein correctly sees Bacon as looking for the renewal of efficient and tactful conciliar control of Parliament with he himself occupying the key maneuvering position. Bacon's royalism had intensified, and Notestein is more correct when he does admit that he did give James advice that "was judicious and often farseeing." Calling him "the English Machiavelli with a difference" is confusing and should have been clarified.

Bacon had served his king faithfully during the turbulent session of 1610. He cannot be blamed for the failure, since he merely helped execute the strategy developed by Salisbury. If Bacon had been more influential, he would have tried to persuade James to behave like a king in effecting a bargain. Whatever he would have advised could hardly have been less successful than the course so tactlessly pursued. Bacon would reveal his opinion of the 1610 fiasco only after the death of his cousin two years later. An analysis of these ideas shows that he supported the contract solely out of loyalty, and not because he believed in the wisdom of the policy.[72] In a very real sense, Bacon was an unfortunate victim of the tragedy of the session. Having reached officialdom, he would have wanted to use the prestige of his office to help James deal more effectively with Parliament. Whether Bacon could have helped the Crown in 1610 had he not merely been in Salisbury's functionary is, of course, questionable. There are, however, degrees of failure. While the atmosphere of 1610 was not conducive to solving major problems, it is conceivable that the kind of open confrontation that so badly estranged Crown-Parliament relations might have been prevented. While Bacon worked desperately toward this end, he was in no position to advise James against Salisbury's "contract." He was still a frustrated political man.

With the failure of 1610, Francis Bacon completed his first "tour of duty" as a servant of James I. He had worked diligently and often brilliantly in efforts that had dealt him continual frustration. Although he was Solicitor-General of England, there was cold comfort in that office as an end in itself. There was still the perennial rivalry with Coke and the twisted shadow of his cousin to plague him as he tried to look to the future. Although he was not without hope, as a man approaching fifty, he could only be uncertain about his political future.

1. Gardiner, *History of England*, I, 194.

2. Willson, *King James . . .* , 243-49. Willson describes James's notion of Parliament as one which "came from the Parliament of Scotland" which was, "for all its age, a weak, primitive and feudal body."

3. Theodore K. Rabb, "Sir Edwin Sandys and the Parliament of 1604," *American Historical Review* (April 1, 1964), 646-70.

Although Rabb refers frequently to an "opposition" group as having existed in 1604, he does not say that it was a closely knit or well-organized party. It organized itself for specific issues and did not attempt to claim sovereign powers for Parliament. Rabb shows that on one issue, that of monopolies, the "opposition" was motivated by specific economic interests. In a larger work, Williams M. Mitchell, *The Rise of the Revolutionary Party in the English House of Commons 1604-1629* (New York, 1957), the problem of tracing the growth of the opposition is dealt with in detail. Mitchell agrees that the "opposition" in 1604, although at times well organized, could hardly be called a party. He expresses the view that an opposition developed between 1604 and 1610, and that this development was due largely to the increased pressure of business, and to the use of new legislative methods. He believes that these two factors, together with loss of power and prestige by the Privy

Councillors (a fact well known because of the work of Notestein and Willson) were important in the development of an opposition. He does not reveal clearly, however, just how much of this development appears to have been conscious, and how much of it to have been the result of increased business and new procedural methods. Although Mitchell uses statistics to show the importance of the increased pressure of business, his conclusions are sometimes contradictory. *See* Mitchell, XV, 26, 38.

4. I have stressed Bacon's role as a mediator in this first parliamentary session in "Francis Bacon: Mediator in the Parliament of 1604," *The Historian* (February, 1968), 219-37.

5. Great Britain, *Journals of the House of Commons*, 1604-1610 (London, 1803), I, 149, 151, 934.

6. *Ibid.*, 158, 938.

7. *Ibid.*, 157-58.

8. Wallace Notestein, *The House of Commons, 1604-1610* (New Haven, 1971), 70.

9. CJ, I, 939.

10. *Ibid.*

11. *Ibid.*, 160, 162, 163, 941.

12. *Ibid.*, 168, 944.

13. *Ibid.*, 153-55, 935, 937.

14. Purveyance, like wardship, is a holdover from the feudal era. It concerned the right of the Crown to purchase goods below the normal market price. Purveyors were royal officials who not only forced people to sell their products at crippling prices, but often requested more than the quantity needed and returned the excess only after extorting a handsome payment. Such practices, although clearly distasteful, were resorted to by the Crown because of the constant need for revenue.

15. *Letters and Life*, III, 181, 187. Bacon wrote out a few of his speeches beforehand. In this instance, however, he not only did so but personally corrected a second copy (the one probably delivered to James).

16. *Ibid.*, 183.

17. CJ, I, 192, 960-61. Although Bacon's report of James's reaction is fragmented in the Journal, the King's apparent willingness to cooperate is clearly shown.

18. *Ibid.*, 232, 253, 895, 1002.

19. *Ibid.*, 242, 244, 994, 996.

20. Notestein points out that the statement in the Apology about purveyors appears based on Bacon's remarks on that subject made earlier in the session. He also tells us that the statement on the Church reflects the tone of Bacon's "Certain Consideration . . ." of 1603. The language of the Apology, however, hardly suggests Bacon had a hand in its writing. Although Notestein feels it is conceivable that Bacon might have assisted in writing it in the hope of toning it down, there is no evidence to support such a claim. His closeness to the Crown makes his opposition to the document understandable. *See The House of Commons. . .* , 136-37.

21. CJ, I, 180, 953; *Letters and Life*, III, 193-95.

22. CJ, I, 184-85, 957.

23. The "Commission for Union" met from October 29 to December 6, 1604.

24. *Letters and Life*, III, 218-34. Although the document is not dated, it was obviously written shortly after the commission ended its session.

25. *Ibid.*, 234.

26. *Ibid.*, 303-304; CJ, I, 324-25.

27. The commission felt those born before the accession (*antenati*) should be naturalized by law but barred from holding any government office.

28. *Letters and Life*, III, 307-24.

29. *Ibid.*, 312-13.

30. *Ibid.*, 314-15.

31. *Ibid.*, 323.

32. CJ, I, 340. In referring to this speech, Notestein makes the following comment: "One would be glad to learn the impact of this persuasive speech upon members. Like Woodrow Wilson three centuries later, Bacon could hit upon arresting and memorable combinations of words; like Wilson, he could lift the debate to what seemed a high level until sometimes, when one thought it over afterward, one asked questions." *See The House of Commons . . .* , 224. I must admit I am not able to grasp the subtlety of this remark.

33. *Letters and Life*, III, 329-30.

34. CJ, I, 345.

35. *Letters and Life*, III, 334-35.

36. *Ibid.*, 335-36.

37. *Ibid.*, 344. *See* also D. H. Willson, ed., *The Parliamentary Diary of Robert Bowyer, 1606-1607* (Minneapolis, 1931), 313.

38. It is true that the atmosphere of the 1605-1606 session was basically harmonious due to the temporary unity provoked by the Gunpowder Plot. Bacon's role here again shows him trying to preserve a cooperative attitude in the House. *See* Epstein, "The Parliamentary Career . . . ," 158-77.

39. *Letters and Life*, III, 362.

40. It is also significant to note that in the same year as the *postnati* case Bacon published another tract on union. The work, "Of the True Greatness of Great Britain," based on Bacon's parliamentary speeches of 1606-1607, popularized the view that a united kingdom was the key to world greatness. His purpose was obviously to generate national support for a cause that had been thwarted by Parliament. Although it is not clear whether the document preceded the *postnati* decision, it is quite possible that one of Bacon's main objectives in writing it was to prepare public opinion for acceptance of a legal victory for the Crown concerning naturalization. *See ibid.*, IV, 16-17; for the text of the work. *See* also *Bacon's Works*, XIII, 221-55.

41. *Bacon's Works*, XV, 200.

42. *Ibid.*, 198-200.

43. *Ibid.*, 200-201.

44. Elizabeth R. Foster, ed., *Proceedings in Parliament 1610*, 2 vols. (New Haven, 1966), II, 29. The "Great Contract" called for an annual parliamentary grant of £200,000 in return for concessions that included the abolition of purveyance and wardship.

45. *Letters and Life*, IV, 155. For two other versions of this report, *see* CJ, I, 395-96; and Samuel R. Gardner, ed., *Parliamentary Debates in 1610* (London, 1862).

46. *Letters and Life*, IV, 160-61.

47. CJ, I, 402.

48. *Letters and Life*, IV, 165.

49. *Parliamentary Debates . . .* , 26.

50. *Bowyer's Diary*, 65-66. By asserting that the King's right to render justice was part of his inseparable prerogative, Bacon was in agreement with the other leading royalists of his day. In a work, "Jurisdiction of the Council of Wales" (1607),

97

he differentiated clearly between an inseparable right and one which the king could voluntarily relinquish without altering his status. Bacon thus showed that his support for the prerogative did not make him rigidly opposed to constructive change. See also Letters and Life, III, 371.

51. Letters and Life, IV, 167.

52. Ibid., 169-76; CJ, I, 422-23.

53. Proceedings in Parliament . . . , II, 94.

54. Ibid., II, 98. Mrs. Foster gives the date of this speech as May 18, 1610. See also Letters and Life, IV, 177-80.

55. I have dealt with this issue more thoroughly in "Francis Bacon and the Challenge to the Prerogative in 1610," Journal of Historical Studies (Winter, 1969-70), 272-83.

56. Aside from Parliament's brief outcry against the decision in 1606, there was no strong protest at the time the case was heard. See William Cobbett, ed., A Complete Collection of State Trials (London, 1809-28), II, 371.

57. History of England . . . , II, 76.

58. Ibid., 75.

59. Judson, 227.

60. Letters and Life, IV, 191-200; Parliamentary Debates . . . , 66-72.

61. Parliamentary Debates . . . , 62, 66, 98.

62. Letters and Life, IV, 192, 196, 198.

63. Ibid., 198-200.

64. Notestein discusses Bacon's argument thoroughly. While he gives the Solicitor credit for making some good points, he feels his argument "was farfetched" and "disingenuous!" He solidly backs up his contention that Bacon misinterpreted the history of imposition in the 1340's. Notestein then asks, "Was he possibly taking a chance that the opponents of royal imposition would never find out that he was misusing the Rolls of Parliament? It is more charitable to assume that he had not read them with sufficient attention or had used an assistant to read them." See The House of Commons . . . , 363-65, 558-59.

65. For the arguments of these two individuals, see State Trials, II, 407-76, 478-519.

66. Judson, 227-28.

67. History of England, II, 78. For a brief but useful account of Hakewill's use of precedent, see Judson, 230-32.

68. Judson, 230.

69. Ibid., 235-37. My remarks on Whitelock's ideas reflect the views stated in these pages.

70. For a discussion of Bacon's persistent efforts to persuade the House to soften its position and grant financial aid, see Epstein, "The Parliamentary Career . . . ," 223-29. After the Commons' total rejection of the contract in early November, the Crown made one final appeal for aid in the traditional manner. Bacon again played an important role in this endeavor.

71. The House of Commons . . . , 558.

72. Letters and Life, IV, 369, 371. Bacon spoke his mind on the mistakes of 1610 only after Salisbury's death in May, 1612. He told James that the practices employed in 1610 were "almost contrary to the frame of monarchy." For a monarch to succeed with Parliament, he must "put off the person of a merchant and contractor, and rest upon the person of a King." Bacon was emphatic in his condemnation of the contract idea.

CHAPTER VII

POLITICAL SUCCESS, I: ATTORNEY GENERAL

As early as 1611, Bacon made clear to James his desire to become Attorney General. The office, he wrote, was "but the natural and immediate step and rise which the place I now hold hath ever in a sort made claim to, and almost never failed of."[1] Early in 1612 (after the current Attorney, Hobart, had become seriously ill), he wrote to Salisbury again expressing interest in the office.[2] As Solicitor, his restlessness to advance was obvious even though he realized that he would have to be patient until the position fell vacant.[3] While no vacancy would occur until 1613, he viewed the death of Salisbury in May, 1612, as removal of a major obstacle to his advancement.

Bacon's real feelings toward his cousin could now be openly expressed. Necessity had always dictated that he keep a cautious silence about the Cecils, even though they had always frustrated the progress of his political career. At last, he could unleash the bitterness he had harbored so long. "Your Majesty hath lost a great subject and a great servant" he wrote James, but added:

> If I should praise him in propriety, I should say that he was a fit man to keep things from growing worse but not a very fit man to reduce things to be much better. For he loved to have all the eyes of Israel a little too much upon himself, and to have all business still under the hammer and like clay in the hands of the potter, to mould it as he thought good.[4]

Such criticism could be considered polite and cautious, but Bacon was less reserved when he published the essay "Of Deformity" in 1612. Sardonically, he stated that "Deformed persons are commonly even with nature; for as nature hath done ill by them, so do they by nature; being for the most part (as the Scripture saith) void of natural affection; and so they have their revenge of nature." "Deformity," he added, "is an advantage to rising," but Kings' "trust toward them (deformed persons) hath rather been as to good spials and good whispers; then good Magistrates, and officers."[5] Robert Cecil was gone and Bacon could no longer cloak the animosity he had engendered for so long.

From the time of Cecil's death until 1615 (after there had been another disastrous Parliament in 1614), Bacon poured out political advice to James. The ideas expressed during that period constitute a part of Bacon's political thinking, and will be treated later.[6] He was primarily concerned with spelling out Salisbury's mistakes of 1610 and advising the King just how Parliament should be managed. To be certain, there was a self-seeking motive behind such endeavors. Apparently, Bacon decided upon Salisbury's death to pursue a different course of advancement. Both the offices of Secretary of State and Lord Treasurer were vacant, and he sought the former post together with its accompanying place on the Privy Council. He hoped James would be impressed with his insights on handling Parliament, and allow him to manage it directly for the Crown. What he sought was a return to the approach last used in the final two Elizabethan sessions when Salisbury (then Robert Cecil) "managed" the Commons as Principal Secretary. Bacon had of course served under Cecil and tried to convince James to return to this method. He wrote the King shortly after his cousin's death suggesting that he might best serve by being removed "to business of state," but declaring openly that he would "be ready as a chessman to be wherever your Majesty's royal hand shall set me."[7] Whether Bacon's ideas about reinvigorating the Elizabethan way of handling Parliament were realistic anymore is a question that will be subsequently discussed. What is of interest here is that he immediately seized upon the occasion of his cousin's death to offer himself to fill the void left in the government. Bacon's thirst for advancement was tremendous. He believed he had the correct advice to help his politically and financially troubled King and gave it extensively, hoping that James would listen. While he did not rule out advancement to Attorney General, he pursued this other course with greater diligence. Apparently, he felt closer to political power than ever before and was determined to succeed.

Bacon's efforts to become a Privy Councillor via the Secretary-ship were not successful. "Perhaps," as Willson suggests, "Salisbury's distrust of Bacon was still present in James's mind," and that "diplomacy and administration, rather than the law, for which James had no great liking, were the usual stepping stones to the secretaryship." The same author further contends that the King passed up "one of the most interesting possibilities of the reign" to alleviate his estranged relationship with Parliament.[8] Whether Bacon could have been very successful in this capacity in 1614, and whether he could have persuaded James to handle Parliament successfully is, of course, quite doubtful. Bacon had much to say about handling Parliament during this period and continued to advise James during 1614, even though he was not in a position to "manage" Parliament. Any sustained effort at implementing Bacon's views would have required royal leadership, of which James was incapable. Bacon's ideas on the Crown-Parliament relationship must be evaluated with this in mind, together with the fact that he himself did not fully understand his King's political incapacity.

Bacon's advancement would proceed via the path of the legal profession. Chief Justice Fleming died in August, 1613, and Bacon immediately suggested to James reshuffling plans that would see him made Attorney General. He pleaded in earnest and desperation: "I have served your Majesty above a prenticehood, full seven years and more, as your solicitor, which is, I think, one of the painfulest places in your kingdom, specially as my employments have been; and God hath brought mine own years to fifty-two, which I think is older than ever any Solicitor continued unpreferred."[9] Attorney Hobart, he felt, should be made Chief Justice, thus making room for his own advancement. Shortly afterwards, however, he revised his plans for reshuffling and advised making Coke Chief Justice of England; Hobart, Chief of Common Pleas; and himself, Attorney. This was to be Bacon's masterstroke that would in time propel his own career and set in motion the process that would bring his arch-enemy down. Coke, he felt, would be bridled in this new post since his closeness to the Crown would prevent him from obstructing the prerogative. Moreover, Coke will crave a place on the Privy Council "and thereupon turn obsequious." Bacon spelled it out to James. With himself as Attorney, Lord Coke could be closely watched and prevented from opposing "the King's causes." "It is not to purpose for the judges to stand well disposed, except the King's counsel, which is the active and moving part, put the judges

101

well to it; for in a weapon what is a back without an edge?"[10] Coke knew his rival sought to see him safely tucked away upstairs and hardly relished such a prospect. Bacon hoped that good behavior would be demanded as a price Coke would have to pay for a seat on the Privy Council. The latter was made Chief Justice and a Councillor at once, however, and his behavior would hardly prove complacent. Bacon's advice had been followed for the most part with his rival seemingly shelved at the top. With Coke's appointment came Bacon's promotion to Attorney in October, 1613.[11] A new phase of his political career was beginning.

Bacon was Attorney General from 1613 until his promotion to Lord Keeper four years later. He had finally reached high officialdom and would for the first time be directly involved in major affairs of state. For the first time, he would be part of the inner workings of government. Although not yet a Privy Councillor, Bacon would utilize his position to lay effectively the basis for his future rise to the Council. His main concern was, of course, the law. Bacon would work vigorously to gain ascendancy for his legal ideas and would inevitably clash with Coke. Having already been instrumental in the move to "contain" his enemy, he would now oppose him more strongly than ever. Lord Coke's continued obstructionism coupled with Bacon's efforts against him would culminate in Coke's fall in 1616. This major struggle, which may be termed both personal and professional, highlighted Bacon's tenure as Attorney. In this conflict, as well as in his cases and legal writings, Bacon would reveal his views on royal justice. He would be very much of an activist as Attorney General.

Before the important cases and the struggle against Coke, there would be the business of Parliament. Bacon's political life had thus been spent primarily in the Commons, and despite his elevation to Attorney, he continued to advise James on this delicate subject. The short, dismal session of 1614 would mark Bacon's finale as a member of the Lower House.[12] He had for some time been concerned about James's relationship with Parliament, and his interest hardly diminished. Bacon knew the Crown's financial situation was deteriorating rapidly, and hoped James would convene another Parliament before it reached the point of utter desperation. Unfortunately, for reasons that reflect James's inability to govern successfully, the decision was put off until the Crown's needs were too great to warrant further postponement.[13] As preparations for

102

the session were being made, Bacon feared the King would again resort to bargaining with the House. He reacted strongly against the governmental plans that were being made by the controversial Henry Neville. Bacon distrusted Neville, who had been on good terms with the opposition in 1610, and who Willson feels would have been a good choice for Secretary of State.[14] He wrote James warning him "not to buy and sell this Parliament, but to perform the part of a King, and not of a merchant or contractor."[15] He was apparently convinced that Neville's policy would inevitably lead James into this approach again. Although not in a position to play a direct role in formulating royal policy in this matter, the new Attorney remained a much concerned royal official. He sensed another fruitless effort by the Crown that could only lead to deeper political stagnation.

Bacon went so far as to advise the King what to say in his opening address to Parliament.[16] It was vital to tell the House immediately that the practice employed in 1610 would never again be used. Assistance in important matters of state should be given as the main reason for the session, with supply mentioned as the second reason. The King should emphasize his heavy expenses, but avoid giving details about his debts, and refrain from attaching any concessions or threats to the report. Bacon had earlier advised great restraint in asking for money and had even implied that James must try not to appear too desperate. The King must attempt to convince Parliament that he would convene it in the future when he was not in need of money. Although Bacon realized that it would be difficult to convince a Jacobean Parliament of the sincerity of such a pledge, the effort had to be made. While no immediate turnabout in the Crown-Parliament relationship was realistic in 1614, Bacon hoped that the King might at least show good faith. James should be majestic, but show sensitivity to accumulated grievances. He should clarify that he would not "for all the treasure in the world, quit any point of his sovereignty and monarchy." He would promise to use his prerogative tactfully, however, without injury to his subjects, and would recognize that grievances had to be dealt with as they arose.[17] Furthermore, he would point out his "affection for the holding of Parliaments" and his hope that it may become a yearly practice.[18]

This advice, on the eve of the session, represents a continuation of the thinking Bacon had echoed earlier. He continued to stress

103

his Tudor approach to Parliament, still hoping that such practices might be reinvigorated. Furthermore, as Attorney General, he sought to gain immediate influence with the King. Parliament was a subject that he knew well, and he truly believed the ideas of Henry Neville would lead to disaster. What better way was there to begin a new position favorably than by impressing the King with important advice? Bacon would again sit in Parliament as a governmental official and did not want to witness a repetition of 1610. He wrote as if he expected James not only to be receptive to his suggestions but also to comprehend thoroughly the urgency of implementing them. Francis Bacon never appeared to be aware of the futility of his endeavors at counseling his King.

The so-called "Addled" Parliament would be a total failure. It would also mark an unpleasant ending to Bacon's career in the Commons. The historian of this Parliament claims James's opening speech "showed Bacon's influence in almost every line."[19] He changed his approach a few days later, however, when in a second speech he "largely abandoned Bacon's ideas in favour of Neville's advice."[20] James retreated to a policy based largely on concession and immediately provoked mistrust. Bacon had failed to influence James sufficiently, and would again find himself forced to support another misguided effort. His position would immediately become difficult since his seat was challenged on the grounds that no Attorney General had ever served as a member of the House.[21] It is doubtful whether the action was meant as a personal assault against Bacon. The lack of precedent for seating an Attorney was purely accidental, and the move was an open display of hostility against the Crown. Bacon absented himself during the lengthy debate on the subject, and despite some vehement opposition to his eligibility, still had friends and admirers among the membership.[22] He was finally admitted with the stipulation that in the future no Attorney General was ever to sit in the House.[23] His admission was a personal exception made by an already defiant Commons. The incident constituted a defeat for both the Crown and Bacon. His standing in the House had been shaken, and the precarious nature of his tenure would cause him to scrutinize his conduct on the floor of the House. Championing the Crown as much as possible under the circumstances, he pleaded an ill-timed request for supply, despite the fact that he had strongly urged James against immediately asking for money from a House that was already hostile. The Attorney spoke discreetly, trying to dignify the Crown's appeal. He did his best to disassociate James from Neville's policies, disavowing bargaining and stressing "mutual affection." Furthermore, he still defended the prerogative, although in language that was discreet and inoffensive.[24] It was a bold performance for someone who had almost been expelled from the House days before. He was determined to show James his willingness to help despite the circumstances.

The two-month session saw continued hostility and noncommunication between the government and the House. Bacon labored tirelessly, again acting as a channel to the Crown, and trying to reverse the mood of the session.[25] When impositions were again debated, he avoided direct involvement. He obviously realized the futility of again arguing the Crown's position on this issue, particularly since his own standing in the House was precarious.[26] The Parliament was terminated in early June with Bacon's warnings having fallen on deaf ears. He had persevered for James anyway, and had even retained a measure of the Commons' respect. Despite his visions of restoring governmental harmony, he could only observe helplessly the further deterioration of the Crown-Parliament relationship. And yet, Bacon did not give up hope. "For nothing is to a man either a greater spur or a greater direction to do over a thing again," he wrote to the King in 1615, "than when he knows where he failed, and I am of the same opinion in this matter of Parliament; in which subject I ought not to be novice-like or ignorant having now served full twelve Parliaments."[27] Bacon sharply attacked Neville and his policies of 1614, reiterating what he said before. When Parliament met again, James should maintain "an utter silence . . . of matters of money or supply, or of the King's debts or wants; they are things too well known. The authority of the King which heretofore hath suffered . . . will ever suffer as long as money is made the mere object of Parliament."[28] James, Bacon advised, must also stop making frequent speeches to Parliament. After the opening address the King "is in the right if he speak no more; except it be upon some occasion of thanks or other weighty particular."[29] James's habit of making long, threatening speeches to Parliament had helped make that body increasingly aware of the dangers of royal absolutism. Bacon knew that the prerogative must be used discreetly and not publicized in Parliament. Another problem of concern to Bacon was James's

105

difficulties with the various factions at court. Court intrigue had delayed the summoning of the 1614 session and had greatly hampered the efforts of Neville and Winwood.[30] Bacon warned that "his Majesty be pleased according to his great wisdom and absolute power to extinguish, or at least compose for a time, the divisions in his own house, which otherwise, as did the last time, will be sure to have such influence and infusion into the House or perhaps the Houses of Parliament as we shall only grow and profit in inconveniences."[31] Such advice was consistent with Bacon's professed distrust of factions in government. Had James been able to overcome this problem (prevalent since the outset of the reign), he would have ruled more strongly from the beginning. The King, however, had virtually no control over the influence of others, and there was little reason to believe he would suddenly acquire such ability.

What is perhaps most important about these suggestions is that they show that even as late as 1615 Bacon failed to realize James lacked capacity for strong leadership. His faith in the King was still strong, and he continued to believe that James might listen to him about Parliament. Bacon's views on speeches to Parliament, and on factionalism were sound, and while he had no illusions that the Crown's financial problems could be easily solved, his advice to try and defuse the money issue with the Commons was thoughtful. He felt that as Attorney he would finally be able to sustain influence with the King. By asking that James learn from his mistakes, he was attributing ability to his monarch that was never recognizable in the latter's personality. Gardiner says that the "failure to recognize that it was impossible to bring James and the House of Commons to work together . . . was a failure, the causes of which lay in Bacon's moral as well as his intellectual nature, and led to the great catastrophe of his misused life."[32] This statement remains muddled, but suggests that Bacon was a weak judge of character. His subsequent career, particularly his tenure as Chancellor, perhaps validates this contention. Bacon still felt that James would respect him as one scholar respected another. Despite the failure of The Advancement of Learning to ignite the King intellectually, the Attorney persisted in his belief that James's mind might be penetrated. This flaw in Bacon's judgment, in evidence at this stage of his life, shows a deficiency in him as a political man. Carelessness and naiveté in his behavior as Lord Chancellor would lead to his downfall.

Bacon did score with James as an influential Attorney General. He championed the power of the prerogative in some important cases and pushed vigorously for acceptance of his legal ideas. Shortly after the dissolution of Parliament, the Crown, still greatly in need of money, asked for "benevolences" from various groups and individuals. A benevolence was a royal exaction of funds asked for in times of need. It was cloaked as a "voluntary" contribution, but had long been called a kind of arbitrary taxation. It marked another use of the prerogative power under the ambiguous constitution. One Oliver St. John, when asked for a contribution, replied in writing that such an exaction violated Magna Carta and other well-known statutes. He also implied that the King perjured himself in his oath by going against statute.[33] Such a charge was a direct attack upon the King, and St. John was summoned before the Star Chamber. There Bacon, in the absence of the Chancellor, prosecuted the case. His argument was involved and well thought out. Apparently, St. John had also claimed in his letter that Parliament was being attacked in the Council for its refusal to help James financially. Bacon stood up for Parliament, claiming that it was dissolved too hastily. There "was in that House a general disposition to give and give largely. The clocks in the House perchance might differ; some went too fast, some went too slow, but the disposition to give was general."[34] He went on to describe Parliament as "the great intercourse and main current of graces and donatives from the King to the people, from the people to the King." A benevolence was asked for because Parliament had been dissolved before it could grant aid. He referred to the benevolence "as an after-child of the Parliament" and sharply differentiated it from an arbitrary "exaction called a benevolence."[35] Every man thus "had a prince's prerogative, a negative voice." St. John was not being tried for refusing to pay, but for his harsh attack upon the King.[36]

In this part of his argument Bacon had in fact criticized the government's policy of failing to try to work harmoniously with Parliament. Indirectly, he was advocating another effort at doing just this.[37] Bacon argued hard that the Crown was not resorting to arbitrary taxation. He knew the image of "Benevolence" and tried his best to persuade that the defendant here was not being persecuted for refusing aid. Much of the speech was devoted to defending the Crown. St. John's charge was sharply refuted, and James was called the "constant protector and conservator" of "the liberties, laws, and customs" of England. "I conceive this consisteth

107

in maintaining Religion and the true Church: in maintaining the Laws of the kingdom, which is the subject's birthright; in temperate use of the Prerogative; in due and free administration of Justice; and conservation of the peace of the land."[38] Bacon echoed his brand of royalism in this statement. Maintenance of the prerogative was crucial; its use had to be moderate since it ran "within the ancient channels and banks" and "overflows do hurt the channel."[39] James was extolled as the wise, cautious King that Bacon mistakenly still believed he could become.

There were other significant cases. The Attorney General took the occasion of the case of one William Talbot, a Roman Catholic accused of supporting tyrannicide of Protestant kings, to reiterate his belief that royal prerogative power is derived directly from God.[40] The Popes had tried to usurp this authority, trying "to make sovereign princes as the Banditti and to proscribe their lives, and to expose their kingdoms to prey." These powers were "the prerogatives of God alone and of his secret judgments." God alone could "poureth contempt upon princes."[41] Bacon was echoing briefly the philosophic foundation for his belief in a strong monarchy.

A similar case was that of John Owen. This individual was charged with high treason before the King's Bench for advocating that it was lawful for any man to kill an excommunicated King. Owen claimed that he was speaking generally and was not directing his remarks against the King of England. Bacon refuted this attempt at distinction and vigorously argued the charge of treason against the accused.[42] "You are indicted, Owen, not upon any statute made against the Pope's supremacy, or other matters that have reference to religion; but merely upon that law which was born with the kingdom, and was law even in superstitious times when the Pope was received." He compared Owen's writings to the Anabaptist desires for "the pulling down of magistrates," and the binding of "Kings in chains and their nobles in fetters of iron." An attack on a King was making "God author of evil," and making him look like "the prince of darkness."[43] Bacon had again vehemently defended the divine basis of monarchy. His charge against Owen was much stronger than that made against Talbot. This was a clear case of treasonable statements, while Talbot had merely approved of subversive political theory. Owen was, in fact, sentenced to death, but was kept in prison for three years and then allowed to leave England.

The case involving a Puritan minister, Edmond Peacham, first came up in early 1615, and precipitated events that led to the open confrontation between the Crown and Edward Coke. As Attorney General, Bacon would continuously oppose his enemy of long standing. Coke, now Chief Justice, would prove more of an obstructionist than ever before. The struggle involved more than just the renewal of a personal rivalry. The two men's conflicting views on the law would confront each other, making for a personal-professional battle that was as intense as it was dramatic. In a larger sense, it involved the culmination of Coke's efforts to use the Common Law against the Crown. Bacon used all his power and prestige to oppose these efforts in 1615-1616, and played a key role in Coke's final removal from the judiciary. By so doing he laid the basis for his own elevation to the Council and his eventual rise to the Lord Chancellorship.

The actual details of Peacham's case may be omitted. Here the matter assumed constitutional significance when James asked Bacon to confer separately with the judges of the King's Bench to ascertain their opinions before hearing the case. Coke alone objected to this, declaring in Bacon's words "that such particular and (as he called it) *auricular* taking of opinions was not according to the custom of this realm."[44] The Chief Justice, finding himself alone in his resistance, finally gave a written opinion in the case. He did not, however, drop his opposition to the Crown's practice of consulting separately with judges. It may be that James did not look at this practice of consultation with the judiciary as tampering with justice. He had never become sensitive to English governmental and legal institutions. Furthermore, there had never been an Edward Coke in Scotland. This case unleashed Coke against the Crown, and put the Common Law and the prerogative into direct confrontation. Bacon would defend the prerogative as the cornerstone of the English legal system and would attack Coke's activities against equity and try to promote the ascendancy of his own ideas. The Attorney General would flourish as he refuted Coke, and helped purge him from the judiciary.

The complexity of Coke's motivations for behavior that hardly appears consistent over a long career has attracted much interest. He too was a "political man" or perhaps a "judicial-political man." The obvious temptation of weaving into the narrative an in-depth comparison with Bacon will be avoided since the scope of this study

109

precludes any lengthy joint treatment of these two important figures. The emphasis must be on Bacon's reactions to Coke. This shows us how skillfully he maneuvered for power, and exposes us to some of his major legal ideas.

The details of Coke's final showdown with the Crown are well known. After Peacham's case, the Chief Justice intensified his defiance of royal authority. He annulled a Patent for making writs in the Common Pleas granted by James to a member of his Bedchamber.[45] More significant was his renewal of the struggle with Chancery that he had first waged while head of Common Pleas. Again, Chancery's power to stop judgment in the Common Law courts was at issue. Early in 1616, King's Bench rendered favorable a judgment to two fraudulent jewel merchants. The victims of the swindlers appealed to Chancery and obtained a reversal of the decision. Edward Coke then moved against Chancery with praemunire. This fourteenth-century law had been used to prevent appeals from English courts to Rome. Coke reinterpreted it, claiming it forbade appeals to any other court except the High Court of Parliament. He secured indictments of praemunire against the man who had appealed to Chancery and against every officer in that court involved in the case. The King eventually threw out the action, provoking strong anger from Coke and the other King's Bench judges.

The principles involved were most important. Coke may have stood for his own egoism, but he also stood for the supremacy of the Common Law. "Danger to the common-law courts was real," writes Coke's biographer. "Coke did not imagine it. He had struck in passion, using a wrong weapon, and the blow redoubled on himself. . . ."[46] Since becoming a judge, Coke had fought and had written for complete supremacy of the Common Law and for its independence from Royal Control. To him, it was the main instrument protecting the subject from the abusive power of the Crown. The King, however, was the fountain of justice, and the question of whether he could be controlled by law or not would ultimately be determined only by revolution. To Francis Bacon, there was never any question that the Crown stood supreme at the head of the legal system. His reaction against Edward Coke was vehement. "I account this a kind of sickness of my Lord Coke's" he wrote James, referring to the justice's use of praemunire against Chancery.[47] "This great and public affront, . . . To your high court of

Chancery, which is the court of your absolute power, may not . . . pass lightly . . . but use is to be made thereof for the settling of your authority and strengthening of your prerogative according to the true rules of monarchy."[48] As for Coke, Bacon advised that this was "a just and fit occasion to make some example against the presumption of a judge in causes that concern your Majesty whereby the whole body of those magistrates may be contained in better awe; and it may be this will light upon no unfit subject of a person that is rude and that no man cares for."[49] He saw no reason to restrain his strong feelings. Coke was tampering with the King's justice and such behavior must not be tolerated. He advised further in the same letter:

> But two things I wish to be done: The one, that your Majesty take this occasion to redouble unto all your Judges your ancient and true charge and rule, that you will endure no innovating the point of jurisdiction, but will have every court impaled within their own precedents, and not assume to themselves new powers upon conceits and inventions of law; The other, that in these high causes that touch upon State and Monarchy, your Majesty give them strait charge, that upon any occasions intervenient hereafter, they do not make the vulgar party to their contestations by public handling them, before they have consulted with your Majesty, to whom the reglement of those things only appertaineth.[50]

The attitude toward Coke was clear. Bacon was merging personal and professional opposition into a potent assault.

In "Of Judicature," he expressed his views on the relationship between the Crown and the Judiciary most succinctly and eloquently:

> Judges ought, above all, to remember the conclusions of the Roman Twelve Tables; Salus populi suprema lex; (The supreme law of all is the weal of the people;) and to know that laws, except they be in order to that end, are but things captious, and oracles not well inspired. Therefore it is an happy thing in a state when kings and states do often consult with judges; and again when judges do often consult with the king and state: the one, when there is matter of law intervenient in business of state; the other, when there is some consideration of state intervenient in matter of law. For many times the things deduced to judgment, may be meum and tuum, when the reason and consequence thereof may trench to point of estate: I call matter of estate, not only the parts of sovereignty, but whatsoever introduceth any great alteration of dangerous

111

precedent: or concerneth manifestly any great portion of people. And let no man weakly conceive that just laws and true policy have any antipathy; for they are like the spirits and sinews, that one moves with the other. Let judges also remember that Solomon's throne was supported by lions on both sides: let them be lions but yet lions under the throne; being circumspect that they do not check or oppose any points of sovereignty. Let not judges also be ignorant of their own right, as to think there is not left to them, as a principal part of their office, a wise use and application of laws.[51]

"Lions under the throne" are, of course, the most famous words from the essay. They reinforce his belief that the Crown stood supreme in justice, while still assigning to judges positions of crucial power. The theme that runs through this essay most strongly is harmony. Bacon had craved what proved to be an unattainable harmony between Crown and Parliament. The notion that order and harmony within the state was vital if human progress is to be realized is fundamental in his thinking. "Just laws and true policy" were "like the spirits and sinews." Political and judicial cooperation were not merely desirable, but necessary for the health of a state. Later, in one of the legal Aphorisms in *De Augmentis Scientiarum* (1623), he again stressed this need for harmony: "Let judgments, as well as answers and opinions, proceed from the judges alone; . . . . And let not these opinions, whether public or private matters, be demanded from the judges themselves, (for that were to turn the judge into an advocate); but from the king or state. Let the king or state refer them to the judges."[52] It is clear how important cooperation between the judges and the Crown was, to Bacon. Coke's behavior continued to run contrary to such spirit.

The case of Commendams of 1616 marked the climax of the crisis between Coke and the Crown. Once again the issue involved the Crown's policy of consulting with the judges of the King's Bench before they decided the case. An involved struggle ensued that eventually saw all the judges of this court submit to the King and admit their errors.[53] Coke, however, justified his conduct by claiming that the King had, in fact, delayed justice by having required a postponement of the case. Bacon, who had been the channel through which the Crown's order to delay was originally made, was at this time made a Privy Councillor.[54] He was now in a stronger position to refute Coke effectively before a king who wanted no more insolence from his Chief Justice. He told James before the

Council that "the putting off of the day in manner as was required by his Majesty (to his understanding) was without all scruple no delay of justice, nor danger of the Judges' oath." He then remarked that it was part of the Judges' oath "to counsel his Majesty when they are called." Coke disagreed caustically, claiming that an Attorney General was supposed to "plead before Judges and not dispute with them." Bacon then said that he found the exception strange; for that the King's learned counsel were by oath and office . . . without fear of any man's face to proceed or declare against any the greatest peer or subject of the kingdom; and not only any subject in particular, but any body of subjects or persons, were they Judges, or were they an upper or a lower house of Parliament, in case that they exceed the limits of their authority, or take anything from his Majesty's royal power or prerogative."[55] Francis Bacon had again shown where he stood. He received full support from James for his refutation of Edward Coke.

Within a few weeks of this dramatic confrontation, the King suspended Coke from the Privy Council. Soon afterwards, James decided to remove him from office completely and requested that Bacon prepare an explanation of why this should be done. We can assume that Mr. Attorney did so with great satisfaction. He mentioned among other things Coke's "perpetual turbulent carriage, first towards the liberties of his church and the state ecclesiastical; then towards his prerogative royal, and the branches thereof; and likewise towards all the settled jurisdictions of his other courts. . . ." Furthermore, Coke "had made himself popular by design only in pulling down government."[56] These and other reasons were presented bluntly and concisely.[57] Shortly after preparing this document, Bacon wrote James the following words: "I send your Majesty a form of discharge for my Lord Coke from his place of Chief Justice of your Bench."[58] It was mid-November, 1616. Francis Bacon had fought and won his toughest struggle to date as a political man.

Bacon looked forward to a decline of Coke's legal influence and the rise of his own. He saw his rival's reports as being full of distortions, and loathed Coke's excessive exaltation of the Common Law. Bacon had long been interested in the reform of English law. He had spoken in Parliament of the need for it, and, as early as 1597, had written a detailed analysis of the workings of the system, *The Maxims of the Law*.[59] Perhaps the most famous of his legal

113

writings were the ninety-seven Aphorisms found in the eight books of *De Augmentus Scientiarum*. These concise statements of legal principles are Bacon's suggestions for a legal system based on flexibility and fairness, rather than on the rigidity of rules. They were written in 1623 by a man who could look back at a lifetime of studying and practicing English Law, and who thus felt he could express his beliefs with eloquent brevity. He did.[60]

Bacon also compiled an important plan for legal reform at the very time that Coke was falling. There could be no more opportune time to impress James with his own ideas on law. The "Proposition to his Majesty. . . . Touching the Compiling and Amending of the Laws of England" was written sometime between June, 1616, and March, 1617.[61] Bacon began by offering himself "as a workman" for "the reducing and recompiling of the laws of England." He proposed to give existing law "rather light than any new nature." The system was cumbersome; it saw a multiplicity of suits, honest subjects oppressed, absolute judges, and an overloaded Chancery due to the failure of the Common Law to remedy many problems.[62] The need for reform was great and Bacon defended innovation. "All purgings and medicines, either in the civil or natural body, are innovations; so as that argument is a common-place against all noble reformations. . . . The work which I propound tendeth to praying and grafting the law, and not to ploughing up and planting it again; . . . the entire body and substance of the law shall remain, only discharged of idle and unprofitable or hurtful matter."[63]

Turning to specifics of reform, Bacon suggested a "digest or recompiling of the common laws," and a "digest" of statutes. For the common laws there would be three goals: First, there must be a book "De antiquitatibus juris." This would be a compilation of documents including cases that are of the most value. They would "be used for reverend precedents, but not for binding authorities."[64] Secondly, he called for "the reducing or perfecting of the course or corps of the common laws." This involved compiling yearbooks from the time of Edward I on, but omitting outdated cases, repetitious cases and "idle queries." Contradictory cases should be specially cited and lengthy ones should be abridged.[65] Thirdly, he suggested "introductive and auxiliary books touching the study of laws." These would deal with legal institutions, rules, and terms. The work on institutions would serve as "a model towards a great

114

building." The book of legal rules he held "the most important to the health as I may term it, and good institution of any laws: it is indeed like the ballast of a ship, to keep all upright and stable. . . . The naked rule or maxim doth not the effect: It must be made useful by good differences, ampliations, and limitation, warranted by good authorities; and this not by raising up of quotations and references, but by discourse and deducement in a just tractate." Bacon then added in confidence, "I do assure your Majesty, I am in good hope, that when Sir Edward Coke's Reports and my Rules and Decisions shall come to posterity, there will be (whatsoever is now thought,) question who was the greater lawyer?"[66]

With respect to statute law, Bacon called for the removing of obsolete laws from the books; repeal of "all statutes which are sleeping and not of use, but yet snaring in force;" mitigating harsh penalties called for in many laws; and finally "the reducing of concurrent statutes heaped one upon another, to one clear and uniform law." Bacon ended by reminding James that this reform must be accomplished by Parliament.[67]

This "Proposition" stands as Bacon's most earnest effort to turn his legal ideas into a blueprint for change. He offered them at a time that seemed ripe for the purging of Coke's influence. His plans might have become the basis for a badly needed reform of a cumbersome system. Had Bacon been retained as Attorney General and been given the backing to carry out his ideas, he might be remembered as the great reformer in English legal history. His career in politics would have been more constructive and undoubtedly would have had a happier ending. But James I again showed he lacked the capacity to recognize the need for constructive change. Bacon's recommendations had no effect, and the Crown passed up an opportunity to allow its gifted Attorney General to serve usefully. To be sure, Francis Bacon would reap great personal benefits from this long episode in politics. He would soon be elevated to the head of Chancery. There he himself would learn how easy it was for a judge to misuse his power.

---

1. *Letters and Life*, IV, 242. Spedding feels this undated letter to the King was probably written in early 1611.

2. *Ibid.*, 245-46.

3. Bacon was, in fact, active as Solicitor-General. He was instrumental in the

creation of a new prerogative court, "the Court of the Verge." In writing the patent for the new court he showed his belief in a strong prerogative dispensing equitable justice. Here, Bacon reflected some of his ideas for legal reform. For an account of some of his other duties as Solicitor *see ibid.*, 244-75, 314-57 (proceeding vs. James Whitelock, 3450571).

4. *Ibid.*, IV, 278-80. This letter was written on May 31, 1612. Salisbury died on May 24.

5. Bacon's Works, XII, 354. The 1625 edition of the essays differs slightly from the original version.

6. *See* below Chapter X.

7. *Letters and Life*, IV, 281-82. Spedding feels this letter was written close to the one in which Bacon criticized Salisbury.

8. D. H. Willson, *Privy Councillors in the House of Commons, 1604-1629* (Minneapolis, 1940), 135.

9. *Letters and Life*, IV, 379.

10. *Ibid.*, 381-82.

11. *Ibid.*, 382.

12. See Thomas L. Moir, *The Addled Parliament of 1614* (Oxford, 1958).

13. *Ibid.*; Willson, *Privy Councillors* . . . , 137-41. The Privy Council decided in February, 1614, to convene Parliament that April.

14. *Privy Councillors* . . . , 136-41. The new secretary, Sir Ralph Winwood, had no parliamentary experience and was not given any opportunity to prepare for the session.

15. *Letters and Life*, V, 1-2.

16. *Ibid.*, 21-30. The document, "Memorial of Some Points Which May Be Touched in His Majesty's Speech to Both Houses," was probably written shortly before the opening of the session on April 5, 1614.

17. *Ibid.*, 27-28.

18. *Ibid.*, 30.

19. Moir, 82-83.

20. *Ibid.*, 88-89.

21. CJ, I, 456.

22. Moir, 85-88.

23. CJ, I, 460.

24. *Ibid.*, 462.

25. I have treated Bacon's activities in 1614 in greater detail in "The Parliamentary Career . . . ," 250-73.

26. *Ibid.*, 270-72.

27. *Letters and Life*, V, 177. The idea of calling of new Parliament was again being considered in 1615.

28. *Ibid.*, 184.

29. *Ibid.*, 190.

30. Willson, *Privy Councillors* . . . , 137-43.

31. *Letters and Life*, V, 188.

32. DNB, I, 808.

33. *Letters and Life*, V, 132-34.

34. *Ibid.*, 137.

35. *Ibid.*, 138-40.

36. *Ibid.*, 140. St. John was in fact sentenced to a short imprisonment and a hearty fine. He apologized and the fine was remitted. He did, however, spend some time in the Tower.

37. Bacon would advise the calling of another Parliament in 1615. *See ibid.*, 175-91.

38. *Ibid.*, 142.

39. *Ibid.*, 143.

40. Talbot was an Irish member of Parliament who had supported the view of the Jesuit philosopher, Francisco Suarez, that all heretics, including Protestant monarchs, were tyrants and could be legally killed. Talbot was called before the Star Chamber where he recanted, affirming his loyalty to James. Bacon called his action the "repenting and relapsing" of a coward. Talbot was given a small fine and released from the Tower (he had already spent four months there). The case was heard in January, 1614. *See ibid.*, 5-12.

41. *Ibid.*, 6.

42. *Ibid.*, 154-68. Owen was tried in May, 1615.

43. *Ibid.*, 155-56, 158.

44. *Ibid.*, 100. This took place in early 1615.

45. The case involved one John Murray. Bacon was involved, protesting on Murray's behalf and helping effect a compromise whereby Murray's patent was allowed. No one in the future, however, was to be issued such a patent. *See ibid.*, 96-98, 125, 169-70.

46. Catherine D. Bowen, *The Lion and the Throne* (Boston, 1957), 363.

47. *Letters and Life*, V, 251. This important letter was written on February 21, 1615.

48. *Ibid.*, 252.

49. *Ibid.*, 252-53.

50. *Ibid.*, 253.

51. *Bacon's Works*, XII, 269-70.

52. *Ibid.*, IX, 340. This excerpt is from Aphorism, 92.

53. For the details of this case *see* Bowen, *The Lion and the Throne*, 370-90.

54. The date of his admission to the Council was June 9, 1616. *See Letters and Life*, V, 349.

55. *Ibid.*, 366-67.

56. *Ibid.*, VI, 95-96.

57. *Ibid.* Bacon also criticized Coke's behavior in Peacham's case and reminded James that the Chief Justice had been given time to reform his reports, "wherein there be many dangerous concerts of his own uttered for law, to the prejudice of his crown, parliament, and subjects." "After three months time," Bacon went on, ". . . he had offered his Majesty only five animadversions, being rather a scorn than a satisfaction to his Majesty."

58. *Ibid.*, 97.

59. Bacon's first plea in Parliament for legal reform came in a speech in February, 1593. During the debates over union in 1607, he stressed the fact that any union of laws must be preceded by reform of English law. "I think there cannot

be a work that his Majesty can undertake . . . more politic, more honourable, nor more beneficial to his subjects in all ages."

For the complete text of the *Maxims of the Law, see Bacon's Works*, XIV, 179-276.

60. For the full text of the Aphorisms *see ibid.*, IX, 311-44.

61. *Letters and Life*, VI, 57. Spedding calculates this as the period during which this work was written.

62. *Ibid.*, 62-64.

63. *Ibid.*, 67.

64. *Ibid.*, 68.

65. *Ibid.*, 68-69.

66. *Ibid.*, 69-70.

67. *Ibid.*, 70-71.

CHAPTER VIII

POLITICAL SUCCESS, II: LORD CHANCELLOR

Bacon made the following statement about judges' behavior in "Of Judicature":

> Above all things, integrity is their portion and proper virtue . . .
> it is the unjust judge that is the capital remover of landmarks,
> when he defineth amiss of lands and property. One foul sentence
> doth more hurt than many foul examples. For these do but cor-
> rupt the stream, the other corrupteth the fountain. . . . The
> place of justice is an hallowed place; and therefore not only the
> bench, but the foot-pace and precincts and purprise thereof,
> ought to be preserved without scandal and corruption.[1]

In "Of Great Place" he wrote that "power to do good is the true
and lawful end of aspiring. . . . Reform therefore, without bravery
or scandal of former times and persons"; he added, "but yet set it
down to thyself as well to create good precedents as to follow them."[2]
It is appropriate to cite these statements as one begins discussion
of his Lord Chancellorship, since it can hardly be said that Francis
Bacon practiced his own philosophic advice.

As we reach the period of Bacon's greatest political success it
is important to explore this remark and perhaps clarify it. Bacon's
career as a political man saw him struggle for high office most of his
life. He was fifty-two when he became Attorney General and fifty-
six when he ascended to Chancery as Lord Keeper; (Bacon became
Lord Chancellor a year later). He would serve four years as Lord

Keeper-Chancellor before being permanently removed from political life. For much of his long career Bacon tried earnestly to harmonize his convictions with positions that were politically necessary. His service in Parliament, together with various efforts to advise two monarchs, illustrate this clearly. Bacon constantly walked a very tight political rope, knowing full well how easy it was to lose one's balance. If we accept this contention that Bacon was the political realist, how then do we accept the well-documented view that he was primarily concerned with the intellectual, scientific, and economic progress, that well-directed power might bring? It is certainly clear that he believed power should be used for progress. His belief in progress in learning and legal reform, together with his comprehensive philosophical commitment to utopianism, would certainly have us believe that Bacon meant what he said in "Of Great Place." A recent provocative study of his political philosophy argues that Bacon directed all his efforts toward building "the ship that would take man to the New Atlantis."[3] All his other beliefs and commitments (including his royalism and support of the church) were merely provisional, and were necessary to help man achieve an utopian condition. (I will discuss this thesis more thoroughly in Chapter X.) For Bacon the philosopher, this work argues, a radically different future was what really mattered. J. G. Crowther (see Ch. I) contends that Bacon entered politics "primarily for scientific ends."[4] Fulton Anderson believes strongly that Bacon always hoped to revolutionize learning by the use of political power.

It is not the purpose here to dispute any of these interpretations. What I do suggest, however, is that Bacon's ideas on the use of power must be studied independently of his career as a royal official. In a sense the "intellectual man" must be separated from the "political man." There is no period in his career when this distinction is clearer than during his four years of greatest power, 1617-1621. Bacon as Lord Chancellor was thoroughly political. His behavior in this period hardly exemplified the philosophic statesman using "power to do good." His main concern seemed to lie in utilizing the intricacies of court politics to his own advantage, and in buttressing his status and financial condition. By the time Bacon reached Chancery his zeal for reform seemed depleted. As the historian of the Parliament of 1621 tells us: "The Chancellor's original perception of the abuses in his court were gradually blurred by identification, and an unmistakable note of bureaucratic complacency crept into his attitude. Presented now with the opportunity of making a grand review of the grievances of the kingdom, he found remarkably little to suggest."[5] And yet in 1620, while Chancellor, Bacon published the *Novum Organum*. In the years after his disgrace there appeared *De Augmentis Scientiarum* (an expanded *Advancement of Learning* written in Latin), and, of course, *The New Atlantis*. Bacon had reached his peak as thinker, and showed his most profound insights into the human capacity for progress. As a political animal himself, however, he could not avoid misusing power and facing the ultimate consequences.

This introduction to my discussion of Bacon as Chancellor in no way seeks to label him with the charge of hypocrisy. The distinction between him as a political man and an intellectual man is, I believe, perfectly understandable and even logical. I would prefer to leave fuller evaluation of these terms to the conclusion. As one studies Bacon enjoying his greatest material success, one sees an aging and mellowing individual determined to enjoy the power that was so long in coming. Frustration in politics had become a way of life for him, and the struggle against it had been long and difficult. It is thus quite understandable that the high officialdom of Chancery became a prize to be cuddled, nurtured, and used to every possible advantage. Although Bacon's political behavior as Lord Chancellor was less than admirable, it is not to be hastily condemned. Political men are molded by their careers, and are usually understandable products of such careers. So it was with Lord Bacon.

Bacon first showed his interest in the Chancellor's office in 1616 when serious illness to Lord Ellesmere created the possibility of a vacancy. "I hope I may be acquitted of presumption if I think of it," he wrote the King, "both because my father had the place, which is some civil inducement to my desire . . . and chiefly because since the Chancellor's place went to the law, was ever conferred upon some of the learned counsel, and never upon a Judge."[6] Ellesmere recovered temporarily in 1616, but resigned as a dying man in March of the following year. Bacon was immediately given the Great Seal of England with the title of Lord Keeper. He had finally achieved the office once held by his father; the prize had been long in coming.

In his first speech in Chancery (May, 1617), Bacon showed some of the enthusiasm of a reformer.[7] He hoped "that justice might pass with as easy charge and expense, and all manner of exactions mought be rooted out so far as mought be." "For, my Lords," he remarked, "the Chancery is ordained to supply the law, and not to subvert the law." Bacon spelled out "the excess or tumor" of Chancery and proposed his remedies. He would convene the court more regularly and do his best to reduce the backlog of cases. "Justice is a sacred thing and . . . I shall by the grace of God . . . add the afternoon to the forenoon, and some fortnight of the vacation to the term, for the expediting and clearing of the cases of the court." The over-all need to avoid delays in justice was made explicit. The new Lord Keeper charged himself with making Chancery a more efficient court.

Even more significant, however, was the strong moral tone of Bacon's speech. His power would be exercised moderately, "for surely the health of a court, as well as of a body, consists in temperance." He promised not to abusively use injunctions against the common law. A "point of excess," he believed, "may be the over-frequent and facile granting of injunctions for the staying of the common law, or the altering of possessions." Bacon pledged himself to a more discreet use of this weapon of Chancery. Most interesting were his words about fees. "I shall," he said, "be careful there be no exaction of any new fees, but according as they have been heretofore set and tabled." He promised furthermore not to interfere with lawyers' fees, declaring that he would "leave it to the conscience and merit of the lawyer, and the estimation and gratitude of the client." Bacon assured honest efficiency in Chancery and his words ring with sincerity. "Now because the law roots so well in my time," he concluded, "I will water it at the root. . . ."[8]

Bacon seemed most anxious to face the challenges of his new position. The speech marked a noble investiture for the new Lord Keeper. His plans for conducting the court were consistent with his professed belief in simpler, more equitable justice. Now after years of striving Bacon had the opportunity to function as a judicial reformer. True, Chancery was but one arm of royal justice. Bacon could hardly effect the comprehensive changes he had philosophized about from this one office. He himself had promised not to meddle in the Common Law. He could, however, use his power to exemplify judicial wisdom. Chancery might become an example of the application of equity in English Law. It was headed by a man not only rich in legal experience, but by someone who possessed the intellectual capacity to grasp the need for the constructive use of power. Potentially, Bacon could have brought greatness to his office.

His record of service would never approach such potential. Bacon soon showed that status and power mattered more to him than did any commitment to principles. It is true that he worked hard at first to clean up the backlog of cases he inherited. He would write to George Villiers (Earl of Buckingham) in early June that he had "made even with the business of the kingdom for common justice. Not one case unheard. The lawyers drawn dry of all the motions they were to make. Not one petition unanswered." "I know men think I cannot continue," he added, "if I oppress myself with business. But that account is made. The duties of life are more than life."[9] Such words suggest Bacon was approaching his new office with conscientious vigor. In July, with James in Scotland, the new Lord Keeper delivered the charge to the judges before they embarked on their summer circuits:

> First, you that are the Judges of Circuits are as it were the planets of the Kingdom (I do you no dishonor that name). . . . Do therefore as they do; move always and be carried with the motion of your first mover, which is your Sovereign. A popular Judge is a deformed thing: and *plaudite's* are fitter for players than for magistrates. Do good to the people, love them and give them justice. But let it be, as the Psalm saith, *nihil inde expectantes*; looking for nothing, neither praise nor profit.[10]

This excerpt from a serious and thoughtful speech again suggests Bacon was assuming his new duties with a dedication to judicial integrity. Such an attitude was, however, not sustained. Bacon was now far more than a judge. He was a power on James's council and would soon integrate himself into the political fabric of that council. He would function in the King's little world of court favorites. In short, he would find that his new office was in reality more political than judicial. It offered Bacon the opportunity for the status and wealth that he had craved all his life. Resisting such a craving would be difficult for most men, and for Bacon would prove impossible. The words he had spoken about judicial integrity faded out of his daily perspective. The inner segment of James's court was hardly conducive to idealism and Bacon would respond to his new surroundings.

Since his elevation to Attorney General, Bacon had been close enough to James's court to learn its working. The King had always depended excessively on "favorites" to help him in what seemed to be an overburdening struggle to manage the affairs of state. These individuals were always young, attractive men, and they provided James with the escape he needed from the conciliar, parliamentary, and judicial conflicts of his reign. Such men could hold great influence over the King during their period of "favor," and cultivating their friendship was a useful political tool. Bacon read this situation perceptively and utilized two such people to gain advantage. The first of these was Robert Carr, Viscount Rochester and eventually Earl of Somerset. Carr, a handsome, physically developed Scot, had been a page to James in Scotland. He rose rapidly, gaining knighthood in 1611 and earldom two years later. Carr had the power to sell offices and did so quite profitably. When Bacon sought the Mastership of the Wards in 1612, he made the request by writing Carr.[11] Carr also tried to act as Bacon's patron when the latter was seeking the Attorney Generalship. Bacon acknowledged that the royal favorite "thrust himself into the business for a fee."[12] Carr was made the Earl of Somerset around the time Bacon became Attorney, and promptly married one Frances Howard, recently divorced from the third Earl of Essex. Somerset and his new Countess quickly plunged themselves into a scheme of treachery and murder. They moved against a personal enemy, one Thomas Overbury, by having him put in the Tower on a false charge; then they had him murdered. As Attorney, Bacon played a key role in the involved prosecution of the pair. They were both ultimately convicted.[13] The case was a "juicy" scandal that would have delighted the masses had modern media existed in seventeenth-century England. Bacon wisely stopped befriending Somerset when the storm broke, and loyally served the Crown in the case. "I am far enough from opinion that the reintegration or resuscitation of Somerset's fourtune can ever stand with his Majesty's honour or safety," he wrote to James's succeeding favorite, Sir George Villiers.[14] The Attorney shrewdly switched his "friendship" to this new and more enduring courtier.

Bacon's relationship with Villiers was of greater importance. The latter's rise at court may be traced from 1614. Villiers was a likable and intelligent individual, who was both politically adept and intellectually sensitive. He learned quickly the ways of the King and rose meteorically. In 1615 he was knighted; a year later he became a Viscount; in 1617 he was made an Earl; and in 1618 a Marquis. He became the Duke of Buckingham in 1623. James was completely captivated by this "seductive young man." He told his Council in 1617: "You may be sure that I love the Earl of Buckingham more than anyone else and more than you who are here assembled. I wish to speak in my own behalf and not to have it thought to be a defect, for Jesus Christ did the same and therefore I cannot be blamed. Christ had his John, and I have my George."[15] Anyone spoken of in such a manner by a king was worth befriending.

While Attorney, Bacon began courting such a friendship. It soon paid off. Villiers helped secure Bacon's elevation to the Privy Council and Sir Francis thankfully told George, "You are the man my heart ever told me you were."[16] Shortly afterwards, Bacon wrote the King describing Villiers as having "a safe nature, a capable mind, an honest will, generous and noble affections, and a courage well lodged; anyone that I know loveth your Majesty unfeignedly, and admireth you as much as is in a man to admire his sovereign upon earth."[17] Villiers read this commendation and immediately regarded Bacon with fondness and respect. He recognized the Attorney General as a man rich in wisdom and experience and sought his advice in political matters.

Bacon advised Villiers extensively, cautioning him against corruption and the abuse of power. "I do not see but you may think your private fourtunes established," he wrote, and "therefore it is now time that you should refer your actions chiefly to the good of your sovereign and your country."[18] In the same year, while still Attorney, Bacon wrote the first version of a detailed "Letter of Advice" to Villiers. In it he spelled out many constructive uses of power in such matters as religion, justice, foreign affairs, and economic policy. In a second, and longer version of this "Advice" written in 1618, Bacon further documented his thoughts on these and other important issues.[19] It is clear from these letters that Bacon still grasped intellectually the necessity of using "power to do good." He echoed his views that progress depended on a basis of civil and religious peace and that a stable monarchy was the best insurance of such a peace. He also again pleaded strongly for judicial integrity. In the second "Advice," while already Lord Chancellor, he wrote:

125

Because the life of the laws lies in the execution and administration of them, let your eye, in the first place, be in the choice of good Judges. These properties they have need to be furnished with; to be learned in their own profession; patient in hearing; prudent in governing; powerful in their eloquence to persuade and satisfy both parties and auditors; just in their judgement; and to sum up all, they must have these three attributes; (1) they must be men of courage, (2) fearing God, (3) and hating covetousness; an ignorant man cannot, a coward dares not, be a good judge.[20]

He retained a strong ideological commitment to the need for an impeccable judiciary.

The statements of "Advice" constitute an expression of some of Bacon's fundamental political thoughts. By playing the sage, Bacon could at least go through the motions of channeling Villiers along the path of constructive statesmanship. The latter individual, however, was incapable of responding to such counseling, and increasingly misused his enormous power. At best, Bacon succeeded in restraining the dashing courtier to some degree. "Villiers," Anderson writes, "would probably have sold justice itself, the law, and the constitution, had Bacon, as a mentor and a holder of high office, not stood in his way."[21] While Bacon enjoyed counseling Villiers, and certainly hoped his advice might have some influence, his motives were predominantly self-seeking. Villiers was already too corrupted by power to utilize it for the public good. Whether or not Bacon fully understood this when he wrote the first "Advice" is uncertain. The first letter was written, however, before Bacon's promotion to Lord Keeper. Upon his appointment, he expressed his gratitude to Villiers for the latter's help in securing the position. "In this day's work you are the truest and perfected mirror and example of firm and generous friendship that ever was at court. And, I shall count every day lost, wherein I shall not either study your well doing in thought, or do your name honour in speech, or perform you service in deed."[22] The new head of Chancery had learned well the temper of the royal court. He knew Villiers might well appreciate his playing the role of the wise elder statesman. Having done so well with this most powerful of James's favorites, he appeared determined to strengthen his hold on power. He was in fact integrating himself into the undistinguished inner circle of Jacobean politics.

126

With a friend of such a stature and the title of Lord Keeper, Francis Bacon felt more secure politically than ever before. He was determined to enjoy power to the fullest. The opportunity to do so arose when James went on a progress through Scotland in the spring of 1617 and left his new Keeper as regent of England. Bacon, in office only a short time, did not hesitate to exercise royal authority. In fact, he appears to have exercised it a bit too freely. He withheld a royal proclamation to the Council ordering the nobles out of London during James's absence. This order interfered with the liberty of Englishmen, and apparently Bacon saw no need to enforce it since most nobles were leaving the city anyway. He thought such discretion on his part would be admired by the King. It was not. James resented this countermanding of his authority and sent word to the Council "that obedience is better than sacrifice, and that he knoweth he is King of England."[23]

A short time later, while the King was still away, Bacon again overstepped his authority and demeaned himself in the process. He "meddled" in the crisis between Coke and his wife over their daughter's marriage. It is no pleasure for a biographer to depict a man of Bacon's stature trying to benefit from the personal troubles of his lifelong enemy. Bacon "meddled" in this matter because he calculated it would be politic to do so; he was now very much the political man.

The affair proved rather messy. Coke, in an effort to win back favor, arranged a marriage between his fourteen-year old daughter and Sir John Villiers, George's older brother. Lady Hatton, bitterly opposed to her husband, "kidnapped" her daughter, only to see Coke "rescue" her with the help of armed men. Bacon sided completely with the woman he had once sought for his own. He went so far as to charge Coke in Star Chamber with "riot and disturbance."[24] He mistakenly thought that the King and Buckingham (George Villiers) would approve of this thwarting the marriage. Soon he realized his miscalculation. The Villiers family was not to turn down Coke's promise of a large dowry.[25] James was not to tolerate a regent overstepping the bounds of his authority.

Bacon was rebuked by both the King and his favorite. Painfully, he accepted admonishment. James told him that it was hardly unlawful for a father to recover his own child. Clearly, he would not condone Bacon's attempt to move legally against Coke for such an act. The King rebuked the Lord Keeper for the bad manners and

127

disrespect he had shown in handling the matter. "For if you had willingly given your consent and hand to the recovery of the young gentlewoman," James wrote, "and then written both to us and to him what inconvenience appeared to you to be in such a match, that had been the part indeed of a true servant to us and a true friend to him, but first to make an opposition and then to give advice by way of friendship is to make the plough to go before the horse." "We fear," added the King, "that you shall prove the only phoenix in that jealousy of all the kingdom."[26] Bacon, humiliated and rebuked by his master, begged for forgiveness: "I shall easily subscribe to your Majesty's censure . . . humbly craving pardon for troubling your Majesty so long; and most humbly praying your Majesty to maintain me in your grace and favour, which is the fruit of my life upon the root of a good conscience." "I hope verily," he wrote in another letter, "to approve myself not only a true servant to your Majesty, but a true friend to my Lord of Buckingham."[27] Bacon apparently begged Buckingham's forgiveness in person. The Earl replied to the Lord Keeper:

> For I do freely confess that your offer of submission unto me . . . battered so the unkindness that I had conceived in my heart for your behavior towards me in my absence, as out of the sparks of my old affection towards you I went to sound his Majesty's intention how he means to behave towards you, specially in any public meeting.

James was still quite upset, and Villiers claimed to have begged "upon my knees" that Bacon suffer "no public act of disgrace." The King finally promised, Buckingham told Bacon, "that he would not so far disable you from the merit of your future service, as to put any particular mark of disgrace upon your person." Bacon, greatly relieved, thanked the Earl with total humility:

> It is the line of my life, and not the lines of my letter, that must express my thankfulness: wherein if I fail, then God fail me, and make me as miserable as I think myself at this time happy by this reviver, through his Majesty's singular clemency, and your incomparable love and favour.[28]

Bacon's behavior in these submissions is pathetic. As one biographer concludes: "The subtlest mind in England strained to twist upon itself, undo what was done, retract from a course in which both retreat and victory were unworthy."[29]

The Lord Keeper's pleas for forgiveness indicate his willingness to crawl in order to avoid falling from favor. His indiscretion had indeed brought humiliation to him. He bowed because he wanted so much to remain in the high circle of politics.

Francis Bacon was fortunate. James, unlike his predecessor, was quick to forgive. Bacon was restored to favor, and in January, 1618, was made Lord Chancellor. The promotion was accompanied six months later by his elevation to peerage with Lord Bacon, Baron of Verulum, his new complete title. Lord Verulum, as he was now most commonly known, had surpassed his father's highest official status and would, for the next three years, flourish in his greatest power. He functioned close to the heart of power, championing the prerogative, and making certain his conduct would only please the Crown. These were years of purely conciliar government; Parliament had not met since 1614 and no new session was being contemplated. Bacon had no reason to fear scrutiny from below.

The Lord Chancellor's life style was excessively lavish.[30] He spent large sums to establish the luxury he had apparently craved all his life. York House, where he had been born, was his official residence as Chancellor. He spent much money repairing it and even had a pipe laid in to pump in fresh water. In St. Albans stood his "escape" residences. The magnificent Gorhambury, his father's mansion, now served as his winter retreat. One mile away he built Verulum House as a haven for summers. These houses were all magnificently furnished and fully staffed. Of even greater interest than the ways in which he spent money, was his apparent inability to control it. Spedding feels that he acquired the habit of recklessly borrowing money early in his career. He had never developed any fiscal responsibility, but instead "a very easy liberality in the spending" and "a carelessness in the keeping of it."[31] His habits with money border on the absurd. One story has it that at Gorhambury, servants liberally helped themselves to money kept in open drawers. "Whilst his Lordship was gone," recalled an observer, "there comes into the study one of his Lordship's gentlemen, and opens my Lord's chest of drawers wherein his money was, and takes it out in handfuls and fills both his pockets, and goes away without saying any word to me." "Another servant then did the very same thing. When Bacon returned and was told what happened, he shook his head" and replied, "Sir I cannot help myself."[32] Even if this incident is somewhat exaggerated, such behavior on his part is believable. Never having learned frugality, he always

129

accustomed himself to a style above his means. As Lord Chancellor, with the fees and bribes flowing into his hands, he had no instinct to hold on. He was a sixty-year old man who felt that luxury was his birthright; he now enjoyed it uncontrollably. We may perhaps compare him to the modern child of credit cards and unpaid bills. Status and ostentation were what counted.

Lord Chancellor Bacon enjoyed these years of high office. As Villiers continued to flourish both in wealth and power, he utilized Bacon's services in Chancery. Buckingham, as he was now called, used the courts to outmaneuver his main rivals, the Howards. Bacon, while not distorting justice, cooperated fully with Villiers in legal matters that were of interest to the favorite. The London merchant, Sir Lionel Cranfield, Master of the Wards, was also an important figure during this period. Cranfield efficiently managed several departments of government, including the Treasury, and was instrumental in increasing revenue from imports. His policies helped the depleted royal treasury and Bacon supported them.[33] The latter admired Cranfield's skills in governmental management even though he appears to have had contempt for his humble origins. Cranfield's performance was referred to by Bacon "as more statesmanlike than he should have expected from a man of his breeding."[34] Cranfield resented Bacon's attitude and was to help effect the Chancellor's downfall in 1621. In 1624 he himself would be impeached.

It was as champion of the Royal Prerogative that Bacon was most outspoken. "The King's prerogative and the law are not two things," he said in the Exchequer, "but the King's prerogative is law, and the principal part of the law; the first born . . . of the law; and therefore in conserving and maintaining that, you conserve and maintain the law. There is not in the body of man one law of the head, and another of the body, but all is one entire law."[35] Bacon again echoed his belief in a legal harmony preserved by royal power. The King perpetuated justice with the aid of his judges. The judges were crucial in this task, but depended on the prime mover of the kingdom who himself depended on God. It was not for a judge to use his place for any individual power or gain. Bacon had said this before. Ideally, he believed it. As Lord Chancellor he spoke often of prerogative power put to constructive use. Wisdom and integrity were essential for anyone holding high office. Bacon believed in these standards; he proved too weak, however, to uphold them.

130

The culmination of Bacon's Chancellorship was his sixtieth birth-day party, January 22, 1621. It was on this occasion, during a great feast at York House, that Ben Jonson spoke his famous lines about his host:

England's High Chancellor, the destin'd heir
In his soft cradle of his father's chair
Whose even thread the Fates spin round and full
Out of their choicest and their whitest wool.

There is something about this often described occasion that seems most fitting. Bacon celebrating a grand sixtieth birthday in one sense symbolized an old man living to enjoy the fruits of a life of many struggles. While one cannot admire his character in this period, it is wrong to begrudge him this lofty celebration. Although this feast very much characterized his excessive life style, Bacon was in fact enjoying the rewards of a career for the last time. Five days after this birthday he received his last title, Viscount St. Alban (St. Albans lies three miles from Gorhambury House). A few days later James convened the Parliament of 1621. The political man was about to fall.

1. *Bacon's Works*, XII, 265-69.
2. *Ibid.*, 113.
3. *See* Howard B. White, *Peace Among the Willows* (The Hague, 1968), 91.
4. *Francis Bacon: The First Statesman of Science*, 16.
5. Robert Zaller, *The Parliament of 1621* (Berkeley, 1971), 20-21.
6. *Letters and Life*, V, 242. This was in February, 1616.
7. *Ibid.*, VI, 182-93.
8. *Ibid.*, 190-92.
9. *Ibid.*, 208-9.
10. *Ibid.*, 211.
11. *Ibid.*, IV, 342.
12. *Ibid.*, 393.
13. *Ibid.*, V, 208-11, 228-33, 292-343. Lady Somerset confessed; she was, how-ever, pardoned a year later. The Earl maintained his innocence but was convicted and kept in the Tower by the succeeding "favorite," George Villiers. James even-tually pardoned him. Richard Weston, underkeeper of the Tower, and the man who delivered the poison to Overbury, was less fortunate than his "employers." He was hanged.
14. *Ibid.*, 285. This was in May, 1616.
15. Willson, *King James* . . . , 384. The words "seductive young man" are Willson's. He also thoroughly discusses Buckingham's rise (378-98).

16. *Letters and Life*, V, 348. This was in early June, 1616.

17. *Ibid.*, VI, 7-8. This was in August of the same year.

18. *Ibid.*, 6. This was also in August, 1616.

19. The first version of this famous "Advice" was written sometime in 1616, although Spedding cannot be certain of the exact date. A somewhat enlarged second version was apparently written two years later. *See ibid.*, 9-56.

20. *Ibid.*, 33.

21. *Francis Bacon, His Career* . . . , 195.

22. *Letters and Life*, VI, 152.

23. *Ibid.*, 161-62.

24. *Ibid.*, 227.

25. In the end Coke paid a total of £30,000. The marriage went through and Coke also received his seat back on the Privy Council. He was not, however, returned to the bench.

26. *Letters and Life*, VI, 244-45.

27. *Ibid.*, 241-42, 245.

28. *Ibid.*, 251-53.

29. Bowen, *Francis Bacon* . . . , 159.

30. Mrs. Bowen's description of Bacon's elegant living is worth reading. *See Francis Bacon* . . . , 159-62.

31. *Letters and Life*, VII, 563.

32. *Ibid.*, 563-64. Spedding admits that this story is hearsay. It is "but the recollection in 1691, of a conversation overheard by a shop-boy in 1655, relating to a matter which took place not later than 1620." Spedding feels, however, that it sounds plausible. "The answer attributed to Bacon," he says, "seems so much more likely to have been remembered than invented."

33. For a good discussion on the relationship between Bacon and Cranfield *see* Robert C. Johnson, "Francis Bacon and Lionel Cranfield," *Huntington Library Quarterly* (August, 1960), 201-20. Johnson traces carefully the governmental relationship between the two, which he says began around 1612. Cranfield's personality reflected the tough, competitive business world. He was "brusque and outspoken, he possessed little tact, and he frequently lost his temper over petty matters." Bacon was naturally arrogant toward such an individual. They did, however, work constructively together. Since Bacon relied heavily on Cranfield's advice, particularly in the area of international trade, Johnson feels they became more antagonistic toward one another as they both rose politically. They both identified with Villiers and were forced into close cooperation. Together they helped put through reforms in the household, wardrobe, ordnance, and the navy. Actually, Cranfield was more the reformer and resented the fact that the Chancellor used his eloquent pen to claim most of the credit and give him mere "casual mention." Much of their quarreling was petty, but the bitterness plaguing their relationship is significant as one looks at Cranfield's role in Bacon's fall.

34. *Letters and Life*, VI, 272.

35. *Ibid.*, 203. This was in May, 1617.

CHAPTER IX

1621: THE FALL OF THE POLITICAL MAN

> *"Those that will strike at your Chancellor, it*
> *is much to be feared will strike at your crown."*
>
> Bacon to James I (sometime in early 1621).

The story of Bacon's impeachment has often been told. There are no new findings to alter the essence of the script detailing his sudden fall from high officialdom. Even though one cannot challenge the conclusion that admits the Chancellor's technical guilt, his trial and conviction must be seen as a political act against the royal prerogative. Bacon's "corrupt" behavior as a judge was hardly unusual for the times. He fell from power because he stood as an ideal scapegoat, sacrificed to a Parliament looking for the vulnerability of royal power. That such conclusions are basically valid must be admitted, and this study pretends to offer no new radical interpretation of Bacon's political defeat. It will merely attempt to survey the major events in that defeat by focusing on a political man facing his last crisis. Francis Bacon had walked a tight political rope for all of his career. He was no stranger to the burdens of office-holding. He perceived the dangers conveyed by "great place" and would accept defeat with a kind of tranquillity and resignation. Bacon had traversed a political road that had almost always been difficult. The nature of his career's finale almost seems predictable.

Bacon's political disgrace came suddenly. The process by which Parliament indicted and convicted him, removed him from office, and threw him at the mercy of James transpired in less than two months. His rise in politics had been slow and agonizing; the end was to be swift and decisive. Lord Chancellor Bacon was created Viscount St. Alban on January 27, 1621. He wrote the King expressing appreciation: "For this is now the eighth time, that your Majesty hath raised me. . . . I shall offer . . . care and diligence, and assiduous endeavor . . . your Majesty shall have the best of my time, which I assure myself shall conclude in your favour and survive in your remembrance."[1] Little did he realize that the Parliament that convened three days after he wrote these words would end his "time" in officialdom.

For Bacon, this was his first and only Parliament in which he participated as a member of the Lords. His parliamentary career had been spent entirely in the Commons, and he had always maintained the trust and respect of that house. As a spokesman for the Crown, he had become familiar with controversy and confrontation. He had often been uneasy serving as representative of the Houses to the Crown, since he tried relentlessly to persuade his colleagues to accept royal policies. The struggles had been intense and often bitter. They engendered a feeling of frustration in Bacon that grew stronger as his relationship with the Crown grew closer. His tenure in Parliament had been anything but tranquil, and yet it had been dignified. Bacon had been respected as a gifted orator and his eloquence had won him general recognition. Moreover, his patience and skill as he conducted joint conferences and generally attempted to work out difficult compromises, had gained the praises of even those who often opposed him. He had functioned in Parliament over a course of forty years, and was a seasoned product of its workings. Now, however, he was cast in a different role. As Chancellor, he stood as the official closest to the Crown. Accordingly, it was for him to address both Houses after the King's opening speech, and lend strong support to the royal message. Bacon had been a familiar speaker in the Commons and had spoken to the Peers in committee on many occasions. He had never, however, formally addressed both houses.

"You have heard the King speak," he began, "and it makes me call to mind what Solomon saith, who was also a king: *The words of the wise are as nails and pins driven in and fastened by the mas-*

134

ters of assemblies. The King is the master of this assembly, and though his words in regard of the sweetness of them do not prick, yet in regard of the weight and wisdom of them, I know they pierce through and through; that is, both into your memories and into your affections. And there I leave them."[2] "There is a great expectation now at the beginning of this Parliament," he added, "and I pray God there may be as great satisfaction in the end."[3] While Bacon had in the past stressed his belief in royal control of Parliament, he had never been so emphatic in his affirmation of the King's preeminence. His speech was, in fact, a command that Parliament obey the Crown. No longer was he playing the mediator or peacemaker. He spoke for the Crown as an arm of its authority. Momentarily, at least, he stood at the pinnacle of his power.

Bacon proceeded to administer the Chancellor's duties toward Parliament. He replied to the Speaker's traditional "excuse" by informing the newly chosen official, Serjeant Richardson, of the King's acceptance of his election; he then offered a detailed reaction to Richardson's "oration." While he maintained firmness on the Crown's superior position, his tone was harmonious. James had been pleased with the Speaker's statement, and Bacon's reply indicated a desire for a cooperative session. He remarked that the King thought "your eloquent discourse" contained "much good matter and much good will." He then acknowledged the Speaker's commendation of monarchy, stated his belief in Parliament as an institution important in the "perfection of monarchy," and vaguely mentioned the Crown's desire to redress grievances. Bacon avoided making any specific commitments, and cautioned Parliament to show restraint. "Ye are to represent the people: ye are not to personate them. . . . Therefore, contain yourselves within that moderation as may appear to bend rather to the effectual ease of the people, than to a discursive envy or scandal upon the state."[4] What he was, in fact, suggesting was that as long as Parliament did not provoke the Crown by raising controversial issues, all would be well. The Chancellor glossed over the subject of grievances by assuring cooperation as long as the grievances had a "decent and reverent form and stile" and were "without pique or harshness." Furthermore, parliamentary privilege should not be "used for defrauding of creditors and defeating of ordinary justice." "Liberty of speech" should "turn not into licence, but be joined with that gravity and discretion, as may taste of duty and love to your sov-

135

ereign, reverence to your own assembly and respect to the matters ye handle."[5] With his customary eloquence, Bacon presented the Crown's desire for harmony on its own terms. While in the past, he had suggested to his colleagues in the House that they should rightfully accept their status as a junior partner of the Crown, he was now telling Parliament it must accept this position. His words still showed a desire to use tact, but he spoke as a man sure of his power. Disaster hardly appeared to be on the horizon.

The historian of 1621 feels that while Parliament was "alarmed by the restriction on debate suggested in the speeches of James and Bacon," it "bent over backward to avoid serious contention with the King." "The Commons' most positive gesture of goodwill," he remarks, "was a speedy grant of two subsidies, an amount— estimated at £160,000—greater than any ever levied on England in one year before."[6] The granting of such aid must certainly be interpreted as a display of good faith by the Lower House. The narrative of the early days of the session shows that despite uneasiness with the Crown's official posture, there was hope of avoiding a repeat of the direct collision course of 1614. As events were to prove, however, this Parliament would be too conscious of the potential threat to its claimed privileges and too concerned with both the grievance of monopolies and the issue of James's foreign policy to preserve an atmosphere of calm. As it launched into consideration of the perennial grievance of monopoly patents, the temporary peace of the session faded quickly. The cultivation of this issue became the first major concern of the Commons and served as the catalyst that would soon expose Lord Chancellor Bacon to wholesale attack.

While this attack mounted gradually only after the session began, Bacon's potential vulnerability should be noted. During the fall of 1620, the Chancellor had headed a special commission to study the major problems and grievances of the Kingdom. He wrote to Buckingham mentioning the need for "commonwealth bills" that would constitute "good matter to set the Parliament on work, that an empty stomach do not feed upon humor."[7] Bacon certainly recognized the major economic problems. He saw among other things the need to invigorate the cloth trade, the need to regulate corn supply, and the importance of checking the outflow of precious specie.[8] "There were few matters the Parliament of 1621 would find to complain of" remarks Zaller, "which had not already been remarked by Bacon."[9] And yet, the Chancellor was no longer fit for the role of a reformer. While he had spoken of the need to reform Chancery upon assuming leadership of that court, and had always espoused the cause of fundamental legal reform, his impetus for practical accomplishment had expired. The years of power had bred self-seeking complacency. The sixty-year old Bacon was now very much part of a prerogative power that had always resisted change. His mind was still vibrant and was still to conceive profound futuristic philosophy. As a political man, however, his constructive ability had waned. Bacon still might perceive England's problems, but was not to present the Parliament of 1621 with any major program of reform.[10] He saw the patent system as something to be tidied, but not abolished. He had tried in vain to persuade Buckingham to sanction reform by correcting some of his own actions. When he reported on the commission's efforts to the Council in December, 1620, he cautioned that Parliament might exploit the patent issue and neglect its "main errand." The indication is that he sensed the potential explosiveness of monopolies, and hoped the Crown might agree to some concessions on the revocation of patents.[11] No strategy was conceived and to quote Zaller, "The bomb was left to tick away, the dust to settle where it would."[12]

Buckingham was the major obstacle to any royal effort at monopoly reform in 1621. It is true that Bacon persisted in trying to influence his former political pupil to give way on this issue. He assured the Marquis "that if way be given . . . to the taking away of some of them, it will sort to your honour."[13] Such pleas were to no avail. While the Chancellor expected problems from Parliament, he anticipated no major crises. He again wrote Buckingham: "I have broken the main of the Parliament business into questions and parts, which I send. It may be, it is an overdiligence; but still methinks there is a middle thing between art and chance: I think they call it providence or some such thing; which good servants owe to their sovereign, specially in cases of importance and straits of occasions. And these huffing elections, and general license of speech, ought to make us better provided."[14] His words suggest satisfaction with his preparatory work and even hope that the session might be managed successfully. Was Bacon overly naive in expressing even cautious optimism? Was he unable to anticipate difficulties with Parliament without vacillation of his own perspective? On the one hand, he sensed the potential of trouble, while on the other he felt as Chancellor he could subdue most problems. Such questions must be raised along with a related one. As a high-ranking royal official, Bacon had been part of the system protecting monopolies. He had sanctioned patents as a referee, and as late as December, 1620, had helped certify a patent for none other than Buckingham himself.[15] Did Bacon therefore not realize that he, himself, might be exposed to open attack? With such protagonists as Coke and Cranfield in Parliament, should not the Chancellor have sensed the danger to himself that cultivation of the monopolies issue might bring?

These are valid questions to raise as one examines the rather sudden nature of Bacon's fall. If the Lord Chancellor approached the session of 1621 naively and underestimated the dangers, then perhaps such behavior is best explained by Bacon's own political character itself. This study has already depicted the Chancellorship as a rather undistinguished period in his career. His greatest concern was to enjoy to the fullest the status that had been so long in coming. Although such a situation was regrettable, it may be seen as understandable, given the nature of his political career. He had become complacent and with such complacency, his political perception had deteriorated. The Bacon that officially prepared for the Parliament of 1621 was a different individual from the man who had once warned James about the complications that union might face in the Commons. In the past, he had shown an understanding of the problems of managing Parliament, and had diligently advised the King. He was concerned that the Crown show tact and discretion in its techniques. Constructive control of Parliament by a strong but temperate prerogative had always been at the heart of his advice. Such advice had been given by a man striving for political success, and at times hoping for the opportunity of managing Parliament. In 1621, however, Bacon was no longer striving. He should have approached this session with at least the same urgency with which he approached the session of 1614, but he did not. Instead, he awaited events in the majestic comfort of the Chancellorship without contemplating that the monopolies grievance might make him vulnerable to open attack. Such thoughts lay beyond the limit of his perspective.

Bacon also appears not to have realized the potential danger from his bitter enemies in Parliament. In Coke and Cranfield, we find skilled antagonists, each of whom had cultivated intense hatred of the Chancellor. Coke's feelings are well known and need no further amplification. The year 1621 marked his return to public life, this time as an ordinary M.P., eager to use Parliament as the new vehicle for his legal assaults against the prerogative. This final phase of his career would begin in this session with his manipulations against Bacon and culminate seven years later with his architecture of the Petition of Right. Although Cranfield's antipathy toward Bacon was not so deeply rooted as Coke's, it too was strong. Despite the fact that Bacon and Cranfield worked constructively together on the Council, mutual affection never abounded between them. Their relationship had deteriorated so much that they "were barely on speaking terms by the autumn of 1620." Cranfield was in fact "the only councillor to present a genuine program of reform to the House of Commons in 1621."[16] His attacks on the Chancellor in Parliament were, says Zaller, "like land mines planted under Bacon's reputation." Both Coke and Cranfield moved against Bacon for different reasons. They did not work or plot together, nor did either conceive of impeachment at the start of the session. They worked along "separate paths" to bring the Chancellor "to the greatest possible discomfiture," and when the possibility of public disgrace presented itself they "seized it gratefully and joyously with both hands."[17] These individuals certainly stand out as Bacon's most potent enemies in 1621. In the Lords, however, there was also feeling against him. There was the Earl of Southampton, who had conspired with Essex and been imprisoned with Bacon's help. There was also Suffolk and his son; Bacon had been instrumental in the former's recent fining and imprisonment in the Tower. The Lords, moreover, were aware of the Chancellor's support of Benevolences and Monopolies and of his championing strong conciliar government in general. They would not initiate actions against him, but when presented with him as a ready-made scapegoat for cumulative grievances against the Crown, they would carry out the sacrifice. Bacon would prove conveniently vulnerable as a means of venting anger and displaying defiance. His enemies would gradually open the door to his exposure for personal corruption. In no way did he anticipate that anything like this was about to happen.

The monopoly issue was raised in a committee on grievances in early February. The mood in which this occurred was not one of

139

open hostility. The Commons quickly passed the subsidy, clearly demonstrating a desire to cooperate with the Crown. The abuse of monopolies, however, was looked upon as a most legitimate grievance; once raised, it was pursued with determination. Cranfield anxiously launched the attack: "What patent hath not had a fair pretence, I know something because I have been a Master of Request." He blamed the Crown's legal servants for sanctioning the most abusive patents. "If the referees be in fault," he said, "can he (the King) do himself more honor than to call them to account?"[18] Bacon had been a referee. A few days later, one William Noy moved to investigate patents. The King, he remarked, was not at fault since he "hath published his Distaste of these importunate Suitors." These individuals should be schooled in "Manners" and "the referees" should be examined.[19] Coke supported Noy. While he would not challenge the King's "indisputable" prerogative power, certain functions were "disputable." Dispensations and the granting of patents could be legally challenged. Grants that were legal but harmful could be challenged in Parliament. Coke also referred to the faults of the referees in the patent system.[20] He was implying, although not strongly asserting, that Parliament should play a permanent role in scrutinizing the entire patent system.

These challenges were enough to open the issue to fruitful exploitation. The patent of Inns held by one Sir Giles Mompesson was next discussed. This was a patent that Bacon urged Buckingham to cancel in November, 1620, having expressed concern that the upcoming Parliament might well be most likely to question the monopolies for inns, alehouses, and casks.[21] Ironically, it was Mompesson's case that paved the way for action against the Lord Chancellor. "Had it not revived the judicial functions of the Lords, Bacon could never have been brought to trial before the Upper House."[22] The patent had given Mompesson and two others the power to license innkeepers, and thus the control of the building and maintenance of inns throughout the realm. "The result," says Zaller, "had been merely a hit-and-run shakedown operation."[23] All the specifics of this case need not concern us here, but the resultant action against Mompesson is significant. Determined to punish this individual, the Commons sought out precedents for judicial action by Parliament. Appropriately, it was Coke who announced historical justification for such procedure, citing precedents of the fourteenth century. Mompesson, he claimed, could be charged by the Commons and tried by the Lords not only for parliamentary offenses, but for grievances of a general, loosely defined nature.[24] While there were medieval precedents for the judicial function of the Lords, it had not heard any criminal cases since the fifteenth century. Coke's proposal to revive and widen this power was clearly a departure from traditional parliamentary practice. It added what was really a new dimension to Parliament's power, and laid the direct foundations for "legal" attacks on the Crown's servants. It was concern over a grievance that led to uncovering this procedure, but it did not take Parliament long to recognize the potency of its new weapon. Coke's efforts in this matter were to bring far more gratifying results than he envisioned when he first conceived of parliamentary judicial action against Mompesson. The latter individual actually never did stand trial. He had been confined in the Tower, but escaped and left England before Coke had finished preparing the case against him. Angrily, the Lords tried him in absentia and sentenced him to life imprisonment. Thus ended the prelude to bigger and more dramatic action.

A foundation for action against Bacon began to develop. While the Commons concerned itself primarily with patents, it also began inquiring into judicial abuses. A committee for courts brought up the matter of abuses in Chancery with both Coke and Cranfield functioning significantly. The latter (Master of the Wards) used the occasion to poison further the feud between his court and Chancery. While not attacking Bacon personally, he called for full-scale judicial reform. Coke had himself already introduced a bill to limit Chancery's power.[25] Thus Chancery was being scrutinized at the same time Parliament was "reviving" its judicial function. Thomas Birch tells us that one Dr. Mead wrote to a friend at this time: "It is said that there are many bills ready to be put up against my lord chancellor."[26]

It was Mompesson's case, however, rather than an immediate inquiry into the activities of Chancery, that most directly helped expose Bacon to attack. Parliament was hardly satisfied with exposure of one abusive patent. The grievance committee decided to investigate others and to examine the referees of the monopolies as well as the holders. Immediately, the patent for gold and silver thread was subjected to examination. Bacon had approved of this patent as a referee, and in 1619, had put it under James's direct

141

jurisdiction. The King, Buckingham, and Sir Edward Villiers (George's older brother) had all profited from the monopoly. By questioning it, the Commons was potentially confronting the King directly, and such behavior was somewhat extreme for the activists of 1621. Action against referees, however, even if they be high royal officials, was not deemed too daring. Bacon's name was linked to this disliked patent. As he emerged as a ripe target for investigation, the two Houses decided on a joint conference to discuss threads and other abusive monopolies. James himself learned that the Commons grievance committee planned to notify the Lords "that they had discovered matters and offences tending to the wrong of his Majesty in his justice, honour, and estate; to the disinheritance of the Commonwealth; and this by a man of quality."[27] They were focusing on the Chancellor. Furthermore, he would be denied admission to the conference and would not be able to reply directly to charges. The King warned Bacon that he might become the subject of some kind of attack. James, however, did not grasp the potential intensity of the assault. Bacon graciously thanked him for the warning, without appearing overly alarmed. He then wrote Buckingham: "I do hear from divers of judgment, that tomorrow's conference is like to pass in a calm, as to the referees. . . . And I do hear almost all men of judgment in the House wish now that way. I woo no body: I do but listen, and I have doubt only of Sir Edward Coke, who I wish had some round *caveat* given him from the King."[28] Such words suggest only moderate concern on Bacon's part. Coke was his perennial nemesis and could be expected to try and provoke trouble. He was not the easiest individual to control, and the King might have to personally intervene to quell him. Bacon did not seem to realize the potential influence Coke might have in the House. There is no indication that he viewed the examination of referees as more than a pesky business that he would just have to endure.

Momentum was building against the Chancellor. The conference with the Lords debated the conduct of referees. Spedding points out that while Bacon was only one of those named, he was "the real object of attack." "When he was overthrown shortly after upon a totally different charge," our compiler adds, "the rest were not pursued any further."[29] Apparently, Bacon spoke in his own behalf before the conference. He admitted this later in the Lords, declaring before his peers that he had done no wrong and was willing to submit to their judgment.[30] At a second joint conference on March 10, Bacon again defended himself. He claimed that referees were not to blame if lawfully conceived patents were unlawfully administered by those holding the grants. He also defended Chancery's imprisonment of individuals who defied the thread patent as justifiable, claiming that these people had been in contempt. Zaller feels that while "no formal charge had yet been placed against him," Bacon already "stood isolated." "With every passing hour," he adds, "his role was being more surely shaped: the victim, the sacrifice, the scapegoat."[31] The impression conveyed is that while Parliament was still primarily concerned with investigating the grievance of patents, it was already aware of its "resurrected" judicial powers, and was being given the opportunity of focusing continuously on the highest ranking royal official. Bacon appeared a third time on March 15, before a joint conference on patents. Again he stood his ground, defending his behavior.[32] It was at this very time that a Commons committee for courts of justice began looking into his general conduct of Chancery. Bacon's presence on one stage was helping make possible his exposure on another. What if Parliament had not restructured its attack at this point in the proceedings? How would Bacon have fared if he had merely been attacked for his role as a referee? Spedding speculates that "he would have come off better than his accusers expected." Unfortunately, he believes, "we shall never know; for before the enquiry reached that stage a very different and much worse matter came out against him."[33]

The investigation into Bacon's conduct as Chancellor began in mid-March, 1621. It was Cranfield who set things in motion. He moved that Parliament look into bills on conformity, claiming they were injunctions that struck at the "roote of every man's estate" and were never sanctioned by the King.[34] He further charged that these measures (they were injunctions issued by Chancery for the staying of debts) were detrimental to trade. Zaller questions whether Cranfield was "carried away by his enmity for Bacon," or whether "the government had decided to throw Bacon to the wolves?" He points out that Cranfield's court also helped issue these injunctions and that the Chancellor himself hoped to abolish them in Parliament.[35] The effect of Cranfield's move was to make Bacon the main center of attention. No sooner had the Master of Wards taken his action, than it was superseded by more serious accusations. Two individuals, Christopher Aubrey and Edward Egerton, each petitioned the committee charging Bacon with accepting bribes. Both petitions claimed the Chancellor had been paid by the petitioners to expedite pending suits in his court. With respect to Aubrey, Spedding says that Bacon was warned in early March "that he was likely to be charged by a discontented suitor with having, about two years and half before, taken a sum of money from him for the better dispatch of a suit which was then in progress." Bacon had tried to quell the matter without success.[36] Egerton's charge surprised the Chancellor, and Bacon tried at the last minute to have it withdrawn.[37] Zaller feels these petitioners were "well sponsored" as they made accusations. He sees a neatly rigged trap for Bacon, suggesting that Coke and Phelips were perhaps the principal architects.[38]

Bacon's immediate reaction was one of shock. On March 14, 1621, the very day these charges were made, he wrote to Buckingham:

> Your Lordship spake of purgatory. I an now in it, but my mind is in a calm; for my fourtune is not my felicity. I know I have clean hands and a clean heart; and I hope a clean house for friends or servants. But Job himself, or whosoever was the justest judge, by such hunting for matters against him as hath been used against me, may for a time seem foul, specially in a time when greatness is the mark and accusation is the game. And if this be to be a Chancellor, I think if the great seal lay upon Hounslow Heath, nobody would take it up. But the King and your Lordship will, I hope, put an end to these miseries, one way or another.

Interestingly, the words, "I hope the King and your Lordship will keep me from oppression" were originally included, then crossed out. Bacon also complained of ill health and wondered if he could physically endure the ordeal. He remarked that if he absented himself because of sickness it would be considered "feigning or fainting."[39] Suddenly, he felt a vise beginning to close around him.

In Parliament, just that was happening. Sir Robert Phelips reported from the committee for courts the initial parliamentary statement against Bacon:

> I am commanded from the Committee for abuses in Courts of Justices to render an account of some abuses in courts of justice which I shall deliver are three parts: 1, the person against whom

it's alleged; 2, the matter alleged; 3, the opinion of the Committee with some desire of further direction. 1, The person is no less man than the Lord Chancellor, a man so endued with all parts both of nature and art as that I will say no more of him because I am not able to say enough. 2, The matter alleged is corruption. The persons by whom this is presented to us are two, Aubrey and Egerton.

Phelips then detailed each of the two charges. Aubrey claimed that he had a case that was delayed in Chancery, when he was "advised by some that are near my Lord" that the way "to quicken" it was "by presenting my Lord with a 100 li." Two intermediaries delivered the money to Bacon and told Aubrey "that my Lord was thankful and assured him of good success in his business." Aubrey said, however, that his matter was still delayed. Egerton apparently mortgaged his estate to come up with 400 li which he sent the Chancellor, also through intermediaries. "My Lord (as they say) started at it at first, saying it was too much, he would not take it but was at length persuaded because it was for favors past and took it." The case was more complex, but the delivery of this sum was substantiated. Phelips concluded his report by asking the House to deal with the matter immediately "because so great a man's honor is soiled with it." The Lords, too, were to be presented with the facts.[40]

The drama continued to unfold. The committee for courts examined the two star witnesses against Bacon—Sir George Hastings and Sir Richard Young. Hastings had delivered the bribes for both Aubrey and Egerton; Young had assisted Hastings in Egerton's case. John Finch, staunchly loyal to Bacon, tried unsuccessfully to discredit Hastings as a credible witness.[41] Further investigation of these individuals led to the recommendation that Bacon's case be presented "single to the Lords . . . without exasperation." This took place on March 17, only three days after the initial petitions had been heard. The Lords should get the case, Phelips argued, "for two Reasons (1) Of Precedent, that in this Course we may followe the stepps of our Ancestours, (2) Of necessitye, which is double, (1) the respect of the person, being a member of the Upper House, (2) our want of that Touchstone whereby truth may be bowlted out."[42] With lightning speed, Bacon was being set up for impeachment.

There were, however, doubts as to whether such drastic action could be taken against so important an individual. For one thing, the Lords had not impeached anyone since 1449. They would now be asked to revive a dormant practice against the Lord Chancellor. Not everyone showed Coke's determination to turn Bacon's case over to the Upper House for immediate action. William Noy remarked hesitantly "that we should discuss the business thoroughly here before we lett it fly abroad." Bacon's corruption was an offense against the King "for as much as in him lyeth he hath broken the king's oathe." "Of necessitie we must goe to the Lords," he said, "But there may be a question whether to them alone and without the Kinge; in one case this was demanded but refused. In Commendinge it to the Lords, not to deliver it as a thinge certeyne, as wee did in Sir Gyles Mompessons case Bust as an Informancion." Noy specified weaknesses in the evidence against Bacon, questioning in particular the credibility of Young and Hastings as witnesses.[43] Edward Sackville and John Stangways also questioned the strength of a case resting solely upon the evidence of these two witnesses. George Culvert questioned Parliament's jurisdictional power against so high a person as the Chancellor, and felt James should be petitioned to hear the case directly.[44] Coke, however, was unshaken in his resoluteness. "It wilbe impossible to prove Bribery if you will not accept of those that carrie the brybe . . . . And therefore we have a rule that if an offence be committed in a Brothel-house, the testimonie of Brothels shalbe admitted." The case, as he saw it, was strong enough. Neither Bacon nor any subject was above being answerable to the law. Bacon's most persistent enemy persuaded his colleagues to proceed without hestitation. "Soe it was ordered to present it to the Lords without prejudice to the cause."[45]

The Upper House listened immediately to the details of the case against Bacon. The Lord Treasurer presented a full report, showing how the charges of Aubrey and Egerton had been substantiated. "They humbly desire," he told his fellow Peers, referring to the Commons, "that, forasmuch as this concerns a person of so great eminency, it may not depend long before your Lordships; that the examination of the proofs may be expedited; and, if he be found guilty, then to be punished."[46] The Lords responded cooperatively. They showed their willingness to handle the case by quickly swearing witnesses, and by appointing three committees to deal with all the specifics. Witnesses were to be examined openly in their House, but Bacon would not be allowed to cross-examine them. They also declared that "no witnesses were to be examined what they received themselves, but only what bribes were given to the Lord Chancellor." It was clear that they considered the terms gratuities and bribes to be synonymous.[47] The prospect of impeaching Bacon rather than frightening the Lords seems to have inspired them to resolute action. Bacon was now their main business and they would not be deterred from trying him. Zaller points out that each house had clarified its function in this Parliament as the Easter recess approached. "The Commons proceeded with their monopolies, the Lords with Bacon. The harmony between the two houses had never been greater, nor apparently had that between Parliament and the King."[48]

How, in fact, did James respond to these events? When confronted with the charges against Bacon, he remarked that "noe Prince could answere for all the faults of his servants, yet he tooke Contentment in this, that his owne honour remayned clear."[49] To be certain, the King would take no major risks to save his Chancellor. He attempted to have Bacon tried by a special commission made up of members of both houses. The houses themselves would determine what individuals should sit on such a body, and the commission would hear the case under oath. Presumably, James thought such an approach was the only way to save Bacon from the stigma and consequences of parliamentary impeachment. The commission's function would actually be merely to investigate and the King himself would judge the Chancellor. Thus, Bacon might be found guilty of wrongdoing and be punished leniently. Parliament might be satisfied with having composed the commission, and more significantly, the judicial weapon of impeachment would be thwarted before its "resurrection." The plan was neat, but unacceptable. Coke saw the obvious threat to Parliament's judicial power and easily convinced his colleagues to reject the proposal. Actually, the plan threatened the Lords most, since it was their judicial authority that would be undermined. The commission scheme was abandoned, however, before the Peers even considered it, and James took no other steps to block impeachment. To confront Parliament head-on, to try to save an official whose guilt appeared obvious, was poor political strategy. The revival of impeachment was a dangerous move, but James felt he had to accept it. A confrontation meant total stagnation, while the sacrifice of Bacon might channel Parliament's energies enough to avoid a crisis over

147

monopolies. Furthermore, James valued his honor and reputation both at home and abroad. He needed support for his venturesome foreign policy and a complete rupture with Parliament was hardly the way to get it. In short, Bacon was expendable, even though he had been a loyal Chancellor. He had been close to the pulse of the Crown, but was still only a royal servant, not the King. James might dislike the impeachment of a Chancellor but might weather the storm with his prerogative power still intact. In the existing situation, Bacon had to be abandoned. The political man was vulnerable from both above and below.

Bacon had been shocked when he first learned individuals had made accusations against him. When it became apparent he would be formally tried, he suffered both physically and emotionally. "With a constitution so delicate and a mind so sensitive," writes Spedding, "it is not surprising that the shock produced by this new and unexpected situation proved too much for Bacon, and that his health gave way."[50] The Chancellor became ill, and wrote the Lords explaining his absence: "It is no feigning nor fainting, but sickness both of my heart and of my back, though joined with that comfort of mind, that perswadeth me that I am not far from heaven, whereof I feel the first fruits." He pleaded that he be judged fairly and be given the right to cross-examine witnesses at his trial. "Whether I live or die, I would be glad to preserve my honour and fame, as far as I am worthy."[51] Bacon was cracking. The once proud Chancellor, who only weeks before had stood at the King's side staunchly defending the prerogative, now pathetically appealed to his peers for leniency. Overcome by illness at the very time the Lords received his case, he tried desperately to retain his balance. On March 25 he wrote the King:

> When I enter into myself, I find not the materials of such a tempest as is cometh upon me. I have been (as your Majesty knoweth best) never author of any immoderate counsel. . . . I have been no avaricious oppressor of the people. I have been no haughty or intolerable or hateful man, in my conversation or carriage. I have inherited no hatred from my father, but am a good patriot born.
>
> . . .
>
> And for the briberies and gifts wherewith I am charged, when the books of hearts shall be opened, I hope I shall not be found to have the troubled fountain of a corrupt heart in a depraved habit of taking rewards to pervert justice; howsoever I may be frail, and partake of the abuse of the times.

148

> And therefore I am resolved when I come to my answer . . .
> to speak to them in language that my heart speaketh to me, in
> excusing extenuating, or ingenuous confessing; praying to God
> to give me the grace to see to the bottom of my faults, and that no
> hardness of heart do steal upon me, under shew of more neatness
> of conscience than is cause.

While not admitting purposeful wrongdoing, Bacon appeared ready to recognize his weakness in partaking "of the abuse of the times." He concluded the letter by throwing himself at James's mercy. "I have been ever your man, and counted myself but an usufructuary of myself, the property being yours: and now making myself an oblation to do with me as may best conduce to the honour of justice, the honour of your mercy, and the use of your service, resting as clay in your Majesty's gracious hands."[52] Bacon was obviously trying to prepare himself for the worst, while still kindling the hope that somehow the King would rescue him. Events had overcome him rapidly and he was already prostrate.

Bacon's case was delayed only by an Easter recess. He himself was at Gorhambury, and was apparently despondent enough about his over-all health to draft a will. "I bequeath my soul to God above," he wrote, "by the oblation of my Saviour. My body to be buried obscurely. My name to the next ages, and to foreign nations." At this time he also wrote a "prayer or psalm" which Joseph Addison viewed as angelic in character:

> The state and bread of the poor and oppressed have been pre-
> cious in mine eyes: I have hated all cruelty and hardness of heart:
> I have (though in a despised weed) procured the good of all men.
> . . . Thousand have been sins, and ten thousand my transgres-
> sions; but thy sanctifications have remained with me, and my
> heart, through thy grace, hath been an unquenched coal upon the
> altar. . . . Be merciful unto me (O Lord) for my Saviour's sake,
> and receive me into thy bosom, or guide me in thy ways.[53]

In the quiet of the St. Albans countryside, Bacon could be contemplative and even spiritual. Upon reading the will and "psalm," one gets the impression that for a short time, anyway, he anticipated the possibility of death and went about making his peace. This retreat to a kind of spiritualism provided a temporary respite from the political agonies that faced him. It was, of course, only temporary. Perhaps, however, this brief interlude in the story of his fall helped buttress his fortitude. Bacon recovered physically, and was able to return to Parliament and face the charges.

When Parliament reconvened on April 17, Bacon's trial began. The Chancellor felt revitalized and appeared determined to offer a defense. While he had little hope of acquittal, he wanted to at least attempt to defend his character. He examined precedents for "bribery" cases and prepared his findings for presentation to the King. "There be," he wrote, "three degrees or cases (as I conceive) of gifts and rewards given to a Judge:"

> The first is, Of bargain, contract, or promise of reward, *pendente lite*. . . . And of this my heart tells me I am innocent; that I had no bribe or reward in my eye or thought, when I pronounced any sentence or order. The second is, A neglect in the Judge to inform himself whether the cause be fully at an end or not, what time he receives the gift; but takes it upon the credit of the party, that all is done; or otherwise omits to enquire. And the third is, When it is received *sine fraude*, after the cause ended which, it seems by the opinion of the civilians, is no offence. . . .

Bacon admitted some negligence in having accepted "gifts," but denied accepting "bribes."[54] His guilt, he felt, was in lapse of discretion, not in any will to pervert justice. He could make such a distinction dramatically to James and perhaps evoke sympathy. Convincing the Lords of the difference between "gifts" and "bribes" was, however, something else.

As it turned out, Bacon did not persist in this defense. He recognized the hopelessness of his case when he learned that forty-one witnesses had testified against him and twenty-eight specific charges had been made. The Chancellor then submitted his resignation to the Lords, hoping they might be satisfied enough and refrain from carrying the trial to a conclusion. "And therefore my humble suit to your Lordships is, that my penitent submission may be my sentence, and the loss of the seal my punishment; and that your Lordship will spare any further sentence, but recommend me to his Majesty's grace and pardon for all that is past. God's holy spirit be amongst you!" Bacon hoped that a "submission" such as this would pacify Parliament enough to stop the formal impeachment proceedings. He made a general admission of guilt: "The greatness of a judge or magistrate shall be no sanctuary or protection of guiltiness. . . . It is like," he added, "that judges will fly

150

from any thing that is in the likeness of corruption (though it were at a great distance), as from a serpent; which tendeth to the purging of the courts of justice, and the reducing them to their true honour and splendor."[55] Bacon was, in fact, pleading the judicial system guilty of corruption more than he was making a personal confession. Perhaps, James might persuade the Lords to accept such a "submission." Bacon tried. He was now, in fact, begging for mercy.

A "general submission," however, would not placate Parliament. While Buckingham and Prince Charles tried to persuade the Peers to accept it and withdraw formal charges, their efforts were in vain. The Upper House clearly recognized that Bacon was trying to avoid confessing specific guilt. His enemies rose to the occasion to voice objection. "The confession is not sufficient," remarked Suffolk, "for he desires to be a judge—to lose his seal, and that to be the sentence: wherefore it is far short of that we expect." "He is charged by the Commons with corruption," added Southampton, "and no word of confession of any corruption in his submission. It stands with the justice and honour of this House not to proceed without the parties' particular confession; or to have the parties' answer." Lord Saye was even more resolute; "If this submission intend a connivance it had been well in the beginning, but coming now after the examinations and proofs, it comes too late. . . . Moved to proceed!"[56] There would be no compromise by the Lords. Bacon would either have to contest the charges and endure what would surely be a painful trial, or submit a full and specific confession. He had made his move to circumvent a direct assault upon himself and failed.

On April 25, Bacon sent the following message to the Lords:

> The Lord Chancellor will make no manner of defence to the charge, but meaneth to acknowledge corruption, and to make a particular confession to every point, and after that an humble submission.
> But humbly craves liberty, that where the charge is more full than he finds the truth of the fact, he may make declaration of the truth in such particulars; the charge being brief, and containing not all circumstances.[57]

The Peers were now satisfied. They agreed to accept Bacon's full confession in writing, thus sparing him the humiliation of a public statement. On April 30, the Upper House received his "Confession

151

and humble Submission." "Upon advised consideration of the conscience, and calling my memory to account so far as I am able, I do
plainly and ingeneously confess that I am guilty of corruption; and
do renounce all defence, and put myself upon the grace and mercy
of your Lordships." Bacon then specified his guilt; to each of the
twenty-eight charges he made an admission. It read almost like a
broken phonograph record:

> I do confess and declare, that soon after coming to the Seal . . .
> the four hundred pounds mentioned in the said charge was de-
> livered unto me in a purse. . . .
> I do confess and declare . . . there were gold buttons about
> the value of fifty pounds . . . presented unto me. . . .
> I confess and declare, that I received at new years' tide an hun-
> dred pounds from Sir John Trevor. . . . I neglected to inquire
> whether the cause was ended or depending. . . .
> I confess and declare, that, as I remember, a good while after
> the cause ended, I received an hundred pounds either by Mr.
> Toybe Matthew, or from Yong himself. . . .

And so it went on. In each case Bacon attempted to qualify his admission of guilt with an explanation. He had no intention of wrongdoing; he had been repeatedly negligent. Perhaps his reply to the
twenty-eighth and final charge best characterizes his pathetic condition:

> To the eight and twentieth article of the charge, *videlicet*, the
> Lord Chancellor hath given way to great exactions by his ser-
> vants, both in respect of private seals, and otherwise for sealing
> of injunctions.
> I confess it was a great fault of neglect in me, that I looked no
> better to my servants.[58]

Upon receiving Bacon's full statement, the Lords dispatched a
committee to him in person to verify his authorship of the document. "My Lords," he told the group, "It is my act, my hand, my
heart. I beseech your Lordships, be merciful to a broken reed." The
King, acting at the request of the Peers, then sent the Lord Treasurer, the Lord Steward, the Lord Chamberlain, and the Earl of
Arundel to fetch the seal from Bacon's person. They found him ill
and when they "wished it had been better with him," he replied:
"The worse the better. By the King's great favour I received the

great seal; by my own great fault I have lost it."[59] With this pitiful statement Bacon's hold on the Chancellorship of England ended. His career as a political man was over.

There remained only the formal sentencing. It came on May 3, 1621, without Bacon present to hear it:

> 1. That the Lord Viscount St. Alban, Lord Chancellor of England, shall undergo fine and ransom of forty thousand pounds.
> 2. That he shall be imprisoned in the Tower during the King's pleasure.
> 3. That he shall for ever be incapable of any office, place, or employment in the State or Commonwealth.
> 4. That he shall never sit in Parliament, nor come within the verge of the Court.

Actually, the punishment could have been more severe. Southampton had in fact favored banishment. The Lords reached near unanimity in passing the actual sentence, however, with Buckingham the only dissenting vote in Bacon's favor.[60] Bacon would spend only a few days in the Tower in late May and early June. He secured a quick release and remitted his fine by putting £40,000 worth of his assets in trust, thereby stifling his creditors.[61]

It appears perhaps that Bacon thought the sentence might be at least partially ignored. On June 4, after his abbreviated stay in prison, he wrote both James and Buckingham thanking them for his early release. "Let me live to serve you," he told the King, "else life is but the shadow of death."[62] He was allowed to remain within the "verge" (twelve miles), until Parliament ended its current sitting. Apparently, James consulted him about Parliament upon his release, and he replied as he had so many times in the past with thoughtful advice. It thus appears that for a few weeks in June, 1621, Bacon still believed he might yet be permitted to remain in public life. If the King still needed him, then perhaps Parliament might be persuaded to revise the sentence. Perhaps he might be allowed to remain within the verge and serve unofficially at court. Any such hopes were dispelled quickly, however, since he was in fact excluded from the verge and left London for Gorhambury on June 23, 1621. Upon arrival in St. Albans he wrote Buckingham:

> I thank God I am come very well to Gorhambury, whereof I thought your Lordship would be glad to hear sometimes; my Lord,

I wish myself by you in this stirring world, not for any love to place or business, for that is almost gone with me, but for my love to yourself, which can never cease in.

Your Lordship's most
obliged friend and
true servant,

Fr. St. Alban[63]

Bacon appeared to breathe a sigh of relief that the struggle was over and seemed ready to accept his forced retirement. While he would regain access to court in March, 1622, in return for selling York House to none other than Cranfield, he would never again return to political life. Thoughts of such a return did, however, linger inside him. By 1623, James had granted him a full pardon. He would still write to the King and Buckingham expressing an interest in returning to politics. He offered James a "digest of the Laws of England" and dedicated his *History of Henry VII* to Prince Charles. Perhaps he hoped his prolific pen would win back royal favor. Bacon's correspondence in the years after his fall shows his continuing interest in affairs of state. Although he adjusted well to a nonpolitical existence, he perhaps always hoped the Crown would express a need for his genius. His removal from officialdom was, however, to prove permanent. Bacon's mind flourished during these final years, but it did so in the gifted "intellectual man" he always was.

What new assessment, if any, can be made of Bacon's fall? One is inclined to agree with standard modern evaluations. Bacon's behavior as a royal official was very much in keeping with the practices of the time. Financial gifts to influential governmental figures were acceptable, and it might be argued, even necessary. Officers of the Crown could not maintain themselves in the style in which they were expected to live, on fixed salaries. Judges always depended on the lucrative help of the fees paid for their services. The line between a "fee" and a "bribe" was blurred, and no one within the system was really interested in focusing on it clearly. Seventeenth-century England had no collective conscience concerned with ethics in government. Bacon's practices were characteristic of the system he helped constitute. They could not be looked upon as criminal.

He fell because he stood as an ideal victim for a Parliament

154

looking to vent hostility against the Crown. He was an assailable symbol of royal power, and there was little risk in attacking him when it became clear James would not stand in the way. With this judgment, that Bacon was, in fact, a convenient scapegoat, it is difficult to disagree. "The cause for Bacon's trial," writes Anderson, "was not the perversion of justice; that was never seriously entertained, even by his most ardent accusers. The charge against the Lord Chancellor was aimed at an official person, a destructive representative and symbol of a regime."[64] Bacon's fall, says Zaller, "was the result of maneuverings as devious as any of his own, but it cannot of itself be called unjust."[65] He indulged in the game of politics and had to risk political failure. As Chancellor, Bacon was involved with large-scale stakes; the failure would also prove grandiose.

Bacon's fall is thus seen as an understandable consequence faced by a vulnerable political figure of the time. I would perhaps disagree with Zaller when he claims it "cannot of itself be called unjust." It cannot be judged "of itself." It was clearly a political act and as such should not be hastily called either just or unjust. From another perspective, it was tragic that an individual so interested in philosophizing about the need for a more enlightened judiciary should have such an undistinguished career as a judge. The reasons for this lie in Bacon's own weaknesses and, given his life, could not have been avoided. Bacon's disgrace was a pathetic spectacle; it should not, however, be evaluated within the traditional categories of justice or injustice.

To this writer, Francis Bacon's failure to embody the reformist spirit he echoed in his writings was more tragic than his actual impeachment. The pity lies in the gifted individual who struggled so long for great place and then behaved in it without distinction. That was sorrowful; his fall was almost logical. Political men often have precarious balances.

Sometime during Bacon's crisis of 1621 (Spedding is not sure exactly when), Bacon made the following statement during a meeting with James: "Those that will strike at your Chancellor, it is much to be feared will strike at your crown."[66] Though facing disgrace, the Lord Chancellor remained well endowed with the gift of prophecy.

1. *Letters and Life*, VII, 168-69.

2. *Ibid.*, 171. *See* also Wallace Notestein, Francis Kelf, Harley Simpson, eds., *Commons Debates, 1621*, 7 vols. (New Haven, 1935), VI, 373-74.

3. *Commons Debates*, VI, 374.

4. *Letters and Life*, VII, 177-78. *See* also *Commons Debates*, V, 430-32. Bacon answered the Speaker on February 3, 1621.

5. *Letters and Life*, VII, 179.

6. Zaller, *The Parliament of 1621*, 37, 47.

7. *Letters and Life*, VII, 116.

8. *Ibid.*, 70-72.

9. *Parliament of 1621*, 20.

10. Zaller remarks that Bacon's "bills of grace were a lusterless lot; little differing from those of 1614, or even 1610." The Chancellor's commission had studied the problem of abusive patents thoroughly and had recommended reform. He was not prepared, however, to alienate Buckingham (sponsor of "the most notorious of patents") nor to cause major dissension within the Council by committing the Crown to reform a practice that brought it much needed revenue. *See Parliament of 1621*, 21-26; *Letters and Life*, VII, 98-99, 133-40, 145-48, 155-56.

11. *Letters and Life*, VII, 151-52.

12. Zaller, 24.

13. *Letters and Life*, VII, 152.

14. *Ibid.*, 155.

15. *Ibid.*, 140-41.

16. Zaller, 21.

17. *Ibid.*, 54-55.

18. *Commons Debates*, II, 90. The date was February 15.

19. *Ibid.*, VI, 249.

20. *Ibid.*, IV, 79-81.

21. *Letters and Life*, VII, 148-49.

22. Zaller, 59-60.

23. *Ibid.*, 57. Zaller carefully treats the details of this case.

24. *Commons Debates*, II, 148; IV, 114-15; Edward, Nicholas, *Proceedings and Debates in the House of Commons in 1620 and 1621* (Oxford, 1766), I, 108-9.

25. This committee met on February 28, even before the absentia sentence was passed upon Mompesson. *See Commons Debates*, VI, 272-75, 292-95; *Proceedings and Debates*, I, 109-12.

26. *Memoirs*, II, 232. Mead wrote this on February 25, 1621.

27. *Proceedings and Debates*, I, 114.

28. *Letters and Life*, VII, 192.

29. *Ibid.*, 197.

30. *Ibid.*, 197-98; Zaller, 70.

31. Zaller, 72-73.

32. *Letters and Life*, VII, 202-3.

33. *Ibid.*, 208.

34. *Commons Debates*, VI, 62-64; V, 296-97; IV, 152-55; II, 221-23; *Proceedings and Debates*, I, 157-60.

35. *The Parliament of 1621*, 75, 204. Johnson feels that while Cranfield's attack on Bacon is "difficult to excuse or to justify, it seems quite clear that his chief motive was not to embarrass a royal minister but rather to prepare the way for positive action to abolish bills of conformity." The evidence, he claims, supports this view—Bills of Conformity were not the actual charges against Bacon. Johnson admits, however, that it was Cranfield who in fact directed the Commons' attention to abuses in Chancery, and never once during Bacon's ordeal, attempted to defend his colleague. *See* "Francis Bacon and Lionel Cranfield." 312.

36. *Letters and Life*, VII, 212.

37. *Ibid.*, 213-14; *Proceedings and Debates*, I, 162. Spedding goes into some of the details of Egerton's case.

38. *The Parliament of 1621*, 75-76, 204.

39. *Letters and Life*, VII, 213.

40. *Commons Debates*, II, 224-26. This report was made on March 15.

41. *Ibid.*, IV, 160-61; V, 44-45, 301-2; VI, 66-68; *Proceedings and Debates*, I, 183-85.

42. *Commons Debates*, II, 237-39; IV, 166-67; V, 306; *Proceedings and Debates*, I, 183-85.

43. *Commons Debates*, IV, 167-68.

44. *Proceedings and Debates*, I, 187.

45. *Commons Debates*, IV, 168. The accusations against Bacon were presented to the Lords on March 19.

46. *Letters and Life*, VII, 223.

47. *Ibid.*, 224.

48. *The Parliament of 1621*, 84.

49. *Ibid.*, 82.

50. *Letters and Life*, VII, 215.

51. *Ibid.*, 215-16.

52. *Ibid.*, 225-26.

53. *Ibid.*, 227-31.

54. *Ibid.*, 237-38.

55. *Ibid.*, 242-45.

56. *Ibid.*, 248-49.

57. *Ibid.*, 250.

58. *Ibid.*, 252-61.

59. *Ibid.*, 262. Bacon surrendered the Great Seal on May 1, 1621.

60. *Ibid.*, 267-71.

61. *Ibid.*, 280-81, 288-91. Spedding claims that he was in the Tower on May 31 and out by June 4. He may have been there only a day or two.

62. *Ibid.*, 281.

63. *Ibid.*, 289-93.

64. *Francis Bacon. . . ,* 226-27.

65. *The Parliament of 1621*, 90.

66. *Letters and Life*, VII, 199-200. Spedding feels the interview during which this statement was made took place when Bacon was being investigated as a referee, but before he was actually charged with corruption.

CHAPTER X

BACON'S POLITICAL IDEAS

This study has centered on Bacon the political activist. I have argued that he must be studied as a political man independently of being analyzed as a thinker. His long and at times tumultuous career in politics seldom made it conducive for him to apply the wisdom he preached in his writings. What place, then, does a discussion of Bacon's political views have in a study of this type? Would it not be more consistent with my interpretation to avoid treating any aspect of his thought, political or other? Perhaps so. I feel sure, however, that no figure of Bacon's scope can be studied merely as a nonthinking functionary. His mind was constantly at work, and he always hoped his ideas would be successfully applied. His many views on monarchy, Parliament, and the law were expressed in various ways. They ranged from speeches and letters of political advice to philosophical treatises. Although it is not the purpose here to attempt a comprehensive analysis of Bacon's political ideas, it is appropriate to include some discussion of these ideas in a political biography. Much of what Bacon thought about political matters was based on the experiences of his long career. Much of what he wrote showed the sincere aspirations of a political man. It is therefore not without justification that some of these views be reflected upon, as one attempts to understand the political side of Francis Bacon.

The first question that must be raised in any effort to study Bacon's political ideas is this: Did he have a systematic political philosophy? Can we consider Bacon a political philosopher of any substance? This is far from a simple problem, and recent scholarship has made it one of interest. What may be termed the "standard view" does not consider Bacon an important political thinker. He is not listed with major seventeenth-century political theorists, and wrote no one work from which an "essence" of political thought can be extracted. J. W. Allen maintains emphatically that Bacon was not a political philosopher. He did have some definite ideas about government and the constitution, but they were at best fragmentary. There was no system to his political thinking.[1] Bacon, Allen feels, believed in government as an instrument of material progress and sought a strong, but enlightened, monarchy, functioning in the public interest. Wisdom was the key to good government and Bacon felt it could be best exercised by the Crown.[2] These views constituted a kind of theory of government but not a comprehensive theory of the state. Bacon never tried to systematize his political ideas. G. P. Gooch also sees Bacon as extolling a kind of enlightened despotism, with the King as the prime mover. Despite this acknowledgment of Bacon's belief in the constructive use of power, Gooch terms his political thought as archaic. With Whiggish condemnation, he charges that Bacon "had no insight into the strength and value of the newer currents that were bearing his countrymen in the direction of a wider and more assured liberty."[3] Although Bacon could not be considered a profound political thinker, Gooch saw the fullest statement of his political thought in the *Essays*.[4]

Margaret Judson, whose ideas have significantly influenced this writer, considers Bacon "more of a political philosopher" than any of his contemporary royalist judges and councillors. She sees him as believing in a balanced constitution, "in a king having great authority, in subjects possessing rights, and in law moulding the body politic together and adjusting and balancing its separate component parts."[5] "To him," she explains, "the King's prerogative, the subject's liberty, and the laws existed side by side, each one complementing and strengthening the others, and all working together to produce a delicately poised and beautifully balanced harmony." His views on these subjects are "the keystone of Bacon's constitutional thinking . . . " and "must always be interpreted in relation to his Renaissance faith in the ultimate harmony of all."[6] Balance and harmony were what Bacon strove to maintain during

159

his many years as a royal servant in Parliament. While Bacon's views on a "balanced constitution" justify higher regard for him as a political thinker than Allen and Gooch are willing to admit, they do not establish him as a major political theorist. Miss Judson feels "that Bacon never really grasped the concept of sovereignty and certainly did not make it a basis of his thought." His main contribution to political thought was "in furnishing and developing ideas concerning the prerogative which the royalists used to justify the legal absolutism they tried so hard to establish in England."[7]

The work that gives us good reason to reconsider our opinions of Bacon's political thinking is Howard B. White's thoughtful and provocative study, *Peace Among the Willows: The Political Philosophy of Francis Bacon.*[8] This highly original work views Bacon's political thought in an entirely new dimension. According to White, Bacon was a profound and unique political philosopher. His thought is understood by distinguishing between what White calls "provisional" and "definitive" thinking. The former embodies Bacon's views on the political and religious problems of the England of his day. His "definitive" thought concerns the utopian condition he hopes man can reach, the *New Atlantis.* The latter is Bacon's final cause and represents the kind of society most desirable for man. Bacon, White argues, was concerned with the major problems such as war, peace, economic growth, and religion. "Any careful and systematic consideration of needs of society, . . . would make Bacon a political philosopher."[9] The *New Atlantis* is thus not merely a scientific utopia; it is a blueprint for man's future social and political condition.

The main problem of course is how to get man to the *New Atlantis.* Peace and stability within the current body politic were the necessary precursors of progress toward utopia. Like the miller of Huntington, Bacon cherished the need for peace. His so-called "provisional" thought concerned itself with creating an atmosphere for scientific and material progress. This setting was one of stability and was grounded on the three main pillars of Bacon's "provisional" politics, Crown, Church, and Empire. Bacon propounded politically conservative ideas because he believed a stable commonwealth free from political and religious strife was necessary for the advancement of science. White contends that Bacon's staunch support of a strong monarchy and unified Church was essentially pragmatic. A strong, cautious monarch such as Henry VII was

160

greatly admired. He had ended civil strife, and ushered in the stability necessary for the reconstruction of a kingdom. Henry was Bacon's model ruler from whom there was much to be learned. White feels Bacon hoped to "use political conservatism as protection for scientific expansion." "If, of course, Bacon is right," he adds, "that the discovery of the nature of man depends on tracking an uncharted wilderness, then the political order that will give man the leisure, the opportunity, the pioneering spirit, and the best available knowledge for getting into that wilderness is provisionally the best political order."[10] That "order" was for Bacon a strong monarchy.

It follows, according to White, that Bacon's belief that traditional monarchy rested in natural right was a "provisional" belief:

> If I am right in insisting that the character of Bacon's teaching on the subject of natural right is intended to be provisional, then the reason for suggesting the preliminary character of its "origins" is clear. As Abraham, David, Moses, Nimrod are preliminary to Christ, so is "natural right" preliminary to Bacon. . . .[11]

White believes that Bacon's statement to James that he was a "perfect and peremptory royalist" summarizes "what we may call Bacon's official view." Yet Bacon's royalism was not unlimited. He distinguished between monarchy and tyranny, and emphasized the constructive use of royal power. Bacon's royalism, White feels, was not a sacred belief, but a pragmatic one. "How should the peremptory royalist counsel," he suggests, "when what he wanted was a state that moved in the direction of science, commerce, mercantilism?" "Bacon may or may not have loved the monarchy partly because it was a monarchy, but he loved it chiefly because it was a modern monarchy, and the monarchy in which scientific and political expansion might take place."[12] Bacon's royalism is seen in a rather unique perspective.

Support for the King meant support for the English Church. Religious peace was crucial if a state was to generate the impetus for scientific development. As Bacon said when he wrote about his miller, "I see that controversies of religion must hinder the advancement of sciences." "Bacon wanted peace among the willows, and it is impossible to stress that fact too strongly. Bacon wanted to run his watermill, the watermill of scientific expansion."[13] The Anglican Church, with a structure that subordinated clerical to

secular power, was well suited to maintain the religious peace necessary for progress. It must be strong, yet tolerant and flexible enough
to absorb heresy without provoking religious strife. As White puts
it, "Bacon certainly thought the Anglican Church well fitted for the
voyage to the New Atlantis."[14]

The third pillar of Bacon's so-called provisional political thought
was the imperial, the need for empire. Bacon's interest in national
greatness through commercial and naval expansion is clear in his
writings. He sought a strong England, dominant in foreign affairs,
and foresaw a great empire based on an expanding capitalism.[15]
His vision of Britain's future greatness proved to be quite prophetic.
The details of Bacon's views on empire and economic growth will
concern us later. What is significant here is White's contention
that Bacon saw the need for England to become a great power.
Such status could be achieved through the development of imperial
power. It would win the respect of the world and serve as a model
of material progress. Bacon was convinced, writes White, "that
Britain was the ship that would take man to the New Atlantis."[16]

Thus, according to this interpretation, the many words Bacon
wrote and spoke about the prerogative power, Parliament, the
law, the English Church, and the need for national greatness compose only his "provisional" political thought. His lifetime of service
in politics then was really a career in "provisional" politics. White
devotes more than half his study to discussing in great detail Bacon's "definitive" political thought. He explores the foundations
of the New Atlantis as well as every important aspect of it. Its
political, cultural, and religious structures are carefully discussed.
White is very much concerned with interpreting the very essence
of Bacon's utopian philosophy. This part of his study is geared to
the scholar primarily interested in Bacon as a philosopher.[17]

White's book is both stimulating and, I must admit, a bit unset-
tling. How is the historian concerned with studying Bacon as a
political man in the real world to react to such an interpretation?
If everything Bacon said and wrote on important matters during his
long tenure in politics was "provisional," then must not career be
viewed in a similar light? In one respect this is true. Bacon's ideal
was always the pursuit of knowledge and he certainly flourished
more in intellectual endeavors than he did as a politician. One cannot dispute the standard view that he would have led a happier and
more noteworthy life, had he the leisure and financial security to

devote himself fully to scholarship. While in politics, he believed in the "power to do good" and tried unsuccessfully to influence his King. A Bacon in politics serving a politically astute, financially secure monarch might have had the opportunity to utilize his "provisional" ideas toward constructive results. But Bacon's hopes remained frustrated, and while he still envisioned scientific and intellectual progress, he pursued power basically as an end in itself. How then does this fact come to terms with White's thesis? The latter is, I believe, argued most thoughtfully and certainly cannot be brushed aside or completely discredited. Bacon as an intellectual man was a philosopher and White makes a strong case by contending that Bacon did construct a political philosophy. I have been concerned with Bacon, the political man, and have maintained that he be studied in a two-fold capacity. Without trying to refute White's interpretation, I feel it is possible to look at Bacon's political views through a different perspective. While Bacon most certainly looked toward the New Atlantis, he functioned in the rather different setting of political reality. He was involved in a multitude of divergent political issues during his career, and often responded to them as a practical politician. The New Atlantis was far off; the problems of Crown and Parliament, and legal reform to name a few, were real issues that had to be faced constructively. Bacon's views on contemporary matters may in one sense be termed "provisional"; however, they can also be studied as the views of a political man seeking to give advice on immediate and often serious problems. We may not call this a political philosophy, since it is fragmentary. Bacon did, however, have some significant political ideas. While they were not expressed systematically, they showed his concern for some of the issues of his day. The political man tried to serve as a pragmatic political adviser.

Bacon best fit this latter role as he attempted to advise James on the problems of handling Parliament. His views on the latter constitute part of his basic ideas on government and the constitution. Without downgrading the importance of the philosophic basis of his thinking on these subjects, I would hold most strongly that much of what he said and wrote was the product of political experience. The Tudor stamp was deeply imprinted upon him, and remained an important basis for his political views. As one biographer aptly puts it: "He was born an Elizabethan and an Elizabethan he remained."[18] Willson writes that Bacon's "political philosophy was essentially Tudor in character, augmented by the sweep of his own rich imagination, and combined with quiet but constant guidance of parliamentary affairs."[19] In advancing her thesis, Miss Judson argues that "the Elizabethan ideal of a balanced government lived on to play an important part in the thinking of men in the early seventeenth century."[20] Bacon, she contends, believed in such a concept. The case for Bacon's adherence to Elizabethan political principles is made with justification. He had both apprenticed and matured in Parliament under Elizabeth. He had witnessed dissent, had briefly engaged in it, and finally helped the Crown attempt to pacify it. The concept of Elizabethan paternalism was woven into his thought and actions. He understood it as standing for a strong but tactful prerogative power that retained its supremacy while still preserving an atmosphere of harmony in government. It was also a flexible instrument to be advanced and relaxed with discretion. Bacon had been conditioned by the Elizabethan method of handling Parliament. One is again prompted to look at his famous speech in 1610 as being most revealing. "The King's Sovereignty and the Liberty of Parliament," he remarked, ". . . though the one be more active the other more passive, yet they . . . strengthen and maintain the one the other."[21] Parliament was the Crown's junior partner in a partnership that had to be preserved to avoid political chaos. Bacon blended this Tudor principle with his more philosophical ideas to construct his reverence for political stability.

The advice to James on Parliament was essentially pragmatic. Parliament occupied a subservient, but significant place in the constitution. Its role as a junior partner had to be recognized by James the way it had been by Elizabeth. Bacon believed that the Commons must be managed the way it had been in 1597 and 1601. The decline of the Privy Councillors' influence in the Lower House had contributed significantly to James's problems with Parliament. Salisbury's efforts at managing had been directed from the Lords, and had been less than spectacular. During the last two Elizabethan sessions, however, this same individual (then Sir Robert Cecil) had successfully guided government policy from the Commons, providing a leadership that avoided conflict, and successfully promoted the Crown's demands. Bacon sought a return to the Elizabethan method, hopefully with himself as parliamentary manager. Any return to the Tudor approach meant a total rejection of Salisbury's bargaining policies of 1610. Such practices, Bacon told James, were "almost contrary to the frame of monarchy." For a monarch to succeed with Parliament, he must "put off the person of a merchant and contractor, and rest upon the person of a King." Even though the matter of Parliament was "a great problem of estate, and deserveth apprehensions and doubts, . . . your Majesty should not descend below yourself."[22] Bacon was emphatic in his condemnation of the contract idea. James's total rejection of it was the most basic condition for a successful change in the Crown-Parliament relationship. A Tudor-like policy called for the reassertion of statesmanlike royal leadership; the King must command respect as he utilized parliamentary assistance in governing the realm. Parliament must never be treated as an equal.

Bacon realized that James's financial troubles, together with his already strained relationship with Parliament, made the task of enhancing the Crown's image difficult. The effort, however, had to be made. "Until your majesty have tuned your instrument you will have no harmony."[23] This meant that the Crown must moderate its financial demands until better relations with the Commons were established. All through his advice Bacon stressed the need for tact and moderation. Let the Crown propose "gracious and plausable laws" to be "handled in Parliament, for the comfort and contentment of the people." Touchy legal matters, such as the right of impositions, must be "buried and silenced."[24] It was the Crown's responsibility to see to it that such issues were not exposed to open debate. A more harmonious atmosphere, Bacon believed, would breed fewer grievances. It was crucial that the Crown work toward such an end.

The elimination of parliamentary factions was also essential to Bacon's concept of governmental harmony. Parliament must function as a unified body and not as the faction-ridden institution of 1610. In the manner of a true Elizabethan, he deplored any practice that might impair the existence of a cooperative spirit. It followed therefore that James must not attempt to pack Parliament with his own party or faction. Such a policy would only serve to "increase animosities and oppositions." The Crown must attempt to gain a majority by exercising "discretion" and an "ability to persuade . . . without labouring or packing."[25] To be certain, Bacon sought a parliamentary membership favorable to the Crown, and had his thoughts on how one might be secured. "The winning or bridling of the lawyers . . . that they may further the King's causes, or at least fear to oppose them" as well as the drawing of "citizens and burgesses," and "of justices of the peace and gentlemen" were steps deemed necessary for the elimination of any potent opposition.[26] Although Bacon warned James against "briques" (underhand soliciting) in elections, he hoped the government could subtly influence elections. The Crown, he believed, should determine "what persons . . . are fit to be brought in to be of the house . . . without labouring or packing" and "what persons . . . are fit to be kept back from being of the house . . . without labouring or packing." He advocated the exertion of both pressure and persuasion for "placing persons well affected and discreet."[27] In actuality, Bacon was advocating the "packing" of Parliament. His approach, however, depended on the use of discretion and on a harmonious atmosphere between Crown and Parliament. The prerogative was supreme, but the survival of this supremacy depended on the Crown's ability to "tune the instrument" of harmony. Bacon's paternalism needed Parliament in its "junior" role.

How realistic were Bacon's political views on the Crown-Parliament situation? When he advised James to stop making frequent speeches to Parliament, he was rendering sound advice. The King's habit of making long, threatening speeches had hardly been a display of tactful absolutism. James should open a session with the customary address stating the proposed business. Afterwards, Bacon believed, "he is in the right if he speak no more; except it be upon some occasion of thanks or other weighty particular." The prerogative must be used without being broadcast. Bacon wrote this advice to James as late as 1615. In the same letter he also wrote: "For nothing is to a man wither a greater spur or a greater direction to do over a thing again, than when he knows where he failed."[28] Bacon's persistent hope that James might behave like a Tudor politician must be considered a major flaw in his political thinking. Willson calls it the "chief defect" in his political thought. "James," he remarks, "could not play the part assigned to him. He was not cast in the Tudor mold."[29] It is doubtful whether Bacon ever fully recognized this defect in the King. His advice on Parliament, the need for legal reform, together with his great hope that James would be impressed by his desire to revolutionize learning, all indicate that Bacon put too much faith in his monarch. He continued to hope James might be capable of the kind of paternalistic ab-

166

solutism that utilized the "power to do good." Bacon pleaded for better monarchy until he himself reached Chancery. Although one must agree that he showed too much confidence in James's abilities, he had little choice if he sought to reform from above. James was the only king and Bacon felt he had no choice but to try continuously to influence him. He tried to advise through Villiers, hoping this favorite might be instrumental in bringing better government. As long as Bacon retained the active impulse to push his ideas at court, he had to express the hope that James might still listen. We may criticize his judgment; we cannot condemn his efforts.

Was Bacon also naive in underestimating the growing intensity of parliamentary opposition to the Crown? Did he, as Allen says, underrate "the strength of an opposition that seemed to him stupidly obstructive?"[30] Did he really believe that even if James could become a good Tudor, the Elizabethan-type control of Parliament could be restored? Bacon's experience made him aware of the presence of an opposition group in Parliament. He believed in 1613 that the opposition party of 1610 was almost entirely split or disbanded. "That opposition which the last Parliament to your Majesty's business," he wrote, "as much as was not expuris naturalibus but out of party, I conceive to be now much weaker than it was, and that party almost dissolved. Yelverton is won; Sandes is fallen off; Crew and Hyde stand to be serjeants; Brocke is dead; Neville hath hopes; Barkley I think will be respective. Martin hath money in his purse; Dudley Digges and Holys are yours." Although Bacon's list of individuals was neither complete nor entirely accurate, he did recognize the existence of a conscious "party" opposing the King.[31] Did he realize that opposition to the Crown was grounded in English society and would not dissolve just because some of its former leaders had lost their potency? He did not. He had too much faith in the capacity of responsible monarchy to prevail in seventeenth-century England. While he recognized that religion and economics were important in society, he did not recognize that religious and economic forces were breeding permanent obstacles to royal power. I would contend, however, that Bacon could not be expected to have analyzed the parliamentary opposition with the perception of a modern observer. In basic agreement, Allen maintains that "no one at that time" recognized the growing strength of the Commons. He does not condemn Bacon for underrating the

167

opposition. "It is comparatively easy," says Allen, "to be wise after the event."[32] The whole question of how rapidly or slowly parliamentary opposition developed, 1603-40, has been one for modern scholars to explore. They have filled volumes trying to analyze the sources of opposition, as well as the strengths and weaknesses of both Crown and Parliament. Bacon was a contemporary viewing politics as a participant. His limited perspective is understandable.

Bacon was thus a political man with definite views on contemporary problems. What about his efforts at developing a political philosophy? If we accept White's argument, then we should not attempt to find anything systematic in his so-called "provisional" ideas. Bacon made many statements about political power in his writings. He did not, however, systematically develop any plan for a political society. Bacon's views are found in selections from letters, speeches, legal writings and philosophic treatises. Cumulatively, they appear to support a belief in a strong, essentially conservative monarchy that insures the domestic stability Bacon felt necessary for progress. White's contention that Bacon sought to "use political conservatism" as a means to scientific progress can be strongly supported by the many statements about political power found in the *Essays*. These are writings of great variance and depth and cannot be considered merely a dictum of political thought. They are often considered the most eloquent example of Bacon's enormous intellectual range. They do, however, contain much on matters political.

"Power to do good is the true and lawful end of aspiring. For good thoughts (though God accept them) yet towards men are little better than good dreams, except they be put in act; and that cannot be without power and place, as the vantage and commanding ground."[33] With these words Bacon showed his fundamental belief in the constructive use of political power. This power was best used by a monarchy, but had to be used with tact and discretion:

> Preserve the right of thy place; but stir not questions of jurisdiction: and rather assume thy right in silence and *defacto*, then voice it with claims and challenges. Preserve likewise the rights of inferior places; and think it more honour to direct in chief than to be busy in all. Embrace and invite helps and advices touching the execution of thy place: . . . The vices of authority are chiefly four: delays, corruption, roughness, and facility.[34]

168

Such words indicate Bacon's adherence to the Elizabethan principles of tact and moderation. They also show his commitment to a sense of balance in government. These views were reinforced by statements in other essays. "Certain it is," he stated in "Of Empire," "that nothing destroyeth authority so much as the unequal and untimely interchange of power pressed too far, and relaxed too much."[35] In "Of Judicature," he advised: "Let no man weakly conceive that just laws and true policy have any antipathy; for they are like the spirits and sinews, that one moves with the other."[36] Cautious and wise government was dependent on the existence of a harmonious atmosphere. It also relied on rulers getting sound advice. "Sovereignty is married to Counsel." "The wisest princes need not think it any diminution to their greatness, or derogation to their sufficiency, to rely upon counsel."[37] Royal government was thus charged with utilizing the virtues of great power and avoiding its vices.

Bacon extolled the strengths of a stable monarchy and cautioned against the problems that could plague it. In "Of Innovations" he echoed his basic conservatism: "It is good also not to try experiments in states, except the necessity be urgent, or the utility evident; and well to beware that it be the reformation that draweth on the change, and not the desire of change that pretendeth the reformation."[38] Perhaps his clearest defense of conservative monarchy came in "Of Seditions and Troubles":

> Also when discords, and quarrels, and factions, are carried openly and audaciously, it is a sign the reverence of government is lost. For the motions of the greatest person in a government ought to be as the motions of the planets under *primum mobile*; (according to the old opinion) which is, that every of them is carried swiftly by the highest motion, and softly in their own motion. And therefore, when great ones in their own particular motion move violently, . . . it is a sign the orbs are out of frame. For reverence is that wherewith princes are girt from God, ...
>
> So when any of the four pillars of government are mainly shaken or weakened (Which are religion, justice, counsel, and treasure), man had need to pray for fair weather.[39]

Bacon saw the monarch as the first mover of his people, drawing his analogy from Aristotelian cosmology. The King's position as the pivotal force in the state was crucial to its ability to function.

169

As order prevailed in the heavens, so must it prevail within the state. It was for the ruler to safeguard the "pillars of government" and maintain them as workable instruments within the body politic. The lions must be kept under the throne. Factional strife and any disrupting forces must be dissipated. "Generally, the dividing and breaking of all factions that are adverse to the state, and setting them at distance, or at least distrust, amongst themselves, is not one of the worst remedies."[40] Monarchs must not only beware of the dangers of disruptive forces, but most maintain their supremacy over all factions or parties. "Kings had need beware how they side themselves, and make themselves as of a faction or party; for leagues within the state are ever pernicious to monarchies: for they raise an obligation paramount to obligation of sovereignty. . . ." "The chiefest wisdom," he wrote in the same essay, "is either ordering those things which are general, and wherein men of several factions do nevertheless agree; or in dealing with correspondence to particular persons, one by one."[41] Bacon truly revered political unity.

Religious unity was also a necessity. In "Of Unity in Religion" he again stressed the importance of religious peace. "Religion being the chief band of human society, it is a happy thing when itself is contained within the true band of Unity."[42] Bacon feared the destructive power of religion upon the state when used by a particular group as a vehicle of protest. He referred to "the massacre in France" and "the powder treason of England." "For as the temporal sword is to be drawn with great circumspection in cases of religion; so it is a thing monstrous to be put into the hands of the common people."[43] He saw religious harmony as an essential ingredient in the maintenance of an orderly commonwealth. The "fruits" of such unity were most beneficial. "As for the fruit towards these that are within, it is peace; which containeth infinite blessings. It establisheth faith. It kindleth charity. The outward peace of the church distilleth into the peace of conscience."[44] Bacon also felt very strongly that religious peace was a necessary condition for intellectual and scientific progress.

The importance of national greatness was also stressed in the *Essays*. Such greatness was achieved by the establishment of imperial and economic power. In "Of the True Greatness of Kingdoms and Estates" Bacon made his case for empire. "In the great frame of kingdoms and commonwealths, it is in the power of princes or estates to add amplitude and greatness to their kingdoms."[45] Showing an admiration for Rome, Bacon justified both arms and war as vehicles for expansion. "For empire and greatness, it importeth most, that a nation do profess arms as their principal honour, study and occupation." "No body can be healthful without exercise, neither natural body nor politic; and certainly to a kingdom or estate, a just and honourable war is the true exercise. A civil war indeed is like the heat of a fever; but a foreign war is like the heat of exercise, and serveth to keep the body in health; for in a slothful peace, both courages will effeminate and manners corrupt."[46] Bacon's defense of a "just war" and his distinction between foreign and civil war were acceptable arguments in his time. A foreign war was seen as a calculated act of diplomacy, embarked upon for a specific purpose. It helped increase national greatness; it might also help insure domestic peace. Bacon craved an empire for England and saw the potential of sea power. "Surely, at this day with us of Europe, the vantage of strength at sea (which is one of the principal dowries of this kingdom of Great Britain) is great, both because most of the kingdoms of Europe are not merely in land, but girt with the sea most part of their compass; and because the wealth of both Indies seems in great part but an accessory to the command of the seas."[47] He saw expansion not as a reckless endeavor, but as a calculated and profitable one. It must be tightly controlled, provide for the extension of citizenship (with rights), and must be economically profitable. The importance of economic and imperial power was stressed in many of his writings.[48]

This brief look at some of the political thoughts reflected upon in the *Essays* has shown how much Bacon valued Crown, Church, and Empire. The *Essays* contain an inexhaustible wealth of ideas, and I do not claim to have extracted everything pertinent to his political thinking. If Bacon was in fact hoping for a voyage to the New Atlantis, the wisdom expressed in these writings constitutes an excellent preparation for such a trip. They may be "provisional" views, but they are indeed profound.

No discussion of Bacon's political ideas can fail to mention his *History of the Reign of Henry VII*. White contends Bacon regarded Henry as the English Solomon. It was he who brought unity and peace to England after a century of civil war. He founded the dynasty that eventually established Anglicanism as the faith preserving royal power.[49] Henry is a logical hero for Bacon. The first

171

Tudor set in motion the political principles that became identified with that dynasty. He exemplified the wise, cautious monarch that Bacon hoped James might become. Henry was "the best lawgiver to this nation after King Edward the First. . . . For his laws are deep and not vulgar, not made upon the spur of a particular occasion for the present, but out of providence of the future; to make the estate of his people still more and more happy. . . ."[50] How very great was this King who led Parliament to constructive achievements. "The lasting fruit of Parliament, which is good and wholesome laws, did prosper and doth yet continue till this day."[51] Henry, of course, seldom convened Parliament during his twenty-four year reign. Bacon thought he used it with discretion and toward the furtherance of harmony.

Bacon's English Solomon provided the ideal model for royal political behavior. The *History* was published in 1622, after Bacon's fall, and was dedicated to Prince Charles. Bacon hoped the work might restore him to favor and erase his disgrace.[52] He also probably hoped his vivid portrait of a successful ruler would help the future King avoid the mistakes of his father. Perhaps, he was looking to the future for the embodiment of his ideas. He would not live long enough to suffer further disillusionment.

1. J. W. Allen, *English Political Thought 1603-1660* (London, 1938), I, 50-52.

2. *Ibid.*, 56-61.

3. G. P. Gooch, *Political Thought in England from Bacon to Halifax* (London, 1915), 19-22.

4. *Ibid.*, 17.

5. *The Crisis of the Constitution*, 168.

6. *Ibid.*, 62-63. Miss Judson supports her statement with the words from Bacon's 1610 parliamentary speech:
"The King's Sovereignty and the Liberty of Parliament . . . do not cross or destroy the one the other, but they strengthen and maintain the one the other. . . ." and the lines from "Of Judicature," "And let no man weakly conceive that just laws and true policy have any antipathy; for they are like the spirits and sinews that one moves with the other."

7. *Ibid.*, 170.

8. White's title was inspired by words in a letter from Bacon to Toby Mathew, written in 1609:
"Myself am like the miller of Huntington, that was wont to pray for peace amongst the willows: for while the winds blew, the wind-mills wrought, and the watermill was less customed. So I see that controversies of religion must hinder the advancement of sciences."
See *Letters and Life*, IV, 137-38.

9. *Peace Among the Willows*, 11.

10. *Ibid.*, 58.

11. *Ibid.*, 60. In his argument in the *postnati* case of 1608, Bacon defended monarchy on the basis of natural right. He stated on that occasion that he could "hardly consent that the King shall be esteemed or called only our rightful sovereign, or lawful sovereign, but our natural *liege sovereign*; as acts of parliament speak: for as the common law is more worthy than the statute law; so the law of nature is more worthy than them both." See *Bacon's Works*, XV, 200-1.

12. *Ibid.*, 62-65.

13. *Ibid.*, 69.

14. *Ibid.*, 67.

15. A fascinating treatment of the influence of Bacon's ideas on capitalistic development is found in Christopher Hill, *Intellectual Origins of the English Revolution* (Oxford, 1965), 85-130.

16. *Peace Among the Willows*, 91.

17. White's approach to Bacon's political philosophy is supported by another scholar in this area, Jerry W. Weinberger. In a thoughtfully written dissertation, "Modern Science and Modern Politics: A Study of Bacon's *Advancement of Learning* and *New Atlantis*" (Harvard, 1972), Weinberger articulates the view that Bacon is "one of the founders of modern political science." Accepting White's contention that Bacon was a major political philosopher, and that his philosophy was utopian, Weinberger concentrates on showing how Bacon developed the connection between natural science and political science. His intention is to return to the "world articulated by natural science in order to understand the relation between science and political things which are part of that world." The ultimate in enlightened political rule was attainable only through the perfection of natural science. The study is a line-by-line analysis of these two major works. Bacon, the author shows, laid the basis for his utopia in *The Advancement of Learning* and perfected his concept in the *New Atlantis*. The latter work is, for Weinberger, too, the expression of what White calls Bacon's "definitive politics." This complex work is a penetrating look at Bacon's thought and should enrich the study of his philosophy.

18. Anderson, 20.

19. *Privy Councillors. . . ,* 132.

20. *The Crisis of the Constitution*, 62.

21. *Letters and Life*, IV, 177.

22. *Ibid.*, IV, 369, 371. These words from an undated letter were written sometime during the spring of 1613.

23. *Ibid.*, 371.

24. *Ibid.*, 366.

25. *Ibid.*, 367-38, 372.

26. *Ibid.*, 366-67.

27. *Ibid.*, 367, 372.

28. *Ibid.*, V, 190.

29. *Privy Councillors. . . ,* 135.

30. *English Political Thought. . . ,* I, 54.

31. *Letters and Life*, IV, 370. For an analysis of Bacon's statement *see* Mitchell, *The Rise of the Revolutionary Party. . . ,* 40-43. Bacon's main error was in claiming that Sandys had "fallen off."

32. *English Political Thought. . . ,* I, 62.

173

33. "Of Great Place," *Bacon's Works*, XII, 113.

34. *Ibid.*, 114.

35. *Ibid.*, 141.

36. *Ibid.*, 270.

37. "Of Counsel," *Ibid.*, 146-47.

38. *Ibid.*, 161.

39. *Ibid.*, 125.

40. *Ibid.*, 130.

41. "Of Faction," *Ibid.*, 254-56.

42. *Ibid.*, 86.

43. *Ibid.*, 91.

44. *Ibid.*, 88.

45. *Ibid.*, 187-88. Bacon reprinted this essay with minor changes in the eighth book of *De Augmentis*.

46. *Ibid.*, 183-85.

47. *Ibid.*, 186.

48. White offers an involved but excellent analysis of Bacon's expansionism. *See Peace. . .* , 75-92.

49. *Ibid.*, 48-57.

50. "The History of the Reign of Henry VII," *Bacon's Works*, XI, 141.

51. *Ibid.*, 129-30.

52. A recently published work, Jonathan L. Marwill, *The Trials of Counsel: Francis Bacon in 1621* (Detroit, 1976) offers a thoughtful analysis of Bacon's history of the first Tudor king. Marwill links Bacon's own career with his writing of the *History*. He emphasizes that Bacon began work on the book in June, 1621, shortly after his release from the Tower. It was, says Marwill, "Bacon's ultimate political testament, a virtuoso work encompassing the thoughts and talents of a lifetime of civil business." Bacon was in fact culminating his own career by writing it. He hoped the book might help him regain official favor and end his banishment from politics. He also hoped it would be an influential political document. Marwill discusses the work carefully, arguing that Bacon used Henry as a vehicle for expressing his own political ideas. He claims that Bacon's Henry "comes close to being a mirror image of Bacon's talents, ideas, and personality." Marwill's argument is scholarly and generally convincing. The claim that Bacon carefully portrayed a politically shrewd Henry to echo his own views appears valid. Although the contention that the work was Bacon's "ultimate political testament" is debatable, Marwill has made a contribution to the scholarship on Bacon's political ideas. *See ibid.*, 152, 194-95.

Marwill also analyzes Bacon's total political career. He studies Bacon's political behavior primarily by studying his writings, with the work on Henry shown as the culmination. Marwill concentrates more on Bacon's written statements than on his actions. He appears to agree that political opportunism was an important motivation in Bacon's career. Although I disagree with his interpretation of Bacon's role in Parliament, his approach to the study of Bacon's career is well researched and thoughtful. I do believe, however, that Marwill is most convincing when he is interpreting Bacon's work on Henry.

174

POSTSCRIPT

Francis Bacon expired on April 9, 1626. The last five years of his life were spent nobly in great intellectual pursuits. Even Bacon's death was linked to his interest in experimentation. The story is well known. In late March, 1626, Bacon "in the course of a drive towards Highgate" "took advantage of an unseasonable fall of snow" to determine "whether it would preserve flesh from putrefaction, as salt does."[1] He stopped at a cottage, purchased a hen from an old woman and stuffed it with snow. Apparently he planned to experiment with snow as a refrigerating agent. He quickly caught a bad chill and was confined to what would prove to be his deathbed. In his very last letter, written to his friend Lord Arundel, Bacon indicated that he wanted "to try an experiment or two, touching the conservation and induration of bodies." The "experiment" "succeeded excellently well; but in the journey . . . I was taken with such a fit of casting, as I knew not whether it were the stone, or some surfeit, or cold, or indeed a touch of them all three." Bacon contracted either bronchitis or pneumonia. He died on Easter Sunday, 1626.[2] Bacon's mind was flourishing right to the end of his life.

Francis Bacon died deeply in debt. Although he designated sums for university lectureships, and for scholarships for poor students, the endowment was bankrupt. It is estimated that Bacon's estate was worth about £7,000; his debts exceeded £22,000.[3] His wife of twenty years, Lady Alice Bacon, was cut off for "just and great causes" and received nothing beyond legal "right."[4] Interestingly enough, Lady Hatton, the woman Bacon had lost to Edward Coke years before received a legacy in his will. Although Bacon never loved any woman, he obviously saw fit to spite his lifelong adver-

175

sary even at the very end. His greatest legacy, his manuscripts, were entrusted to William Rawley, who produced the first compilation, and ensured their survival. His political career bequeathed only poverty; his intellect left a wealth of knowledge for posterity.

1. *Letters and Life*, VII, 549-50.

2. *Ibid.*, 550-1.

3. *Ibid.*, 552.

4. Bacon had married Alice Barnham in 1606, when he was forty-five and she, fourteen. The match apparently brought financial help to Bacon (Alice was a co-heiress to the estate of a wealthy Alderman), being a socially acceptable convenience marriage. Actually Bacon's views on marriage were devastating. He wrote in "Of Marriage and the Single Life," "He that hath wife and children hath given hostages to fortune; for they are impediments to great enterprises. . . . Certainly the best works . . . have proceeded from the unmarried or childless men." Bacon himself married solely for convenience. There were, of course, no children, and we know relatively little about his twenty-year relationship with Alice. Throughout most of that period there were no hints of scandal. Lady Alice apparently did grow weary of her life with the Chancellor and eventually sought other company. She appears to have found it. Bacon cut her off because he suspected her of taking one John Underhill as a lover. She married that gentleman eleven days after Bacon's death.

See ibid., III, 290-1, VII, 539-45. *See* also, Alice Chambers Bunten, *Life of Alice Barnham* (1592-1650), (London, 1928).

176

CONCLUSION: "THE POLITICAL MAN"

The opening lines of Bacon's essay "Of Great Place" read as follows:

Men in great place are thrice servants; servants of the sovereign or state; servants of fame; and servants of business. So as they have no freedom; neither in their persons, nor in their actions, nor in their times. It is a strange desire, to seek power and to lose liberty: or to seek power over others and lose power over a man's self. The rising into place is laborious; and by pains men come to greater pains; and it is sometimes base; and by indignities men come to dignities. The standing is slippery, and the regress is either a downfall, or at least an eclipse, which is a melancholy thing.

The 1625 edition of the same essay ended with these words:

Use the memory of thy predecessor fairly and tenderly; for if thou does not, it is a debt will sure be paid when thou art gone. If thou have colleagues, respect them, rather call them when they look not for it, than exclude them when they have reasons to look to be called. Be not too sensible or too remembering of thy place, in conversation and in private answers to suitors; but let it rather be said, *When he sits in place he is another man.*[1]

Bacon depicted much about his own career with these words. His own "rising into place" was indeed "laborious," and he had found the "standing" to be "slippery." Moreover, his acquisition of "power over others" had been accompanied by a lapse in his self-control. Bacon had perceived these dangers when he first wrote this essay in 1612, years before the period of his greatest power. It is significant that he added new words to the edition of the essay published

177

after his fall. He noted poignantly the necessity of exercising discretion while holding power. The italicizing of the final words shows that he had finally recognized his own political mistakes.

This study has argued that Francis Bacon spent most of his active life as a "political man" whose career was the very product of the politics of his society. Anyone saturated in the politics of a country is likely to have his actions, and to some degree his thinking, determined by the dictums of that politics. The more committed to political life he becomes, the less individual freedom of action he has. Bacon himself admitted this in the lines I have cited. He became involved early, and for several reasons remained immersed until his forced removal from government. Had he enjoyed financial independence early in life, he might never have become deeply involved in politics. He would have been able, at any rate, to control the degree of involvement and withstand political saturation. With Bacon's intellectual interests being what they were, it is not unlikely that he would have chosen scholarship over total political involvement. Given his situation, however, Francis Bacon had little choice but to become political. He saw the logic in it given his familial background, and began his career anticipating early success. The more that success eluded him, the more committed to attaining it he became. Rapidly he engulfed himself in politics, and was soon dedicated to steadfast service of the Crown. His lot was cast early; from the time of his initial suit for Attorneyship in the 1590s he was determined to rise to high officialdom. From then on, he walked a treadmill assuring him total status as a "political man."

The term "political man" is a natural one and is not meant to be derogatory. All partisan government officials in any system or era are conditioned politically. Their behavior is determined by political standards of the system they serve. To be certain, such a contention does not mean that all political acts are to be condoned merely because they may be sanctioned or ordered by a particular regime or administration. The "political man" must always be evaluated with some ethical and moral standards in mind. Despite Hannah Arendt's interesting claim that Adolph Eichmann was a "Law-Abiding Citizen" who merely administered decisions of his government, it remains difficult to accept his actions as those of an ordinary "political man" just doing his job.[2] The "political men" of the Nixon years, including the President himself, engaged in activities that proved both morally and legally unacceptable to American society. Nixon officials claimed that clandestine acts committed for the President should not be considered criminal. Such claims were of course rejected by the courts. While societies must maintain ethical as well as legal standards of political behavior, they often have difficulty in discerning these standards. Many Americans saw the Watergate shenanigans as nothing more than traditional "dirty politics." Are we always capable of judging political behavior objectively? Perhaps not. Political behavior may be unethical, devious, or even, in the eyes of some, immoral. It is often difficult, however, to know when it should be labeled criminal. There will perhaps never be uniform standards by which the official and moral activities of political men can be judged. The complexities of political life often make it difficult to render judgment, and students of history must always struggle with these problems. Should Oliver Cromwell be considered a "butcher" because of Wexford and Drogheda? Was Harry Truman a war criminal because of Hiroshima? The answers to these and countless other similar questions often depend on the perspective of the historical judge. There will never be universal agreement on such evaluations. Whether one studies major historical figures or more ordinary political men, he faces similar problems in rendering judgment. Political men are by no means automatically devious entities. They are human beings in politics and must be so judged both on their merits and faults.

What kind of a "political man" was Francis Bacon? This study has contended that this question has not been treated thoroughly by past biographers. Answering it remains a subjective exercise, and in no way do I claim to offer a definitive evaluation. There remain mysteries about Bacon's character which I do not pretend to have solved. What were the crucial factors in his early years that helped shape his personality? What was the nature of that personality? While there have been many superficial answers to the second question, the truth remains elusive. Studying Bacon's political career does not provide all the answers. If there were serious deficiencies in his character as some have claimed, they are not shown by his political behavior. That behavior was molded by a combination of idealistic and self-seeking motivations. It was neither particularly sinister nor truly distinguished. It provides us with some clues to his personality, but does not really uncover what we might call the "personal man." While Mrs. Bowen has come closer to understanding this "personal" side than anyone, further study of Bacon's personality is needed.

As a "political man," Bacon functioned both logically and predictably. Once he climbed on what I have referred to as a political treadmill he became totally committed to achieving success. That goal took precedence and necessitated the sacrifice of greater scholarly productivity. While Bacon craved the pursuit of knowledge and flourished best as an "intellectual man," politics was always given priority. Ideally, reaching the New Atlantis was what mattered most, but as Bacon functioned in the arenas of government, politics was of primary concern. "Power to do good is the true and lawful end of aspiring," he wrote. Although he always tried to remain committed to this principle, it cannot be said that such words stand as the guide to his political career. I cannot support the view that Bacon's main goal in politics was to use power to promote knowledge and progress. While Bacon the "intellectual man" was dedicated to that goal, the "political man" pursued power, wealth, and status as ends in themselves. Bacon's career illustrates this clearly. The fact that his years of greatest political success produced relatively little intellectual achievement, while the last five years after impeachment were truly "noble" intellectually, justifies the distinction between the "political man" and the "intellectual man" in Francis Bacon. Although he never lost the desire to use power constructively, he became less concerned with this goal as he himself reached greater heights. There was, to be sure, his hope that the *Advancement of Learning* would spark an intellectual revolution at the Jacobean Court. There were his efforts to encourage over-all legal reform, and his ideas in the *Essays* published in 1612, that clearly showed his genius for conceiving the positive ends to which power could be used. Bacon never closed the intellectual compartments in his mind that longed for such goals. He never, however, merged the intellectual and political characteristics of his nature to achieve the kind of paternalistic statesmanship he believed in so strongly.

Had Bacon been stronger or more financially secure, his constructive goals in government would have been pursued more diligently. The fact that they were not is perhaps indicative of a frailty of character. Without indulging in the intense personality probing which is perhaps needed, I would offer a brief evaluation. Bacon's long and arduous struggle to rise fostered an insecurity within him that remained ever present. He clearly recognized the "slippery" nature of officialdom and his own frustrating career made uncertainty a way of life. Bacon was forty-six before achieving the relatively subservient post of Solicitor-General. He was past fifty when appointed Attorney, and close to sixty when he reached the Chancellorship. The fact that success came so slowly, and with such difficulty, stands as most significant. Bacon never really enjoyed stability of position long enough to work seriously at applying his ideals to politics. In competing for status and power, he faced constant uncertainty about his future. When "great place" finally came Bacon had lost his zeal for carrying out reform. The climb to power had been so frustrating that the Chancellor's main concern was to personally thrive in his office. In so doing he became so careless that he exposed himself to charges of corruption. Bacon is a pathetic figure in these years. His inability to control servants helping themselves to his money, and his behavior during impeachment, illustrate this clearly. His insecurity culminated with his inability to withstand being overcome by his very power and position.

What some have claimed was a cold and aloof character was more likely a facade to hide insecurity. To those who knew and befriended him, Bacon was hardly sinister-like. To his rivals and to some who frequently heard him in Parliament, his masterful handling of words conveyed the impression of arrogance. To some, Bacon was a kind of evil genius seeking primarily to deceive others to gain personal power. While it is understandable that he might have appeared less than totally likable to some contemporaries, any careful study of his life dispels the stereotype of the callous political figure. If Bacon was somewhat less than honorable for the role he played in helping prosecute Essex, he was certainly not a demon at work. He had pleaded with Essex to curb his impetuous behavior. Eventually he found himself in the role of official adversary. The role he played in prosecuting the case was one he found himself in as a "political man." There he was as a royal counsel, asked to assist the Attorney in this important case. Bacon had already learned that the way to please Elizabeth was to obey without question. Perhaps a stronger, more independent individual would have shrugged off such a duty regardless of the consequences. Bacon, however, can hardly be condemned for being a dutiful servant. His feelings toward men like Coke and Robert Cecil are also understandable. The sardonic essay "Of Deformity" stands as an eloquent expression of Bacon's bitterness toward a man who helped frustrate the progress of his own career. The mutual hatred he and Coke had for one another was rooted in both personal and philosophic antagonisms. The political climate of the time was a ripe breeding ground for rivalries of this type. In fact, anyone of Bacon's ability could never have functioned politically without incurring the hostility of some contemporaries. He was neither unusually compassionate nor unusually sinister. He was a "political man," functioning in a treacherous atmosphere. The rope he walked was always extremely tight, and he did not lose consciousness of this fact until he became swollen with the power of great place.

To me, Francis Bacon stands as a political figure molded by his times. Despite his brilliance, he never functioned with great distinction in politics. He was, in my view, a "political man," not a statesman. Statesmanship is a status that implies rising above partisan politics to achieve distinction in affairs of state. Although Bacon always conceived of the constructive use of power, he never quite translated his ideas into accomplishments. We do not condemn him for this; statesmanship is a distinction few individuals achieve. This study has attempted to understand him as the "political man" he was. That man was ambitious, energetic, frustrated, resourceful, and eventually pathetic. The mind of that man was always vibrant with creative genius. That it was not put to use more fully over a life span will always be a legitimate lamentation of Bacon's biographers. How well Francis Bacon might have fit into a "think tank," had his society ever conceived such a concept! There he could have pursued the New Atlantis free from the rigors of domestic politics.

1. *Bacon's Works*, XII, 111-15.
2. *Eichmann in Jerusalem* (New York, 1963), 135. Miss Arendt argues basically that the system Eichmann served rather than the man himself was the main bearer of guilt.

EPILOGUE: POLITICS AND THE INTELLECTUAL

Perhaps a reflection on Francis Bacon as an intellectual in politics is in order. That subject has not been the theme of this study, although more general biographies have to some extent portrayed Bacon as the versatile genius who combined scholarship and politics. The emphasis here has been on Bacon, the political man. I have maintained that he successfully compartmentalized his political and intellectual sides so that open conflict between the two was avoided. Bacon's career does not mirror that of the modern intellectual who leaves the campus for government. A political career was, in a very real sense, Francis Bacon's birthright; he pursued such a career diligently at first because he hoped it would afford the financial independence his father's will denied him. Soon, his pursuit of political power became an end in itself. While his public career was long, arduous, and essentially undistinguished, it did not impede his accomplishments as a philosopher. Any analysis of Bacon's writing clearly substantiates his own claim that "all knowledge" was his "province."

Why, then, this "Epilogue?" If Bacon could function in political life and still establish himself as such a renowned thinker, then presumably, he was not adversely affected by such dualism. I would contend, however, that he was affected detrimentally by such a situation. Bacon survived a long time in political life, and while his over-all career may be termed mediocre, he was in no sense a dismal failure. His fall was to a large extent caused by political circumstances beyond his control. It came late in life, forty years after he had sat in his first Parliament. The intellectual who tries politics usually resigns or is removed after a much shorter tenure in government. He enters government expecting a short stay, merely

183

hoping that some of his ideas may imprint themselves on the political system. A Henry Kissinger who can successfully apply his views to the world of international politics is indeed a rarity. Government does not expect such success from intellectuals. In one sense, Francis Bacon did "make it" politically. He strove patiently for power and eventually achieved it. But, he conceived the constructive use of such power and never came close to achieving such a goal. He faced perpetual frustration in the political world of James I and finally succumbed to its rather banal political habits. That he did so, was tragic in itself. For someone of such gifted talents to become relegated to a life of political mediocrity was catastrophic. While it did not impede his intellectual talents, it reduced him as a man and made him susceptible to disgrace and humiliation. A Francis Bacon who could have functioned only as an "intellectual man" would have lived a more noble and satisfying life.

INDEX

Abbott, Edwin, 11-12
Allen, J. W., 159-60, 168
Amboise, Pierre, 5
Anderson, Fulton, 16-18, 57
Andrews, Bishop Lancelot, 4
Arendt, Hannah, 178
Arundel, Earl of, 152
Aubrey, Christopher, 144-6
Aubrey, John, 7

Bacon, Lady Alice (Alice Barnham Bacon, Francis Bacon's wife) 175, 176, n.4
Bacon, Lady Ann (Francis Bacon's mother), 24
Bacon, Francis (1561-1626):
biographical studies of, 1-19; early life, 20-5; marriage, 175-6; death, 175 In Parliament: 1581, 25; 1584-5, 25-6; 1586-7, 27-9; 1589, 29-30; 1593, 37-42, 45, n.21; 1597-8, role in social legislation, 50-1; other activities, 49-52, 62, n.21; 1601, role in monopolies dispute, 52-3; role in social legislation, 55-6; other activities, 52-7; 1604, thoughts about his role in that Parliament, 76-8; role in the Goodwin-Fortescue case, 76-8; role in Union issue, 79-80; other duties 78-9; 1605-6, 97, n.38; 1606-7, role in Union issue, 81-4; 1610, problems of participation in session as Solicitor-General, 86-7; role in "Great Contract," 86-7; role in debate over legality of impositions, 89-92; views on Royal Prerogative, 89-90; 1614, advises James on how to handle the session, 103-4; problems as Attorney-General in Parliament, 104-5; failure of the session, 105; 1621, pre-

pares for, 134; addresses at start, 134-5; views on reform of patent system, 136-7; Bacon's enemies in 1621, 138-9; basis of attack against Bacon, 140-2; investigation of him as Chancellor begins, 143; Bacon charged with bribery, 144-5; case substantiated against him, 146-50; James "abandons" him, 147; Bacon's trial, conviction and sentencing, 150-3; spends a few days in the Tower, 153; aftermath of Impeachment, 154; assessment of Impeachment, 154-5
Political Career: early efforts to rise in government, 24-5; early advice to the Queen on religion, 26; admitted to the bar, 27; establishes friendship with Essex, 35-6; seeks Attorney-Generalship with help of Essex, 37, 42; seeks Solicitor-Generalship with help of Essex, 43-4; relationship with Essex cools, 58-9; role in the Essex case, 59-61; aspirations in 1603, 65-7; becomes Solicitor-General, 84; argues *postnati* case (1608) 84-5; aspires to become Attorney-General, 99-100; aspires to be Secretary of State, 101; becomes Attorney-General, 101-2; advises James on Parliament, 106; activities as Attorney, 107-8; role in Coke's fall from King's Bench, 109-13; tries to assert his legal philosophy, 113-15; aspires to be Lord Chancellor, 121; ideas about Chancery upon becoming Lord Keeper, 121-3; friendship with Villiers, 124-7; meddles in Coke's personal affairs, 127-9; becomes Lord Chancellor, 129; inability to handle

187